SOUS VIDE COOKBOOK

575 Best Sous Vide Recipes of All Time

~ Rachel Collins

Merry Christmas, Scott!
Looking forward to
sharing some tasty
meals.
Love you,
Mom & Dad
2019

Illustrations © James Foster

Cover design by Kim White

Dedication

To John and the kids,

You inspire me not only in the kitchen, but in every part of life. I love to cook, in no small part, because of the excitement and appreciation you have shown for my home-cooked meals all along the way. Our time together in the kitchen and the countless hours we have spent around the table are my favorite memories of all.

To dark chocolate,

my companion through many a long night of writing.

To you (yes, you)!

TABLE OF CONTENTS

Sous Vide Basics

We all enjoy quality food. People will travel thousands of miles just to get a taste of amazing gourmet meals.

A natural instinct draws people to good and quality food. However, it is not possible for us to always enjoy such delicacies, perhaps due to lack of time, lack of knowledge, or the experience to prepare the meals ourselves.

If you are one of these people, I would've told you that the only solution is to make enough free time in your busy schedule to visit a restaurant or ask someone to prepare a nice meal for you.

Things have changed now, thanks to the fact that Sous Vide circulators are available at such affordable prices.

While it is true that there are some pretty amazing cooking appliances—such as the Air Fryer, Instant Pot, Crock Pot, etc.—Sous Vide circulators are in a league of their own.

The best part of Sous Vide, you ask?

Regardless of the level of your experience, you will be able to prepare the "Perfect" meal every single time.

Now, this might sound a little bit difficult to believe at first, but it's actually true.

Before exploring the more than 500 amazing recipes in this book, I would ask you to walk through this in-depth introductory chapter that will introduce you to the basics of Sous Vide cooking and help you master the art.

This book is targeted toward amateurs and new chefs alike, so everything is broken down into very easy to understand sections.

A Brief History of Sous Vide Cooking

Generally speaking, the process of vacuum sealing food in order to extend shelf life has been around for a long time. However, it didn't gain recognition as a cooking method before the 1940s. Even after that, it took a lot of experimentation before people actually started to place vacuum-sealed food in a pot full of boiling water to cook it.

As a cooking method, the origin of the Sous Vide technique, therefore, finds its roots in the mid-1970s, when Chef Georges Pralus tried to develop a cooking technique that would minimize costly shrinkage and help create an optimal cooking environment for cooking Foie Gras.

Needless to say, the technique of Sous Vide cooking was not confined to him. Soon after Pralus introduced the technique to the world, Chef Bruno Goussault took up the technique and refined it further, which allowed him to use Sous Vide to craft meals for the first-class travelers of Air France.

Seeing the hidden potential behind the technique, Bruno worked relentlessly to bring the technique to the mainstream market.

However, despite reaching mass popularity, it still was a costly technique for ordinary people to afford, and it took two years of evolution before it completely broke the barriers and became one of the "Best" cooking technique ever made.

Contrary to popular belief, thanks to a large number of affordable Sous Vide circulators available in the market, anyone can pick up the device and start experimenting with Sous Vide cooking.

The Science Behind Sous Vide Cooking

Despite being popular at present, the Sous Vide cooking technique still creates confusion among beginners.

If you are one of them, let me help you clarify the concept a bit.

Let's start with the fundamental element first:

What exactly does "Sous Vide" mean?

The term "Sous Vide" is the French word for "Under Vacuum."

The name itself is inspired by the process that is used in Sous Vide cooking.

Perhaps one of the major differences between Sous Vide and other traditional cooking methods is that, in terms of Sous Vide cooking, you will be asked to add all of your ingredients to either a zip bag or a canning mason jar and seal them up in such a way that a vacuum is created inside.

This sealed vessel is then submerged under water that is heated to a certain temperature with utmost precision using the Sous Vide circulator, which allows for perfect cooking every single time.

The whole process greatly simplifies "Cooking"—even for amateurs—and allows anyone to create masterpieces in no time.

The Advantages of Sous Vide

The following advantages should inspire you to jump onto the Sous Vide bandwagon.

- It will allow you to create perfect meals every single time, regardless of your cooking experience.
- It will help you infuse your meals with "Gourmet" quality flavors and enjoy restaurant-quality meals at home.
- You do not need to stand in front of the water bath all day long, saving you a lot of time to carry out your day-to-day activities.
- The natural juices and nutrients are preserved in Sous Vide cooking.
- Since there's no risk of overcooking or undercooking, you will be able to cook your expensive meat cuts with ease.

The Health Benefits of Sous Vide Cooking

While the advantages mentioned above focused on the general aspects of Sous Vide, the following will provide you an elaborate outline of the health benefits of accompanying Sous Vide.

- While cooking with Sous Vide devices, you won't need to add any kind of additional fats required in other methods. This immediately eliminates the need for using harmful oils that increase the cholesterol levels of the food, making Sous Vide meals much healthier.

- Exposing ingredients to heat, oxygen, and water causes them to lose a lot of vital nutrients, leading to over-carbonization of meats and vitamin/antioxidant loss in vegetables. The vacuum sealing technique that is implemented while cooking with Sous Vide prevents this from happening, as the food is not exposed to any water or oxygen. As a result, the nutritional contents are preserved to near-perfect levels.

- Sous Vide cooked meals are easier to digest, as it helps to break down the collagen proteins into gelatin, which is easier for our body to digest and absorb.

- Undercooking is very harmful, as it not only leads to unpleasant tasting food, but also causes the foods to be overrun by bacteria and viruses. The vacuum seal of Sous Vide prevents this from happening, and the oxygen that is required for the pathogens to live is sucked out. The precise cooking technique ensures that you are getting perfectly cooked meals every single time.

Essential Kitchen Equipment

As mentioned before, there is a very common misconception amongst people who think that Sous Vide cooking requires a bucket load of expensive equipment and appliances, in order to be pulled off properly.

While it is true that Uber-expensive equipment is available that would allow you to create even more "premium" meals, it is still possible to achieve the same level of satisfaction without burning a hole in your pocket.

Thanks to technological advancements, Sous Vide circulators have become very cheap and affordable (you can get some good ones for as low as 60$), which makes it easier for the mainstream market to penetrate into Sous Vide cooking.

Aside from the circulator itself, you need a few other pieces of equipment, which are readily available for low prices in the supermarket or can even be found at your home.

I will be talking about all of them in a bit, but before that, let me talk a bit about the Sous Vide Circulator itself.

The Sous Vide Immersion Circulator: The Sous Vide circulators are the heart of Sous Vide cooking.

The main purpose of these devices is to simply heat your water bath to a precise temperature with utmost precision and maintain that specified temperature throughout the cooking process.

The circulator also circulates the water to ensure that the heat is distributed evenly.

If you are buying a Sous Vide Circulator for the first time, the following are the best ones available right now:

- **Anova Wi-Fi Precision Cooker:** The Anova Wi-Fi Circulator is the top dog in the Sous Vide business, and it took the world by storm when it launched. Aside from the obvious cooking functionality, other additional features, such as Bluetooth or Wi-Fi connectivity that allows for wireless controlling, make this the complete package, perfect for beginners.
  At the time of writing, the lowest market price was $159.

- **ChefSteps Joule:** While Anova is considered the leading device, the ChefSteps Joule is the pioneer when it comes to the "Smart Kitchen" scene! Back when this device was introduced, aficionados instantly fell in love with the device, thanks to its compact size and robust array of features.
  At the time of writing, the lowest market price was $175.

- **Gourmia Sous Vide Pod:** The Gourmia is the one to go for if you are on a tight budget. This Sous Vide circulator has all of the basic functionalities that you would expect without letting go of the "Cool" aesthetics.
At the time of writing, the lowest market price was $59.

Aside from the circulator itself, the following are some of the other essential items that you would need.

A reasonably large container: You should already know by now that you are going to need a good quality container to prepare your water bath, in order to submerge your vacuum-sealed container and cook the contents. Therefore, it is wise to go for a good quality 8-12-quart stockpot. However, if not possible, then you should go for a 12-quart square, polycarbonate food storage container, just to be safe. Either way, make sure to purchase a container that has the capacity to hold water heated to 203 degrees Fahrenheit.

Resealable bags and jars: Once you are set with the container, the next items you are going to need are the resealable bags and sealing jars.

When considering the bags, you should go for heavy-duty, resealable bags that are capable of sustaining a temperature of up to 195 degrees Fahrenheit. If possible, get bags that are marked "Freezer Safe" and come with a double seal.

For the jars, simply go for mason jars or canning jars that come with a tight lid.

You might notice that throughout the book, we used the "Immersion" method for sealing zip bags and "Finger Tip Tight" technique for tightening cans; both of the techniques are explained below.

Cast Iron Pan: Some recipes will ask you to sear your meal after Sous Vide cooking is done, so keeping a Cast Iron Pan nearby is a good decision.

Alternatively, you may also achieve a brown texture using a blowtorch.

The Basics of using the Sous Vide

While some recipes will call for deviations in the process, the following are the basic steps that you are to follow while cooking, using the Sous Vide Device.

Prepare: Once you have decided which container to use, simply attach the Immersion Circulator to the container and fill it with water. Make sure to keep the height of the water just 1 inch above the minimum water mark of the circulator that you are using.

Dutch oven, plastic storage containers, stockpot, and large saucepans are good options for Sous Vide cooking.

Choose temperature: Set the temperature of your circulator as asked by your recipe.

Pre-heat water bath: Turn the device on and allow the water bath to reach the desired temperature; it should take about 20-30 minutes, depending on your device.

Season and seal the meal: Season your food as instructed by the recipe and vacuum-seal it in either zip bags or canning jars.

Submerge underwater: Once the desired water level has been reached, and you have sealed your bags, submerge the food underwater and cover the container with a plastic wrap.

Wait until cooked: Wait until cooking is complete.

Add some finishing touches: Take your bag out and follow the remaining recipes for some finishing touches.

Getting to Know the Sealing Techniques

While you can most definitely use expensive devices to seal your zip bags automatically, you may simply use the method mentioned below to vacuum-seal bags easily.

Water Immersion Method: This method is also sometimes known as the Archimedes Principle Method. The steps are as follows:

- First, put the ingredients in your bag.

- Gently start to submerge the bag under water, making sure to keep the upper part (the enclosure) above water.

- As you keep on submerging the bag underwater, the pressure from the water will slowly push out all the air that may be present in the zip bag.

- Submerge it just up to the zipper, and quickly lock up the zipper, making sure that no water has entered the bag.

- That's it. Simple as that.

As for canning jars, the Finger Tip Tight Technique is what you need to know.

Finger Tip Tight: The Finger Tip technique is used for tightening jars. For this technique, all you have to do is tighten the lid of your jar gently and stop just at the moment you start to feel the slightest amount of resistance.

This is to ensure that the air is able to escape from the inside once you submerge the jar.

Some General Tips

- If you are planning on saving some time while prepping the foods, then you may purchase meats that are already sliced and cut in the shape that you prefer. Some stores even offer foods that are prepackaged in Sous-Vide sealed plastic bags. Such meats are already prepared and can be put under a water bath without any further preparation.

- If you have a vacuum sealer and want to bring your foods in seconds, simply put the meat in a bowl with brine solution and place it in the vacuum chamber. Turn the device on, and the vacuum sealer will pull all the air out of the meat, which will allow the marinade to instantly bond with the meat and fill up the gaps.

- Putting garlic in Sous Vide meals can often bring out a bitter flavor; to avoid this, try to look for a spice known as "Asafoetida." This particular spice comes from the same family as garlic and onions, but does not infuse your meal with the bitter garlic taste.

- Sometimes, once you have sealed your meals by either using the immersion method or a vacuum sealer, the edges might end up flat, which might distort the shape of some food. This can be tackled easily by adding a couple of flavorless oils, such as vegetable oil, to the bag before sealing it.

- Sous Vide Circulators might take a bit of time to heat your water bath. To speed up the process, a good practice is to add already-heated water to your Sous Vide container, such as from a kettle or boiled on the stove, and insert the Sous Vide circulator afterward. This would allow the water to reach your specified temperature quickly.

- If you cook a lot of vegetables, there remains a possibility of developing brown edges from acid development. A good way to tackle this is to sprinkle a bit of baking soda on before sealing them.

- If the recipe requires you to sear your food, you will be asked to use an extremely hot pan. To ensure that you're able to handle this safely, keep tongs close to your cooking station.

- Once you are done with Sous Vide cooking, make sure to thoroughly dry your meat before searing, grilling, or torching it.

Sous Vide Food Safety Tips

Like all other cooking methods, Sous Vide cooking will also require you to handle and serve food in a safe manner to make sure that everything is perfect.

1. With any food, it is essential to cook the food long enough to ensure that foodborne pathogens are eliminated. Make sure to prepare the meals according to the specified temperature and for the specified period. However, if you are trying something new, then try to find your ingredient in the chart below and cook accordingly.

2. The safest way to Sous Vide is to seal the food and put them directly in pre-heated water. However, when you seal the food in plastic, you should consider the temperature at which they are sealed and for how long you are going to store them. Sealing food creates an oxygen-free environment that allows anaerobic bacteria to grow. You may easily avoid this by making sure that meat and poultries are below 40 degrees Fahrenheit while you are sealing them and Seafood are frozen.

3. Cross-Contamination of food is one of the major ways through which foodborne illness are spread. People often tend to handle uncooked meat, fish, or poultry in unsanitary conditions that lead to contamination. The way to avoid this is to have a completely sanitized cooking station and make sure that the surface and cooking utensils are properly washed with hot water or chlorine solution.

CHAPTER 1 | VEGETABLES & FRUITS

Yogurt & Caraway Soup

(Serves: 4 / **Prep Time:** 25 minutes / **Sous Vide Cooking Time:** 2 hours 8 min)

Ingredients

- 1 tablespoon extra-virgin olive oil
- 1½ teaspoons caraway seeds
- 1 medium onion, diced
- 1 leek, halved and thinly sliced
- Kosher salt as needed
- 2 pounds red beets, peeled and chopped
- 1 bay leaf
- 3 cups chicken broth
- ½ cup whole milk yogurt
- Apple cider vinegar
- Fresh dill fronds

How To

1. Prepare your Sous Vide water bath using your immersion circulator and raise the temperature to 185-degrees Fahrenheit
2. Add the oil in a large skillet and heat it over medium heat
3. When the oil is shimmering, add your caraway seeds
4. Toast them for about 1 minute
5. Put the onion, pinch of salt and leek, and sauté them for 5-7 minutes until the leek and onion are tender
6. Put the bay leaf, beets, and ½ teaspoon of salt into a large bowl and mix them well
7. Divide the mixture between two heavy-duty, resealable zipper bags and seal them using the displacement/water immersion method
8. Submerge the bag under water for about 2 hours
9. Once done, take the bags out and pour the contents to a large-sized bowl or pot.
10. Add the chicken broth and blend the whole mixture using an immersion blender
11. Stir in the yogurt, with some extra water or broth if you want a different consistency
12. Season the soup with some salt and vinegar
13. Serve with a garnish of dill fronds!

Nutrition Values (Per Serving)

- Calories: 189
- Carbohydrate: 16g
- Protein: 9g
- Fat: 12g
- Sugar: 5g
- Sodium: 325mg

Mashed Potato

(Serves: 4 / **Prep Time:** 5 minutes / **Sous Vide Cooking Time:** 1 hour)

Ingredients

- 1 lb. russet potatoes, peeled and sliced
- 8 tablespoons butter
- ½ cup heavy cream
- 1 teaspoon kosher salt

How To

1. Prepare your water bath using your Sous Vide immersion circulator and raise the temperature to 190-degrees Fahrenheit
2. Add the heavy cream, russet potatoes, kosher salt, and butter into a heavy-duty zip bag and seal using the immersion method*
3. Submerge and cook for 60 minutes
4. Pass the contents through a food processor into a large bowl
5. Mix them well and serve!

Nutrition Values (Per Serving)

- Calories: 226
- Carbohydrate: 34g
- Protein: 5g
- Fat: 7g
- Sugar: 3g
- Sodium: 93mg

Miso Roasted Celeriac

(Serves: 6 / **Prep Time:** 30 minutes / **Sous Vide Cooking Time:** 2 hours)

Ingredients

- 1 tablespoon miso paste
- 1 whole celeriac, carefully peeled and cut into small bite-sized pieces
- 6 cloves garlic
- 5 sprigs thyme
- 1 teaspoon onion powder
- 3 tablespoon feta cheese
- 1 tablespoon mustard seeds
- Juice of ¼ a large lemon
- 5 cherry tomatoes roughly cut
- Chopped up parsley
- 8-ounce vegan butter
- 1 tablespoon olive oil
- 8 ounce cooked quinoa

How To

1. Prepare the Sous Vide water bath using your immersion circulator and raise the temperature to 185-degrees Fahrenheit

2. Take a large-sized pan and place it over medium heat, add the garlic, thyme, feta cheese, and dry fry them for 1 and a ½ minute
3. Add the butter and keep stirring until slightly browned
4. Add the onion powder and keep the mixture on the side and allow it to cool at room temperature
5. Add the celeriac to a zip bag alongside the cooled butter mixture
6. Submerge and cook for 1½ to 2 hours
7. Transfer the mixture to a hot pan (place over medium heat) and stirring it until golden brown
8. Season with miso paste
9. Add the oil to another pan and place it over medium heat, add the tomatoes, mustard seeds and re-heat the quinoa
10. Carefully add the lemon and parsley to the previously made tomato mixture
11. Assemble your platter by transferring the celeriac and tomato mix
12. Serve!

Nutrition Values (Per Serving)

- Calories: 200
- Carbohydrate: 5g
- Protein: 12g
- Fat: 15gt
- Sugar: 1g
- Sodium: 36mg

Whiskey & Poached Peaches

(Serves: 4 / **Prep Time:** 15 minutes / **Sous Vide Cooking Time:** 30 minutes)

Ingredients

- 2 peaches, pitted and quartered
- ½ cup rye whiskey
- ½ cup ultrafine sugar
- 1 teaspoon vanilla extract
- A pinch of salt

How To

1. Prepare your Sous Vide water bath using your immersion circulator and raise the temperature to 180-degrees Fahrenheit
2. Place all the ingredients in a heavy-duty zip bag
3. Seal it using immersion method and submerge it in the hot water
4. Let it cook for about 30 minutes
5. Once the timer runs out, take the bag out and transfer it to an ice bath
6. Serve!

Nutrition Values (Per Serving)
- Calories: 656
- Carbohydrate: 162g
- Protein: 13g
- Fat: 3g
- Sugar: 147g
- Sodium: 8mg

Curried Apples

(Serves: 4 / **Prep Time:** 5 minutes / **Sous Vide Cooking Time:** 1 hour)

Ingredients
- 2 tart apples, cored, peeled and sliced
- 1 tablespoon Madras curry powder
- 2 tablespoons coconut cream

How To
1. Prepare your Sous Vide water bath using your immersion circulator and raise the temperature to 185-degrees Fahrenheit
2. Put all the ingredients into a heavy-duty resealable bag and seal it using the immersion method
3. Submerge and cook for 60 minutes
4. Remove the apples and transfer to a large bowl
5. Divide them among the serving plates and serve!

Nutrition Values (Per Serving)
- Calories: 368
- Carbohydrate: 70g
- Protein: 6g
- Fat: 8g
- Sugar: 17g
- Sodium: 450mg

Cardamom Apricots

(Serves: 4 / **Prep Time:** 15 minutes / **Sous Vide Cooking Time:** 1 hour)

Ingredients
- 1 pint small apricots, halved
- 1 tablespoon unsalted butter
- 1 teaspoon cardamom seeds, freshly ground

- ½ teaspoon ground ginger
- A pinch of smoked sea salt
- Fresh basil for garnishing, chopped

How To

1. Prepare your Sous Vide water bath by increasing the temperature to 180-degrees Fahrenheit using an immersion circulator
2. Put the butter, apricots, ginger, cardamom, and salt in a large, heavy-duty plastic bag, and mix them well
3. Carefully seal the bag using the immersion method and submerge it in the hot water
4. Let it cook for 60 minutes and remove the bag once done
5. Put the apricots in serving bowls
6. Garnish by topping it up with basil
7. Serve!

Nutrition Values (Per Serving)

- Calories: 270
- Carbohydrate: 60g
- Protein: 1g

- Fat: 0g
- Sugar: 49g
- Sodium: 33mg

Honey Kumquats

(Serves: 4 / **Prep Time:** 15 minutes / **Sous Vide Cooking Time:** 1 hour)

Ingredients

- 1 lb. kumquats
- ¼ cup honey
- ¼ teaspoon kosher salt

How To

1. Prepare your Sous Vide water bath using your immersion circulator and raise the temperature to 194-degrees Fahrenheit
2. Slice your Kumquats into ⅛ inch thick slices, carefully remove the stems and de-seed them
3. Put the honey, kumquat, and salt in a heavy-duty, resealable bag and seal it using the immersion method/water displacement method
4. Submerge it in the hot water and cook for 60 minutes
5. Prepare an ice bath and put the bag in the bath
6. Cool and serve!

Nutrition Values (Per Serving)

- Calories: 390
- Carbohydrate: 28g
- Protein: 5g
- Fat: 30g
- Sugar: 23g
- Sodium: 118mg

Squash Casseroles

(Serves: 4 / **Prep Time:** 30 minutes / **Sous Vide Cooking Time:** 1 hour)

Ingredients

- 2 tablespoons unsalted butter
- ¾ cup onion, chopped
- 1½ lbs. zucchini, quartered lengthwise and sliced into ¼ inch thick pieces
- Kosher salt as needed
- Ground black pepper as needed
- ½ cup whole milk
- 2 large whole eggs
- ½ cup crumbled plain potato chips for serving

How To

1. Prepare your water bath using your Sous Vide immersion circulator and raise the temperature to 176-degrees Fahrenheit
2. Take 4 x 1-pint canning jars and grease them
3. Take a large skillet and put it over medium heat. Add the butter, melt the butter
4. Add the onions and sauté for 7 minutes
5. Add the zucchini and sauté for 10 minutes and season with pepper and salt
6. Divide the zucchini mix into the greased jars and allow them to cool
7. Whisk the milk, salt, and eggs in a bowl
8. Grind some pepper and mix well
9. Divide the mixture amongst the jars and place the lids loosely on top
10. Submerge underwater and cook for 60 minutes
11. Allow to cool for few minutes and serve over potato chips

Nutrition Values (Per Serving)

- Calories: 319
- Carbohydrate: 29g
- Protein: 10g
- Fat: 19g
- Sugar: 3g
- Sodium: 539mg

Potato Confit

(Serves: 4 / **Prep Time:** 15 minutes / **Sous Vide Cooking Time:** 1 hour)

Ingredients

- 1 lb. small red potatoes
- 1 teaspoon kosher salt
- ¼ teaspoon ground white pepper
- 1 teaspoon chopped fresh rosemary
- 2 tablespoons whole butter
- 1 tablespoon corn oil

How To

1. Prepare the Sous Vide water bath using your immersion circulator and increase the temperature to 190-degrees Fahrenheit
2. Then cut the potatoes in half, carefully season the potatoes with rosemary, salt and pepper
3. Mix the potatoes with butter and oil
4. Transfer them to a heavy-duty, resealable bag and seal using the immersion method
5. Submerge underwater and cook for 60 minutes
6. Once done, add them into a large bowl, add the extra butter and serve

Nutrition Values (Per Serving)

- Calories: 314
- Carbohydrate: 53g
- Protein: 8g
- Fat: 10g
- Sugar: 6g
- Sodium: 306mg

Cauliflower Mash

(Serves: 4 / **Prep Time:** 10 minutes / **Sous Vide Cooking Time:** 2 hours)

Ingredients

- 1 lb. trimmed cauliflower
- ½ teaspoon garlic powder
- 1 teaspoon kosher salt
- 1 tablespoon butter
- 1 tablespoon heavy whipping cream

How To

1. Prepare the Sous Vide water bath using your immersion circulator and increase the temperature to 183-degrees Fahrenheit

2. Add the cauliflower, salt, garlic powder, and heavy whipping cream in a large resealable bag and seal using the immersion method
3. Cook for about 2 hours
4. Pour the contents into a blender and purée
5. Season and serve!

Nutrition Values (Per Serving)

- Calories: 307
- Carbohydrate: 14g
- Protein: 7g
- Fat: 28g
- Sugar: 3g
- Sodium: 206mg

Garlic & Rosemary Mashed Potatoes

(**Serves:** 4 / **Prep Time:** 25 minutes / **Sous Vide Cooking Time:** 90 minutes)

Ingredients

- 2 lbs. Russet potatoes
- 5 pieces' garlic cloves, peeled and mashed
- 8 oz. unsalted butter, melted
- 1 cup whole milk
- 3 sprigs rosemary
- Kosher salt as needed
- White pepper as needed

How To

1. Prepare your water bath using your Sous Vide immersion circulator and raise the temperature to 194-degrees Fahrenheit
2. Rinse the potatoes well under cold water
3. Peel the potatoes and slice them into ⅛ inch thick rounds
4. Put the potatoes, garlic, butter, 2 teaspoons of salt, and rosemary into a heavy-duty, resealable bag and seal using the immersion method
5. Cook for 1½ hours
6. Strain the mixture and pour into a medium-sized bowl
7. Transfer the potatoes to a large-sized bowl and mash them using a potato masher
8. Stir the melted butter and milk into your mashed potatoes
9. Season with salt and pepper
10. Garnish with rosemary and serve!

Nutrition Values (Per Serving)

- Calories: 184
- Carbohydrate: 6g
- Protein: 6g
- Fat: 6g
- Sugar: 3g
- Sodium: 449mg

Persimmon Chutney

(**Serves:** 4 / **Prep Time:** 25 minutes / **Sous Vide Cooking Time:** 90 minutes)

Ingredients

- 2 lbs. fuyu persimmons, peeled and diced into small pieces
- 1 small onion, diced
- ½ cup light brown sugar
- ¼ cup raisins
- 2 tablespoons apple cider vinegar
- 2 tablespoons freshly squeezed lemon juice
- 1½ teaspoons yellow mustard seeds
- 1½ teaspoons coriander seeds
- ½ teaspoon kosher salt
- ¼ teaspoon curry powder
- ¼ teaspoon dried ginger
- ⅛ teaspoon cayenne

How To

1. Prepare your Sous Vide water bath using your immersion circulator and raise the temperature to 183-degrees Fahrenheit
2. Put all the ingredients into a large, heavy-duty resealable bag
3. Seal it using the immersion method and submerge
4. Cook for 90 minutes
5. Once done, remove the bag and transfer it to a storage container
6. Serve cool

Nutrition Values (Per Serving)

- Calories: 313
- Carbohydrate: 79g
- Protein: 2g
- Fat: 1g
- Sugar: 28g
- Sodium: 509mg

Vegetable Frittata

(**Serves:** 5 / **Prep Time:** 35 minutes / **Sous Vide Cooking Time:** 1 hour)

Ingredients

- 1 tablespoon extra-virgin olive oil
- 1 medium onion, chopped
- Kosher salt as needed
- 4 cloves garlic, minced
- 1 small rutabaga, peeled and diced
- 2 medium-sized carrots, peeled and diced
- 1 medium-sized parsnip, peeled and diced
- 1 cup butternut squash, peeled and diced

- 6 oz. oyster mushrooms, roughly chopped and trimmed
- ¼ cup fresh parsley leaves, minced
- A pinch of red pepper flakes
- 5 large whole eggs
- ¼ cup whole milk

How To

1. Prepare your Sous Vide water bath using your immersion circulator and raise the temperature to 176-degrees Fahrenheit
2. Grease your canning jars with oil
3. Take a large-sized skillet and add the oil in it and place over a medium high heat
4. Add your onions to the heated skillet, stir cook for about 5 minutes, season with some salt
5. Add the garlic and stir cook for few more minutes
6. Add the carrots, rutabaga, mushrooms, butternut squash and parsnips, season with some salt and cook for 10-15 more minutes
7. Stir in the pepper flakes and parsley
8. Take a large liquid measuring cup and whisk in eggs and milk, season the mix with salt
9. Divide the egg mixture amongst the jars together with the vegetables
10. Wipe off the tops, using a damp cloth, and tighten the lids using the fingertip method
11. Place the jars in your water bath and cook them for 60 minutes
12. Once done, remove the jars from your water bath and remove the lids
13. Allow to cool and serve!

Nutrition Values (Per Serving)

- Calories: 465
- Carbohydrate: 34g
- Protein: 29g
- Fat: 23g
- Sugar: 5g
- Sodium: 516mg

Peas & Shallots

(Serves: 8 / **Prep Time:** 5 minutes / **Sous Vide Cooking Time:** 1 hour)

Ingredients

- 1 lb. fresh sweet peas
- 1 cup heavy cream
- ¼ cup butter
- 1 tablespoon cornstarch
- ¼ teaspoon ground nutmeg
- 4 cloves
- 2 bay leaves
- Freshly ground black pepper

How To

1. Prepare your water bath using your Sous Vide immersion circulator and raise the temperature to 184-degrees Fahrenheit

2. Put the cornstarch, butter, nutmeg and cream into a small bowl
3. Whisk well until the cornstarch has fully dissolved
4. Put the mixture into a zip bag together with the peas, black pepper, cloves, bay leaves, and seal using the immersion method
5. Submerge underwater and cook for 1 hour
6. Discard the bay leaf and serve!

Nutrition Values (Per Serving)

- Calories: 143
- Carbohydrate: 17g
- Protein: 6g
- Fat: 7g
- Sugar: 6g
- Sodium: 360mg

Apple & Cauliflower Soup

(**Serves:** 8 / **Prep Time:** 30 minutes / **Sous Vide Cooking Time:** 1 hour)

Ingredients

- 2 tablespoons extra-virgin olive oil
- 1 large onion, diced
- 2 garlic cloves, thinly sliced
- Kosher salt as needed
- ⅛ teaspoon crushed red chili flakes
- 1 large cauliflower head, chopped into medium florets
- 1 apple, peeled and diced
- 4-6 cups vegetable broth

How To

1. Prepare the Sous Vide water bath using your immersion circulator and increase the temperature to 183-degrees Fahrenheit
2. Place a medium-sized skillet over a medium heat, add the oil and allow the oil to shimmer
3. Add the onion, ¼ teaspoon of salt, and garlic and sauté for 7 minutes until they are tender
4. Add the chili flakes and stir well
5. Once done, turn-off the heat and allow the mixture to cool
6. Divide the apple, the onion mix, cauliflower, and ¼ teaspoon of salt between two individual resealable bags
7. Seal the bags using the immersion method, submerge and cook for 1 hour
8. Once done, remove the bag and place the contents in a large pot

9. Add the vegetable broth and blend well using an immersion blender
10. Add a bit more broth for a thicker consistency
11. Season with salt and serve

Nutrition Values (Per Serving)

- Calories: 192
- Carbohydrate: 19g
- Protein: 8g
- Fat: 11g
- Sugar: 11g
- Sodium: 11mg

Honey Miso Butter Corn

(Serves: 4 / **Prep Time:** 15 minutes / **Sous Vide Cooking Time:** 30 minutes**)**

Ingredients

- 4 ears of corn
- 6 tablespoons butter
- 2 tablespoons red miso paste
- 1 teaspoon honey
- Togarashi*
- Sesame oil
- 1 scallion, thinly sliced
- 1 teaspoon toasted sesame seeds

How To

1. Prepare the Sous Vide water bath using your immersion circulator and increase the temperature to 183-degrees Fahrenheit
2. First remove the husks, then silk from corn and cut the ears in half
3. Slather 2 teaspoons of butter on each piece of the corn
4. Transfer the corn to sous vide resealable zip bag and seal using the immersion method. Cook for 30 minutes.
5. Add 4 tablespoons of butter, 2 tablespoons of miso paste, 1 teaspoon of honey, the sesame oil, and Togarashi in a bowl
6. Whisk well. Allow to rest for 30 minutes in your fridge.
7. Finally, you can finish the corn with a searzall, blowtorch on the grill to create a nice char and spread the miso honey mixture on top
8. Sprinkle with sesame seeds and scallions.
9. Serve!

Nutrition Values (Per Serving)

- Calories: 238
- Carbohydrate: 36g
- Protein: 5g
- Fat: 11g
- Sugar: 20g
- Sodium: 423mg

(**Togarashi*** - Japanese 7 Spice Blend (Shichimi Togarashi) Spicy Japanese seasoning blend, also known as Shichimi Togarashi, includes chilies, sesame, orange peel, nori and more, is used to flavor soups, noodles dishes, grilled meats and seafood.)

Honey Poached Pears

(**Serves:** 2 / **Prep Time:** 5 minutes / **Sous Vide Cooking Time:** 45 minutes)

Ingredients

- 1 pear, thinly sliced
- 1 lb. honey
- ½ cup of walnuts
- 4 tablespoons shaved Parmesan
- 2 cups rocket leaves
- Salt and pepper as needed
- 2 tablespoons lemon juice
- 2 tablespoons extra-virgin olive oil

How To

1. Prepare your water bath using your Sous Vide immersion circulator and raise the temperature to 158.8-degrees Fahrenheit
2. Put the honey, smeared pears in a heavy-duty resealable bag
3. Seal using the immersion method and submerge
4. Cook for 45 minutes
5. Put the contents of the bag in a bowl
6. Add the remaining dressing ingredients and toss well
7. Serve!

Nutrition Values (Per Serving)

- Calories: 189
- Carbohydrate: 16g
- Protein: 9g
- Fat: 12g
- Sugar: 5g
- Sodium: 437mg

Pear & Walnut Salad

(Serves: 4 / **Prep Time:** 10 minutes / **Sous Vide Cooking Time:** 30 minutes)

Ingredients

- 2 tablespoons honey
- 2 pears, cored, halved and thinly sliced
- ½ cup walnuts, lightly toasted and roughly chopped
- ½ cup shaved parmesan
- 4 cups arugula
- Sea salt and pepper as needed

Garlic Dijon Dressing

- ¼ cup olive oil
- 1 tablespoon white wine vinegar
- 1 teaspoon Dijon mustard
- 1 garlic clove, minced
- Salt as needed

How To

1. Prepare your Sous Vide water bath using your immersion circulator and raise the temperature to 159-degrees Fahrenheit
2. Put the honey in a heat-proof bowl
3. Heat for 20 seconds
4. Put the pears in the honey and mix well
5. Put them in a heavy-duty resealable bag and seal using the immersion method
6. Cook for 30 minutes and plunge the bag into an ice water bath for 5 minutes
7. Chill in your fridge for 3 hours
8. Add all of the dressing ingredients and give the jar a nice shake
9. Leave it in your fridge for a while
10. Serve by placing the walnuts, arugula, and parmesan in a large bowl
11. Add your drained pear slices and the dressing
12. Toss everything well and season with pepper and salt

Nutrition Values (Per Serving)

- Calories: 377
- Carbohydrate: 56g
- Protein: 5g
- Fat: 14g
- Sugar: 35g
- Sodium: 165mg

Red Onions Balsamic Glaze

(Serves: 1 / **Prep Time:** 20 minutes / **Sous Vide Cooking Time:** 90 minutes)

Ingredients

- 3 medium-sized red onions
- 1 tablespoon unsalted butter
- Salt and pepper as needed
- 2 tablespoons balsamic vinegar
- 1 tablespoon honey
- 2 teaspoons of fresh thyme leaves

How To

1. Prepare the Sous Vide water bath using your immersion circulator and raise the temperature to 185-degrees Fahrenheit
2. Peel the skin of the onion, making sure to keep the roots intact
3. Cut the onion into wedges through the root end
4. Put a large skillet over a medium/high heat
5. Add the butter and allow to heat up and melt
6. Add the onion and season with pepper and salt, cook for about 10 minutes until nicely browned
7. Put the balsamic vinegar and simmer on low heat for 1 minute
8. Remove from the heat and carefully stir in the honey
9. Transfer the onions to a large, heavy-duty zipper bag
10. Seal the bag using the immersion method and submerge
11. Cook for 90 minutes
12. Once done, remove from the water and arrange the onions on a serving plate
13. Sprinkle with fresh thyme and serve with pizza or a sandwich

Nutrition Values (Per Serving)

- Calories: 141
- Carbohydrate: 19g
- Protein: 5g
- Fat: 6g
- Sugar: 6g
- Sodium: 87mg

Gnocchi Pillows with Parmesan

(Serves: 2 / **Prep Time:** 20 minutes / **Sous Vide Cooking Time:** 1 hour 30 min)

Ingredients

- 1 pack store-bought gnocchi
- 1 tablespoon unsalted butter
- ½ thinly sliced sweet onion

- Salt and black pepper as needed
- ½ cup frozen peas
- ¼ cup heavy cream
- ½ cup grated parmesan
- Salt and pepper as needed

How To

1. Prepare your water bath using your Sous Vide immersion circulator and raise the temperature to 183-degrees Fahrenheit
2. Put the gnocchi in a heavy-duty resealable bag
3. Seal using the immersion method and cook for 1½ hours
4. Once done, place a cast iron skillet over a medium heat
5. Add the butter and allow to melt
6. Add the onion and season with salt. Sauté for 3 minutes
7. Add the frozen peas and cream, and bring to a simmer
8. Stir in the gnocchi and grated parmesan, to coat with the cream sauce
9. Season with pepper and salt
10. Transfer to a plate and serve!

Nutrition Values (Per Serving)

- Calories: 189
- Carbohydrate: 16g
- Protein: 9g
- Fat: 12g
- Sugar: 5g
- Sodium: 517mg

Momofuku Styled Brussels

(Serves: 8 / **Prep Time:** 20 minutes / **Sous Vide Cooking Time:** 50 minutes)

Ingredients

- 2 lbs. Brussels sprouts, stems trimmed and slice in half
- 2 tablespoons extra-virgin olive oil
- ¼ teaspoon kosher salt
- ¼ cup fish sauce
- 2 tablespoons water
- 1½ tablespoons granulated sugar
- 1 tablespoon rice vinegar
- 1½ teaspoons lime juice
- 12 pieces thinly sliced Thai chilis
- 1 small minced garlic clove
- Chopped fresh mint
- Chopped fresh cilantro

How To

1. Prepare the Sous Vide water bath using your immersion circulator and raise the temperature to 183-degrees Fahrenheit
2. Put the Brussel sprouts, olive oil and salt in a heavy-duty, resealable bag
3. Seal using the immersion method
4. Cook for 50 minutes
5. Put the fish sauce, sugar, water, rice vinegar, lime juice, garlic, and chilis in a small bowl and mix them to prepare the vinaigrette
6. Once done, put the Brussels on an aluminum foil, lined baking sheet and heat up your broiler
7. Broil the Brussels for 5 minutes until they are charred
8. Transfer to a medium-sized bowl and add the vinaigrette
9. Toss well and sprinkle with mint and cilantro

Nutrition Values (Per Serving)

- Calories: 610
- Carbohydrate: 38g
- Protein: 10g
- Fat: 5g
- Sugar: 20g
- Sodium: 684mg

Cauliflower Puree

(Serves: 4 / **Prep Time:** 20 minutes / **Sous Vide Cooking Time:** 45 minutes)

Ingredients

- 1 head cauliflower
- 1 cup chicken stock
- 3 tablespoons unsalted butter
- ¾ teaspoon salt

How To

1. Prepare the Sous Vide water bath using your immersion circulator and increase the temperature to 185-degrees Fahrenheit
2. Remove a few leaves from the bottom part of the cauliflower core and cut into ¼ inch small slices
3. Put the cauliflower, butter and chicken stock in a heavy-duty, resealable bag
4. Seal using the immersion method
5. Submerge underwater and cook for 45 minutes
6. Once cooked, remove the bag and strain the contents through a metal mesh
7. Save the cooking liquid
8. Put the cauliflower to a blender and puree until smooth
9. Add some of the cooking liquid, season with salt and serve!

Nutrition Values (Per Serving)

- Calories: 171
- Carbohydrate: 29g
- Protein: 7g
- Fat: 5g
- Sugar: 4g
- Sodium: 6mg

Sweet Corn Soup

(**Serves:** 4 / **Prep Time:** 15 minutes / **Sous Vide Cooking Time:** 60 minutes)

Ingredients

- 4 ears of corn, shucked*
- 4 tablespoons unsalted butter
- 1 cup whole milk
- 1 bay leaf
- Kosher salt as needed
- Ground white pepper as needed
- 4 slices crispy cooked bacon
- 2 tablespoons minced chives

How To

1. Prepare the Sous Vide water bath using your immersion circulator and increase the temperature to 185-degrees Fahrenheit
2. Put the corn kernels, corn cobs, milk, 1 tablespoon of salt, 1 tablespoon of white pepper, and bay leaf into a heavy-duty, resealable bag and seal using the immersion method
3. Submerge the bag and allow it to cook for 1 hour
4. When ready, discard the corn cobs and bay leaf, and transfer the remaining mix to a blender
5. Puree for about 1 minute
6. Add some milk if you want to change the consistency
7. Season it with salt and pepper and serve with a garnish of bacon and chive

Nutrition Values (Per Serving)

- Calories: 374
- Carbohydrate: 11g
- Protein: 32g
- Fat: 32g
- Sugar: 3g
- Sodium: 592mg

(**Note: Shuck*** - Shucking is the process of removing the surrounding leaves from the corn. Once the corned is shucked, you have to shave off the corn kernels from the corn body.)

Butter Radish

(Serves: 4 / **Prep Time:** 15 minutes / **Sous Vide Cooking Time:** 45 minutes)

Ingredients

- 1 lb. radish, halved
- 3 tablespoons unsalted butter
- 1 teaspoon sea salt
- ½ teaspoon freshly ground black pepper

How To

1. Prepare the Sous Vide water bath using your immersion circulator and raise the temperature to 180-degrees Fahrenheit
2. Put all the listed ingredients into a medium-sized zip bag
3. Seal using the immersion method and allow it to cook underwater for about 45 minutes
4. Once done, remove the bag and transfer the contents to a platter
5. Serve!

Nutrition Values (Per Serving)

- Calories: 248
- Carbohydrate: 56g
- Protein: 1g
- Fat: 1g
- Sugar: 53g
- Sodium: 535mg

Cinnamon Poached Pears

(Serves: 8 / **Prep Time:** 40 minutes / **Sous Vide Cooking Time:** 30 minutes)

Ingredients

- 4 Bosc pears (firm yet ripe)

- 1 cup tawny port
- ½ cup granulated sugar
- 2 wide strips orange zest, 2 inches long and ½ inch wide
- 2 wide strips lemon zest, 2 inches long and ½ inch wide
- ½ teaspoon ground cinnamon
- Ice cream for flavor

How To

1. Set your Sous Vide immersion circulator to a temperature of 180-degrees Fahrenheit, and prepare your water bath

2. Peel the pears and add them in a heavy-duty zip bag, together with the remaining ingredients
3. Seal using the immersion method and cook for 30 minutes
4. Cool for 30 minutes and pour the liquid into a pan. Place it over medium heat and reduce the liquid by 2/3
5. Remove the heat and wait until the liquid is cooled
6. Core the pears diagonally and create fan shapes
7. Carefully transfer the pears to your serving plate and pour the previously prepared sauce on top
8. Serve with a topping of your favorite ice cream

Nutrition Values (Per Serving)

- Calories: 383
- Carbohydrate: 97g
- Protein: 1g
- Fat: 0g
- Sugar: 85g
- Sodium: 12mg

Mexican Street Corn

(Serves: 2 / **Prep Time:** 5 minutes / **Sous Vide Cooking Time:** 30 minutes)

Ingredients

- 2 ears of corn, shucked
- 2 tablespoons cold butter
- Kosher salt as needed
- Fresh ground pepper
- ¼ cup mayonnaise
- ½ tablespoon Mexican style chili powder
- ½ teaspoon grated lime zest
- ¼ cup crumbled Queso Fresco**
- ¼ cup chopped, fresh cilantro

How To

1. Prepare the Sous Vide water bath using your immersion circulator and increase the temperature to 183-degrees Fahrenheit
2. Put the corn ears and butter in a zip bag
3. Season with salt and pepper and seal using the immersion method
4. Cook for 30 minutes
5. Once done, remove the corn
6. Add the mayo, lime zest, and chili powder into a small bag and mix
7. Place the Queso Fresco on a small plate
8. Spread 1 tablespoon of mayonnaise mixture on top of the corn ears, and roll them on the cheese
9. Sprinkle with salt and fresh cilantro and serve!

Nutrition Values (Per Serving)

- Calories: 373
- Carbohydrate: 30g
- Protein: 15g
- Fat: 24g
- Sugar: 9g
- Sodium: 587mg

(**Note: Queso Fresco**** - Queso Blanco, with similar cheeses including queso fresco, is a creamy, soft, and mild unaged white cheese)

Schmaltzy Brussels Sprouts

(**Serves:** 4 / **Prep Time:** 10 minutes / **Sous Vide Cooking Time:** 30 minutes)

Ingredients

- 1 lb. Brussels sprouts
- ¼ cup schmaltz (such as rendered chicken, duck or goose fat)
- ½ teaspoon salt
- Pepper as needed

How To

1. Prepare the Sous Vide water bath using your immersion circulator and increase the temperature to 183-degrees Fahrenheit
2. Trim the Brussels to halve and quarter them
3. Put them in a zip bag and season with salt and pepper
4. Add the schmaltz and mix well
5. Seal the bag using the immersion method
6. Submerge and cook for 30 minutes
7. Remove from the bag and serve!

Nutrition Values (Per Serving)

- Calories: 246
- Carbohydrate: 23g
- Protein: 12g
- Fat: 13g
- Sugar: 4g
- Sodium: 351mg

Green Beans & Mandarin Hazelnuts

(Serves: 9 / **Prep Time:** 5 minutes / **Sous Vide Cooking Time:** 60 minutes)

Ingredients

- 1 lb. green beans, trimmed
- 2 small mandarin oranges
- 2 tablespoons butter
- ½ teaspoon salt
- 2 oz. toasted hazelnuts

How To

1. Prepare the Sous Vide water bath using your immersion circulator and increase the temperature to 185-degrees Fahrenheit
2. Put the green beans, butter, and salt in a zip bag
3. Zest one of the mandarins into the bag and keep the other for later use
4. Cut the zested mandarin in half and squeeze the juice into the bag
5. Use the immersion method to seal the bag
6. Submerge and cook for 60 minutes
7. Pre-heat your oven to 400-degrees Fahrenheit and toast the hazelnuts for 7 minutes
8. Remove the skin and chop roughly
9. Serve by putting the beans on a platter and topping them up with a garnish of toasted hazelnut and the remaining mandarin zest

Nutrition Values (Per Serving)

- Calories: 520
- Carbohydrate: 48g
- Protein: 40g
- Fat: 18g
- Sugar: 8g
- Sodium: 131mg

Sous Vide Cactus

(Serves: 4 / **Prep Time:** 15 minutes / **Sous Vide Cooking Time:** 60 minutes)

Ingredients

- 2 tablespoons freshly squeezed lime juice
- 1 tablespoon canola oil
- 1 clove garlic, thinly sliced
- 1 teaspoon ground coriander
- 1 teaspoon ground cumin
- 1 teaspoon salt
- 4 cactus paddles, thorns removed

How To

1. Prepare the Sous Vide water bath using your immersion circulator and increase the temperature to 175-degrees Fahrenheit
2. Whisk the lime juice, garlic, oil, coriander, cumin and salt in a small bowl
3. Transfer to a zip bag and add the cactus
4. Seal using the immersion method and cook for 60 minutes
5. Once cooked, remove the bag from the water and take out the cactus
6. Discard the cooking liquid
7. Remove the skin from the cactus with a vegetable peeler and slice into thin strips
8. Serve!

Nutrition Values (Per Serving)

- Calories: 59
- Carbohydrate: 11g
- Protein: 2g
- Fat: 2g
- Sugar: 4g
- Sodium: 262mg

Asparagus Vinaigrette

(Serves: 2 / **Prep Time:** 20 minutes / **Sous Vide Cooking Time:** 15 minutes)

Ingredients

- 1 Bunch large asparagus
- Salt and pepper as needed
- ¼ cup extra-virgin olive oil
- 1 teaspoon Dijon mustard
- 1 teaspoon red wine vinegar
- 1 hard-boiled egg, cooled and roughly chopped
- Fresh parsley, chopped

How To

1. Prepare the Sous Vide water bath using your immersion circulator and increase the temperature to 185-degrees Fahrenheit
2. Slice up the fibrous bottom of the asparagus and discard it
3. Peel the bottom three-quarters of the stalks and place them, in a single layer, in a zip bag
4. Season with salt and pepper and seal using the immersion method and cook for 15 minutes
5. For the vinaigrette, put the olive oil, vinegar and Dijon mustard in a bowl and mix them well
6. Season with salt and transfer to a mason jar. Seal tightly and shake until emulsified

7. Remove the bag and transfer to an ice bath
8. Discard the cooking liquid and serve with a topping of egg, parsley, and the vinaigrette

Nutrition Values (Per Serving)

- Calories: 139
- Carbohydrate: 9g
- Protein: 5g
- Fat: 10g
- Sugar: 4g
- Sodium: 469mg

Ma Po Tofu

(Serves: 6 / **Prep Time:** 15 minutes / **Sous Vide Cooking Time:** 90 minutes)

Ingredients

- 1 cup vegetable broth
- 2 tablespoons tomato paste
- 1 tablespoon grated ginger
- 1 tablespoon rice wine vinegar
- 1 tablespoon agave nectar
- 2 teaspoons sriracha sauce
- 3 cloves minced garlic
- 1 teaspoon soy sauce
- 2 boxes cubed silken tofu

How To

1. Prepare the Sous Vide water bath using your immersion circulator and increase the temperature to 185-degrees Fahrenheit
2. Whisk all of the listed ingredients in a bowl, except the tofu
3. Put the tofu in a zip bag and add the mixture
4. Seal the bag using the immersion method and cook for 1½ hours
5. Serve!

Nutrition Values (Per Serving)

- Calories: 560
- Carbohydrate: 83g
- Protein: 33g
- Fat: 14g
- Sugar: 1g
- Sodium: 402mg

Buttered Beets & Orange

(Serves: 4 / **Prep Time:** 15 minutes / **Sous Vide Cooking Time:** 90 minutes)

Ingredients

- 1 lb. medium red beets, peeled and quartered
- 2 tablespoons unsalted butter
- 2 peeled oranges, cut into Supreme
- 1 tablespoon honey
- 3 tablespoons balsamic vinegar
- 4 tablespoons extra virgin olive oil
- Kosher salt and black pepper as needed
- 6 oz. baby romaine leaves
- ½ cup pistachios, chopped and roasted
- ½ cup Parmigiano Reggiano/Parmesan Cheese

How To

1. Prepare the Sous Vide water bath using your immersion circulator and increase the temperature to 180-degrees Fahrenheit
2. Put the beets in a plastic zip bag and add the butter
3. Seal using the immersion method, and cook for 90 minutes
4. Once cooked, take the beets out from the bag and discard the cooking liquid
5. Whisk the honey, oil and vinegar, with a seasoning of salt and pepper, in a bowl
6. Toss the romaine leaves, orange, beets and vinaigrette, and divide the whole mixture amongst four platters
7. Top the servings with pistachio and Parmigiano Reggiano cheese and serve!

Nutrition Values (Per Serving)

- Calories: 130
- Carbohydrate: 17g
- Protein: 3g
- Fat: 6g
- Sugar: 12g
- Sodium: 591mg

CHAPTER 2 | POULTRY

Ginger Marmalade Chicken

(Serves: 4 / **Prep Time:** 7 minutes / **Sous Vide Cooking Time:** 4 hours)

Ingredients
- 2 lbs. bone-in skin-on chicken
- 4 tablespoons marmalade of your choice
- 2 tablespoons minced ginger
- Salt and pepper as needed

How To
1. Prepare your water bath using your Sous Vide immersion circulator, and raise the temperature to 170-degrees Fahrenheit
2. Season the chicken with salt and pepper
3. Put the ingredients (including the chicken) in a heavy-duty, resealable bag and seal using the immersion method
4. Submerge the bag and cook for 4 hours
5. Transfer the cooked chicken to a baking dish
6. Heat the broiler to a temperature of 500-degrees Fahrenheit
7. Arrange a rack, making sure it is 20 cm away from the heat source
8. Place the baking dish to the broiler and broil for 10 minutes until crispy
9. Remove and serve!

Nutrition Values (Per Serving)
- Calories: 726
- Carbohydrate: 9g
- Protein: 64g
- Fat: 48g
- Sugar: 2g
- Sodium: 291mg

Honey Dredged Duck Breast

(Serves: 3 / **Prep Time:** 7 minutes / **Sous Vide Cooking Time:** 3½ hours)

Ingredients
- 1 x 6 oz. boneless duck breast
- ¼ teaspoon cinnamon
- ¼ teaspoon smoked paprika
- ¼ teaspoon cayenne pepper
- 1 teaspoon honey
- Salt and pepper as needed

How To

1. Prepare your water bath using your Sous Vide immersion circulator and raise the temperature to 134.9-degrees Fahrenheit
2. Remove the duck breast from the packaging and pat dry using a kitchen towel
3. Score the skin of the duck breast using a crosshatch pattern - do not cut the flesh, sprinkle some salt over
4. Take a medium sized frying pan/skillet and place it on your stove over medium-high heat
5. Put the breast in the pan and cook for 3-4 minutes, making sure the skin side is facing down
6. Remove the breast from your pan and set it on a surface
7. Add the paprika, cayenne pepper and cinnamon in a small bowl and mix everything well
8. Spread the mixture over the duck breast and season, add some additional salt and pepper
9. Now put the breast in a heavy-duty, resealable bag with a teaspoon of honey and seal the bag using the immersion method and submerge it underwater
10. Cook for about 3½ hours and take it out once done
11. Pat dry and place in a frying pan over high heat to sear for about 2 minutes, make sure you keep the skin side facing down
12. Flip it and sear for another 30 seconds, allow to rest and serve!

Nutrition Values (Per Serving)

- Calories: 304
- Carbohydrate: 25g
- Protein: 18g
- Fat: 15g
- Sugar: 19g
- Sodium: 612mg

Lemon Grass Chicken Dish

(**Serves:** 3 / **Prep Time:** 5 minutes / **Sous Vide Cooking Time:** 45 minutes)

Ingredients

- 1 lb. chicken breast
- 1 stalk of fresh lemon grass, chopped
- 2 tablespoons fish sauce
- 2 tablespoons coconut sugar
- ½ teaspoon salt
- 1 tablespoon chili garlic sauce

How To

1. Prepare your water bath using your Sous Vide immersion circulator and raise the temperature to 150-degrees Fahrenheit
2. Cut the chicken into bite size portions and put them in a bowl
3. Chop the lemon grass and place in a blender

4. Add the fish sauce, sugar, and salt and blend well
5. Pour the marinade over your chicken and mix well
6. Insert skewers into the chicken
7. Keep repeating until all the chicken has been used
8. Place the skewered chicken in a heavy-duty, resealable bag, seal them using the immersion method and submerge and cook for 45 minutes
9. Remove the bag transfer it to a water bath to chill
10. Remove the chicken from the bag and slice it up even more if you prefer
11. Brush with chili-garlic sauce
12. Sear the chicken on a skillet over medium heat and then serve

Nutrition Values (Per Serving)
- Calories: 304
- Carbohydrate: 34g
- Protein: 22g
- Fat: 9g
- Sugar: 7g
- Sodium: 529mg

Special Tips
It is recommended that before placing the skewers inside the bag, you cushion the pointed ends with a piece of meat to make sure the skewers don't penetrate through the bag.

Waldorf Chicken Salad

(Serves: 4 / **Prep Time:** 15 minutes / **Sous Vide Cooking Time:** 120 minutes)

Ingredients
- 2 skinless chicken breasts, boneless
- ½ teaspoon ground black pepper
- 1 tablespoon corn oil
- 1 Granny Smith apple, cored and diced
- 1 teaspoon lime juice
- ½ cup red grapes, cut in half
- 1 stick rib celery, diced
- 1/3 cup mayonnaise
- 2 teaspoons Chardonnay wine
- 1 teaspoon Dijon mustard
- 1 tablespoon kosher salt
- 1 Romaine lettuce head
- ½ cup walnuts, toasted and chopped

How To
1. Prepare your water bath using your Sous Vide immersion circulator, and increase the temperature to 145-degrees Fahrenheit
2. Take the chicken and season it with black pepper and salt. Put the seasoned chicken breast and corn oil in a large, resealable bag and seal using the immersion method
3. Cook for 2 hours and then remove the bag

4. Put the apple slices in a large-sized bowl, add the lime juice, and toss them well.
5. Add the celery and red grapes and stir well
6. Put the mayonnaise, Dijon mustard, and Chardonnay wine in a small bowl and mix well
7. Pour the whole mixture over the fruits and give them a nice toss
8. Remove the chicken breast from the plastic bag and discard the liquid
9. Dice the breast and place in a medium-sized bowl
10. Add some kosher salt and toss well
11. Put the seasoned chicken in with the rest of the salad and toss well
12. Dived your romaine lettuce amongst the salad bowls, spoon the salad on top of the lettuce, and garnish with some walnuts
13. Serve!

Nutrition Values (Per Serving)

- Calories: 304
- Carbohydrate: 34g
- Protein: 22g

- Fat: 9g
- Sugar: 7g
- Sodium: 529mg

Sous Vide Poached Chicken

(Serves: 4 / **Prep Time:** 45 minutes / **Sous Vide Cooking Time:** 6 hours)

Ingredients

- 1 whole bone-in chicken, trussed
- 1-quart low sodium chicken stock
- 2 tablespoons soy sauce
- 5 sprigs fresh thyme
- 2 dried bay leaves
- 2 cups thickly sliced carrots

- Salt and pepper as needed
- ½ tablespoon olive oil
- 2 cups thickly sliced celery
- ½ oz. dried mushrooms
- 3 tablespoons unsalted butter

How To

1. Prepare your Sous Vide water bath using your immersion circulator and raise the temperature to 150-degrees Fahrenheit
2. Add the soy sauce, chicken, stock, herbs and veggies in a heavy-duty zip bag and seal using the immersion method and cook for 6 hours
3. Remove the chicken and strain the veggies
4. Pat dry and season with the olive oil, pepper and salt
5. Roast in your oven for 10 minutes at 450-degrees Fahrenheit
6. Simmer the cooking liquid in a large saucepan
7. Once done, turn off the heat and whisk in the butter

8. Carve the chicken, making sure to discard the skin
9. Divide the veggies and chicken between the platters and serve with the sauce on top

Nutrition Values (Per Serving)

- Calories: 435
- Carbohydrate: 17g
- Protein: 34g

- Fat: 26g
- Sugar: 5g
- Sodium: 342mg

Rare Duck Breast

(Serves: 2 / **Prep Time:** 10 minutes / **Sous Vide Cooking Time:** 120 minutes)

Ingredients

- 2 duck breasts
- ¼ cup olive oil

- 4 sprigs thyme
- Salt and pepper as needed

How To

1. Prepare your Sous Vide water bath using your immersion circulator and raise the temperature to 135-degrees Fahrenheit
2. Transfer the duck breast to a hot pan and sear them for 1-2 minutes per side
3. Place in a zip bag with the olive oil and thyme
4. Cook for 2 hours
5. Sear them again for 1-2 minutes in a hot pan
6. Allow them to rest and slice
7. Sprinkle with salt and pepper and serve

Nutrition Values (Per Serving)

- Calories: 434
- Carbohydrate: 8g
- Protein: 47g

- Fat: 24g
- Sugar: 1g
- Sodium: 645mg

Moroccan Chicken Salad

(Serves: 2 / **Prep Time:** 10 minutes / **Sous Vide Cooking Time:** 60 minutes)

Ingredients

- 6 chicken tenderloins

- 4 cups pumpkin, cubed and roasted

- 4 cups rocket tomatoes
- 4 tablespoons sliced almonds
- Juice of 1 lemon
- 2 tablespoons olive oil
- 4 tablespoons red onion, chopped
- 2 pinches paprika
- 2 pinches turmeric
- 2 pinches cumin
- 2 pinches salt

How To

1. Prepare your water bath using your Sous Vide immersion circulator and raise the temperature to 140-degrees Fahrenheit
2. Add all the spices and chicken in a zip-bag. Coat the chicken well
3. Seal using the immersion method and cook for 60 minutes
4. Sear for 1 minute on each side afterwards
5. Put the remaining ingredients in another bowl and toss well
6. Top them up with the chicken and serve!

Nutrition Values (Per Serving)

- Calories: 261
- Carbohydrate: 6g
- Protein: 19g
- Fat: 18g
- Sugar: 4g
- Sodium: 418mg

Korean Chicken Wings

(Serves: 2 / **Prep Time:** 20 minutes / **Sous Vide Cooking Time:** 2 hours)

Ingredients

- 8 chicken wings
- 2 tablespoons low-sodium soy sauce
- 2 tablespoons rice vinegar
- 2 tablespoons light brown sugar
- ½ teaspoon ginger powder
- ½ teaspoon sesame oil
- 1 tablespoon chili sauce
- A pinch of white pepper
- Salt and freshly ground black pepper as needed
- 1 scallion, finely chopped
- 1 tablespoon unsalted peanuts, toasted and chopped

How To

1. Prepare your Sous Vide water bath, using your immersion circulator and raise the temperature to 147-degrees Fahrenheit.
2. Season the wings with pepper and salt.
3. Put the wings in the Sous Vide zip bag and seal using the immersion method and cook for 2 hours

4. While the wings are cooking, mix together vinegar, sugar, soy sauce, chili sauce, ginger powder, sesame oil, and white pepper in a medium saucepan.
5. Bring to a rapid simmer over medium heat and continue to simmer until reduced by half. Move to a large bowl and set aside.
6. Once the cooking is done, take out the bag from water. Remove the wings and pat dry them. Discard the cooking liquid and heat broiler to high
7. Move the wings to bowl with sauce and toss to coat. Place wings and remaining sauce onto a foil-lined rimmed baking sheet.
8. Broil wings for about 10 minutes or until slightly charred and sauce is sticky
9. Top with scallion and peanuts and serve.

Nutrition Values (Per Serving)

- Calories: 915
- Carbohydrate: 15g
- Protein: 41g
- Fat: 279g
- Sugar: 1g
- Sodium: 813mg

Panko Crusted Chicken

(Serves: 4 / **Prep Time:** 30 minutes / **Sous Vide Cooking Time:** 60 minutes)

Ingredients

- 4 boneless chicken breasts
- 1 cup panko bread crumbs
- 1 lb. sliced mushrooms
- Small bunch of thyme
- 2 eggs
- Salt and pepper as needed
- Canola oil as needed

How To

1. Prepare your water bath using your Sous Vide immersion circulator, and increase the temperature to 150-degrees Fahrenheit
2. Season the chicken with salt, and thyme
3. Place the breast in a resealable bag and seal using the immersion method and cook for 60 minutes
4. Then, place a pan over medium heat, add the mushrooms and cook them until the water has evaporated
5. Add 3-4 sprigs of thyme and stir
6. Once cooked, remove the chicken from the bag and pat dry
7. Add the oil and heat it up over medium-high heat. Add the eggs into a container and dip the chicken in egg wash until well coated.
8. Add the panko bread crumbs in a shallow container and add some salt and pepper. Put the chicken to bread crumbs and coat until well covered.
9. Fry the chicken for 1-2 minutes per side and serve with the mushrooms

Nutrition Values (Per Serving)

- Calories: 394
- Carbohydrate: 71g
- Protein: 19g
- Fat: 5g
- Sugar: 5g
- Sodium: 59mg

Clementine Chicken Breast

(Serves: 2 / **Prep Time:** 30 minutes / **Sous Vide Cooking Time:** 150 minutes)

Ingredients

- 1½ tablespoons freshly squeezed orange juice
- 1½ tablespoons freshly squeezed lemon juice
- 1½ tablespoons brown sugar
- 1 tablespoon Pernod
- 1 tablespoon extra-virgin olive oil
- 1 tablespoon whole grain mustard
- 1 teaspoon fennel seeds
- 1 teaspoon kosher salt
- ¾ teaspoon freshly ground black pepper
- 2 chicken breasts, bone in, skin on
- 1 medium-sized fennel bulb, trimmed, thinly sliced up (reserve the fronds for later use)
- 2 clementines, unpeeled, cut into ¼ inch thick slices
- Chopped parsley for garnishing

How To

1. Prepare your water bath using your Sous Vide immersion circulator and raise the temperature to 146-degrees Fahrenheit
2. Put the lemon juice, orange juice, Pernod, olive oil, fennel seeds, brown sugar, mustard, salt and pepper in a large bowl, give it a good mix
3. Put the chicken breast, sliced clementine and sliced fennel in a large, resealable zip bag and add the orange mixture
4. Seal using the immersion method and cook for 2½ hours
5. Set the broiler to high heat. Prepare a broiler safe baking dish and line it with aluminum foil
6. Once cooked, take the bag out from the water bath and transfer the contents to the baking sheet
7. Broil for 3-6 minutes to char slightly
8. Transfer the juice from the bag into a small saucepan and simmer for about 5-10 minutes

9. Put the chicken and vegetables on a platter and drizzle the sauce all over.
10. Sprinkle with parsley and fennel fronds and serve!

Nutrition Values (Per Serving)

- Calories: 304
- Carbohydrate: 34g
- Protein: 22g

- Fat: 9g
- Sugar: 7g
- Sodium: 519mg

Chicken & Melted Leeks

(Serves: 4 / **Prep Time:** 15 minutes / **Sous Vide Cooking Time:** 45 minutes)

Ingredients

- 4 x 6 oz. skinless chicken breast
- Salt and pepper as needed
- 3 tablespoons butter
- 1 large leek, cleaned and sliced crossways
- ½ cup panko
- 2 tablespoons chopped parsley
- 1 oz. cheddar cheese
- 1 tablespoon olive oil

How To

1. Prepare your water bath using your Sous Vide immersion circulator and raise the temperature to 145-degrees Fahrenheit
2. Take the chicken breast and season it generously on both sides with salt and pepper and put in a zip bag
3. Seal using the immersion method and cook for 45 minutes
4. Take a skillet and add 2 tablespoon of butter over medium heat, allow the butter to heat up and add the leeks
5. Stir to coat them
6. Season with salt and pepper
7. Then, lower down the heat to low and cook for additional 10 minutes
8. Put a clean skillet over a medium heat. Put in a tablespoon of butter
9. Add the panko and toast, and stir well until the panko is hot
10. Spoon the panko mixture from the skillet into a separate bowl and add the cheddar cheese and chopped up parsley, mix well
11. Once the chicken breasts are thoroughly cooked, remove them from the bag and pat dry

12. Heat the olive oil over a high heat and sear the breasts for 1 minute
13. Serve each breast on the melted leek, and top with the toasted panko/cheese mix

Nutrition Values (Per Serving)

- Calories: 803
- Carbohydrate: 11g
- Protein: 51g
- Fat: 61g
- Sugar: 3g
- Sodium: 323mg

Moroccan Chicken Meal

(**Serves:** 2 / **Prep Time:** 15 minutes / **Sous Vide Cooking Time:** 60 minutes)

Ingredients

- 6 chicken tenderloin
- 4 cups pumpkin, cut into cubes and roasted
- 4 cups rocket lettuce
- 4 tablespoons sliced almonds
- Juice of 1 lemon
- 2 tablespoons olive oil
- 4 tablespoons red onion, chopped
- 2 pinches paprika
- 2 pinches turmeric
- 2 pinches cumin
- 2 pinches salt

How To

1. Prepare your water bath using your Sous Vide immersion circulator, and raise the temperature to 140-degrees Fahrenheit
2. Put the chicken and the seasoning in a heavy-duty, resealable bag
3. Seal it using the immersion/water displacement method
4. Submerge the bag and let it cook for about 60 minutes
5. Once done, take the chicken out from the bag and sear the tenderloins in a very hot pan, allowing 1 minute per side
6. Put all the remaining ingredients in a serving bowl and toss them well
7. Cover the chicken with your salad and serve!

Nutrition Values (Per Serving)

- Calories: 304
- Carbohydrate: 34g
- Protein: 22g
- Fat: 9g
- Sugar: 7g
- Sodium: 529mg

Chicken Breast Meal

(Serves: 2 / **Prep Time:** 5 minutes / **Sous Vide Cooking Time:** 60 minutes)

Ingredients

- 1-piece boneless chicken breast
- Salt and pepper as needed
- Garlic powder as needed

How To

1. Prepare your water bath using your Sous Vide immersion circulator, and increase the temperature to 150-degrees Fahrenheit
2. Carefully drain the chicken breast and pat dry using a kitchen towel
3. Season the breast with garlic powder, pepper and salt
4. Place in a resealable bag and seal using the immersion method
5. Submerge and cook for 1 hour
6. Serve!

Nutrition Values (Per Serving)

- Calories: 150
- Carbohydrate: 0g
- Protein: 18g
- Fat: 8g
- Sugar: 0g
- Sodium: 257mg

Special Tips

Remember that the time it takes to Sous Vide chicken breast depends on their size. If the breast is 1 inch in length, it will take 1 hour and if it is 2 inches long, it will take 2 hours, and so on....

Spicy Adobo Chicken

(Serves: 2 / **Prep Time:** 5 minutes / **Sous Vide Cooking Time:** 120 minutes)

Ingredients

- 2 chicken leg quarters
- 2 garlic cloves, crushed
- ¼ teaspoon whole black peppercorns
- ½ tablespoon molasses
- ¼ cup dark soy sauce
- Salt as needed
- 1 tablespoon canola oil
- ½ Worcestershire sauce
- 1 bay leaf
- ¼ cup white vinegar

How To

1. Mix the soy sauce, Worcestershire, peppercorns, molasses, garlic, bay leaf and salt.
2. Add the chicken legs in a Sous Vide bag with the marinade and refrigerate for 12 hours or overnight.
3. Prepare your Sous Vide water bath, using your immersion circulator, and raise the temperature to 165-degrees Fahrenheit
4. Submerge the chicken and cook for 2 hours
5. Remove the chicken legs from the bag and air dry for 10-15 minutes.
6. Sear over medium heat in a nonstick pan with canola oil
7. Add the sauce from the bag to the pan and keep cooking until you have reached the desired consistency
8. Serve the chicken with sauce!

Nutrition Values (Per Serving)

- Calories: 320
- Carbohydrate: 33g
- Protein: 16g
- Fat: 14g
- Sugar: 3g
- Sodium: 255mg

Ginger Duck Breast

(Serves: 2 / **Prep Time:** 20 minutes / **Sous Vide Cooking Time**: 120 minutes)

Ingredients

- 2 boneless duck breasts
- Kosher salt and pepper as needed
- 1-inch fresh ginger, peeled and sliced thinly
- 2 garlic cloves, thinly sliced
- 1½ teaspoons sesame oil

How To

1. Prepare your water bath, using your Sous Vide immersion circulator, and raise the temperature to 135-degrees Fahrenheit
2. Season the duck breasts with pepper and salt
3. Put the breasts in a zip bag and add the ginger, sesame oil and garlic
4. Seal using the immersion method, and cook for 2 hours
5. Remove the duck and discard the garlic, ginger and cooking liquid
6. Place the duck breast in a cold, non-stick skillet and put it over a high heat
7. Cook the breast with the skin side down for about 30 seconds, flip, and cook for another 30 seconds

8. Then place the breasts on a cutting board to rest for 5 minutes
9. Slice the breasts and serve with your desired side dishes

Nutrition Values (Per Serving)

- Calories: 365
- Carbohydrate: 19g
- Protein: 18g
- Fat: 25g
- Sugar: 13g
- Sodium: 63mg

Greek Meatballs

(Serves: 4 / **Prep Time:** 20 minutes / **Sous Vide Cooking Time:** 120 minutes)

Ingredients

- 1 lb. ground chicken
- 1 tablespoon extra-virgin olive oil
- 2 garlic cloves, minced
- 1 teaspoon fresh oregano, minced
- 1 teaspoon kosher salt
- ½ teaspoon grated lemon zest
- ½ teaspoon freshly ground black pepper
- ¼ cup panko bread crumbs
- Lemon wedges for serving

How To

1. Prepare your Sous Vide water bath, using your immersion circulator, and raise the temperature to 146-degrees Fahrenheit
2. Add the garlic, olive oil, chicken, oregano, lemon zest, salt, and pepper in a medium-sized bowl
3. Mix well everything using your hands and gently mix in the panko bread crumbs
4. Form the mixture into 14 balls
5. Put the balls in a resealable bag and seal using the immersion method
6. Submerge the bag and cook for 2 hours
7. Remove the bag and transfer the balls to a baking sheet (lined with foil)
8. Set your broiler to high heat
9. Broil the balls for 5-7 minutes until they turn brown
10. Serve with lemon wedges

Nutrition Values (Per Serving)

- Calories: 238
- Carbohydrate: 3g
- Protein: 8g
- Fat: 21g
- Sugar: 2g
- Sodium: 332mg

Jamaican Jerk Chicken

(**Serves:** 3 / **Prep Time:** 5 minutes / **Sous Vide Cooking Time:** 190 minutes)

Ingredients

- 2 lbs. chicken wings
- 2 tablespoons jerk seasoning
- ¼ cup fresh cilantro for garnishing, chopped

How To

1. Prepare your Sous Vide water bath using your immersion circulator, and increase the temperature to 145-degrees Fahrenheit
2. Put the chicken and jerk seasoning in a resealable, heavy-duty plastic bag and seal the bag using the immersion method
3. Carefully transfer the bag under the pre-heated water bath and allow to cook for about 3 hours
4. Once done, take the bag out from the water and remove the wings, pat the wings dry with kitchen towel
5. Heat up your grill to high, and put the wings under it
6. Lower down the heat of your grill to medium and cook the chicken until crispy and slightly brown
7. Remove from the grill and add some jerk paste
8. Garnish with chopped cilantro
9. Serve

Nutrition Values (Per Serving)

- Calories: 330
- Carbohydrate: 4g
- Protein: 24g
- Fat: 23g
- Sugar: 1g
- Sodium: 311mg

Bacon Wrapped Chicken

(**Serves:** 2 / **Prep Time:** 15 minutes / **Sous Vide Cooking Time:** 3 hours)

Ingredients

- 2 chicken breasts
- 2 strips bacon
- 2 tablespoons Dijon mustard
- 1 tablespoon grated parmesan cheese
- ½ teaspoon salt

How To

1. Prepare your water bath using your Sous Vide immersion circulator, and raise the temperature to 145-degrees Fahrenheit
2. Season the chicken with salt and spread Dijon mustard on both sides
3. Sprinkle with parmesan cheese
4. Wrap the bacon around the chicken breast and place in a zip bag
5. Cook for 3 hours
6. Remove the chicken and pat dry
7. Sear until crispy
8. Serve!

Nutrition Values (Per Serving)

- Calories: 284
- Carbohydrate: 5g
- Protein: 18g
- Fat: 21g
- Sugar: 2g
- Sodium: 563mg

Chicken Caprese

(Serves: 2 / **Prep Time:** 5 minutes / **Sous Vide Cooking Time**: 45 minutes)

Ingredients

- 2 chicken breasts, boneless, skinless
- Salt and pepper as needed
- 2 teaspoons unsalted butter
- 4 cups lettuce
- 1 large tomato, sliced
- 1 oz fresh mozzarella, sliced
- 2 tablespoons red onion, diced
- Fresh basil leaves
- 1 tablespoon extra-virgin olive oil
- 2 lemon wedges for serving

How To

1. Prepare your Sous Vide water bath, using your immersion circulator, and raise the temperature to 145-degrees Fahrenheit
2. Season the chicken with pepper and salt
3. Add them in a large zip bag and seal using the immersion method and cook for 45 minutes
4. Once cooked, remove the chicken from the bag and discard the cooking liquid
5. Place a large skillet over a medium/high heat
6. Add the butter and allow to heat
7. Add the chicken breasts and sear until they turn golden brown
8. Transfer to a serving platter

9. Divide the lettuce among the breasts and top up with tomato, red onion, mozzarella, and basil
10. Season with pepper and salt and then drizzle the olive oil over the top
11. Serve with lemon wedges

Nutrition Values (Per Serving)

- Calories: 440
- Carbohydrate: 5g
- Protein: 30g

- Fat: 33g
- Sugar: 3g
- Sodium: 524mg

Stuffed Cornish Hen

(**Serves:** 5 / **Prep Time:** 45 minutes / **Sous Vide Cooking Time**: 4 hours)

Ingredients

- 2 whole Cornish game hens
- 4 tablespoons unsalted butter plus 1 tablespoon extra, melted
- 2 cups shitake mushrooms, thinly sliced
- 1 cup leeks, finely diced
- ¼ cup walnuts, coarsely chopped
- 1 tablespoon fresh thyme, minced
- 1 cup cooking wild rice
- ¼ cup dried cranberries
- 1 tablespoon honey

How To

1. Prepare your water bath using your Sous Vide immersion circulator, and raise the temperature to 150-degrees Fahrenheit
2. Take a large sized skillet and place it over medium heat
3. Once the skillet is hot, add 3 tablespoons of butter and allow the butter to melt
4. Add the mushrooms, thyme, leek and walnuts and cook for 5-10 minutes
5. Stir in the rice, cranberries and remove from the heat, allow to cool for 10 minutes
6. Divide the stuffing between the hen cavities
7. Truss the legs together tightly and put the hens in a zip bag
8. Seal using the immersion method and cook for 4 hours
9. Remove the hens and pat dry
10. Set your broiler to high heat
11. Add the honey and the extra tablespoon of melted butter in a small bowl

12. Brush the mixture over the hens
13. Broil for 2 minutes and then serve

Nutrition Values (Per Serving)

- Calories: 1196
- Carbohydrate: 70g
- Protein: 69g
- Fat: 72g
- Sugar: 11g
- Sodium: 523mg

Five Spice Chicken Breast

(Serves: 4 / **Prep Time:** 20 minutes / **Sous Vide Cooking Time**: 75 minutes)

Ingredients

- 1½ lbs. chicken breast, boneless and skinless
- ¼ cup onions, finely chopped
- 2 tablespoons soy sauce
- 1 tablespoon honey
- 1 teaspoon sesame oil
- 1 clove garlic, minced
- ¾ teaspoon Chinese five spice powder
- Coconut basmati rice for serving

How To

1. Prepare your Sous Vide water bath, using your immersion circulator, and raise the temperature to 146-degrees Fahrenheit
2. Add the chicken, onions, honey, soy sauce, sesame oil, garlic and five spice powder into a zip bag
3. Seal using the immersion method and cook for 75 minutes
4. Heat your broiler
5. Once cooked, remove the chicken from the bag and broil for around 5 minutes until it turns golden brown
6. Cut the chicken into medallions and serve on top of coconut basmati rice

Nutrition Values (Per Serving)

- Calories: 936
- Carbohydrate: 11g
- Protein: 82g
- Fat: 64g
- Sugar: 5g
- Sodium: 407mg

Chicken Mint Pea Feta

(Serves: 8 / **Prep Time:** 10 minutes / **Sous Vide Cooking Time**: 75 minutes)

Ingredients

- 6 chicken breast tenderloins, boneless
- 4 tablespoons extra virgin-olive oil
- Salt and pepper as needed
- 2 cups green peas, blanched
- 1 cup mint, freshly torn
- ½ cup crumbled feta cheese
- 1 tablespoon freshly squeezed lemon juice
- 2 teaspoons honey
- 2 teaspoons red wine vinegar

How To

1. Prepare your water bath, using your Sous Vide immersion circulator, and increase the temperature to 140-degrees Fahrenheit
2. Put the chicken and 2 tablespoons of olive oil in a zip bag
3. Season with pepper and salt
4. Seal using the immersion method, and cook for 75 minutes
5. Add the peas, feta cheese and mint in a large bowl
6. Whisk the lemon juice, red wine vinegar, honey and 2 tablespoons of olive oil in a small bowl
7. Season with salt and pepper
8. Once cooked, take the chicken out from the bag and chop it into bite sized pieces
9. Discard the cooking liquid and toss the salad with the chicken and the dressing
10. Serve!

Nutrition Values (Per Serving)

- Calories: 252
- Carbohydrate: 29g
- Protein: 16g
- Fat: 8g
- Sugar: 10g
- Sodium: 534mg

Duck Breast with Calamansi Sauce

(Serves: 2 / **Prep Time:** 15 minutes / **Sous Vide Cooking Time:** 120 minutes)

Ingredients

- 2 duck breasts
- 1 teaspoon ground coriander and ginger powder
- 1 teaspoon of garlic powder

- Salt and pepper as needed
- 2 tablespoons olive oil

For Sauce
- 1 tablespoon butter
- 1 sprig of thyme
- 1 garlic clove, minced
- 1 small shallot, minced
- 3 tablespoons calamansi juice
- Cooking juice (from the Sous Vide bag)

How To

1. Prepare your Sous Vide water bath using your immersion circulator, and increase the temperature to 134-degrees Fahrenheit
2. Take a knife and score the skin of the duck breast in a cross-hatch pattern and season it with coriander, garlic and ginger powder
3. Place the breasts in a sous vide bag and seal using the immersion method
4. Submerge and cook for 2 hours
5. Put some oil in a pan, place it over medium heat
6. Add the duck and sear until crispy, flip and sear the other side for 1 minute
7. Use the same pan for the sauce ingredients. Add all the sauce ingredients and simmer until thickened.
8. Slice the duck and drizzle the sauce over
9. Serve!

Nutrition Values (Per Serving)

- Calories: 373
- Carbohydrate: 15g
- Protein: 41g
- Fat: 16g
- Sugar: 5g
- Sodium: 420mg

Chicken Roulade

(**Serves:** 2 / **Prep Time:** 30 minutes / **Sous Vide Cooking Time:** 90 minutes)

Ingredients

- 1 x 8 oz chicken breast
- ¼ cup goat cheese
- ¼ cup julienned roasted red pepper
- ½ cup loosely packed arugula

- 6 slices prosciutto
- Salt and pepper as needed
- 1 tablespoon oil for searing

Tools Required: Plastic wrap, wine/vinegar bottle

How To

1. Prepare your water bath, using your Sous Vide immersion circulator, and raise the temperature to 155-degrees Fahrenheit
2. Drain the chicken breast if needed, and place it between plastic wrap. Pound it using a mallet or the side of wine bottle, until it gets ¼ inch thick
3. Cut in half and season both sides with pepper and salt
4. Spread 2 tablespoons of goat cheese on top and top each half with roasted red peppers
5. Top with half the arugula
6. Roll both breasts like sushi
7. Place 3 layers of prosciutto on your work surface (overlapping each other)
8. Put the rolled chicken at the base of the prosciutto and roll it all up to enclose the roulade
9. Place in a zip bag and seal using the immersion method and cook for 90 minutes
10. Take out of the bag and sear
11. Slice and then serve

Nutrition Values (Per Serving)

- Calories: 513
- Carbohydrate: 6g
- Protein: 47g
- Fat: 32g
- Sugar: 2g
- Sodium: 527mg

Sous Vide Turkey Breast

(Serves: 6 / **Prep Time:** 15 minutes / **Sous Vide Cooking Time:** 180 minutes)

Ingredients

- 1 (3 lbs.) turkey breast half, boneless with skin on
- 1 tablespoon extra-virgin olive oil
- 1 tablespoon garlic salt
- 1 teaspoon freshly ground black pepper

How To

1. Prepare your water bath, using your Sous Vide immersion circulator, and increase the temperature to 145-degrees Fahrenheit

2. Season the turkey breast with garlic, salt and pepper
3. Put the seasoned turkey in a heavy-duty, resealable zip bag
4. Add the olive oil to the bag
5. Seal, using the immersion method, and submerge underwater. Cook for 3 hours
6. Remove the bag and pat the breast dry using a kitchen towel
7. Place an iron skillet over a high heat
8. Put the turkey breast in the skillet and sear for about 5 minutes until it turns golden brown and serve!

Nutrition Values (Per Serving)

- Calories: 178
- Carbohydrate: 6g
- Protein: 24g
- Fat: 6g
- Sugar: 5g
- Sodium: 453mg

Special Tips

While searing the breast, it is highly recommended you keep the "skin" side down in order to achieve maximum flavor in your meal.

Mushroom Sauce & Chicken Breast

(**Serves:** 2 / **Prep Time:** 20 minutes / **Sous Vide Cooking Time:** 4 hours)

Ingredients

For Chicken

- 2 skinless boneless chicken breast
- 1/8 teaspoon salt
- 1 teaspoon vegetable oil

For Mushroom and Cream Sauce

- 3 finely chopped French shallots
- 2 finely chopped garlic cloves
- 1 teaspoon olive oil
- 2 tablespoon butter
- 1 cup sliced mushrooms
- 2 tablespoon port wine
- ½ a cup chicken stock
- 1 cup cream
- ¼ teaspoon cracked black pepper

How To

1. Prepare the Sous Vide water bath using your immersion circulator, and raise the temperature to 140-degrees Fahrenheit
2. Season the breast with salt and transfer them to your zip bag, seal using the immersion method
3. Submerge under water bath and cook for 4 hours
4. Remove the bag and transfer to an ice bath, allow it to chill for few minutes and dry off
5. Place a non-stick skillet on medium-heat, add the oil and allow the oil to heat up
6. Add the shallots and stir cook for 2-3 minutes, add the butter, garlic and stir for 1 minute more
7. After 1 minute, carefully increase the temperature to medium-high heat and add the mushrooms, cook until they release the liquid
8. Then, add the port wine, chicken stock and cook for 2 minutes, add the cream
9. Keep cooking over medium heat until the sauce thickens, add the pepper and salt
10. Heat up a grill pan to smoking hot, take out the chicken breast from the bag and put oil on both sides
11. Cook on your grill pan giving 1 minute to each side
12. Serve with the sauce!

Nutrition Values (Per Serving)

- Calories: 334
- Carbohydrate: 9g
- Protein: 34g
- Fat: 17g
- Sugar: 4g
- Sodium: 428mg

Pheasant Breast

(Serves: 2 / **Prep Time:** 15 minutes / **Sous Vide Cooking Time**: 45 minutes)

Ingredients

- 2 pheasant breasts, bone in
- Kosher salt as needed
- Fresh ground black pepper to taste
- 2 tablespoons unsalted butter
- 3 sprigs of thyme
- 1 tablespoon extra-virgin olive oil

How To

1. Prepare your Sous Vide water bath, using your immersion circulator, and raise the temperature to 145-degrees Fahrenheit
2. Season the pheasant breast with pepper and salt and place them in a zip bag
3. Add the butter and thyme
4. Seal using the immersion method and cook for 45 minutes
5. Once done, remove the pheasant and pat dry
6. Discard the cooking liquid
7. Place a large, non-stick skillet over a medium heat and add the oil
8. Once the oil is heated, add the pheasant, skin side down, in the skillet
9. Sear for 2 minutes and serve!

Nutrition Values (Per Serving)

- Calories: 283
- Carbohydrate: 3g
- Protein: 17g
- Fat: 21g
- Sugar: 71
- Sodium: 145mg

Fried Chicken

(Serves: 4 / **Prep Time:** 10 minutes / **Sous Vide Cooking Time:** 1 hour)

Ingredients

- 8 pieces chicken, legs or thighs
- Salt and pepper as needed
- Lemon wedges for serving

For Wet Mix
- 2 cups soy milk
- 1 tablespoon lemon juice

For Dry Mix
- 1 cup plain, high protein flour
- 1 cup rice flour
- ½ cup cornstarch
- 2 tablespoons paprika
- 2 tablespoons salt
- 2 tablespoons ground black pepper

How To

1. Prepare your sous vide water bath to a temperature of 154.4-degrees Fahrenheit, using your immersion circulator
2. Season your chicken pieces well with pepper and salt and seal them in a resealable bag using the water immersion method

3. Cook them in the water bath for 1 hour
4. Remove the chicken and place it to one side. Allow it to sit for 15-20 minutes
5. Take a pan and place it on the stove, pour in some oil and pre-heat to a temperature of 400-425-degrees Fahrenheit
6. Take a large-sized bowl and add the soy milk and lemon juice, whisk them well
7. Use another bowl to mix the protein flour, rice flour, cornstarch, paprika, salt and ground black pepper
8. Gently dip the cooked chicken in the dry mix, then dip into the wet mixture
9. Repeat 2-3 times then place the prepared chickens on a wire rack
10. Keep repeating until all the chicken has been used
11. Fry the chicken in small batches for about 3-4 minutes for each batch
12. Once done, allow the chicken to cool on the wire rack for 10-15 minutes
13. Serve with some lemon wedges and sauce!

Nutrition Values (Per Serving)

- Calories: 251
- Carbohydrate: 10g
- Protein: 28g
- Fat: 11g
- Sugar: 4g
- Sodium: 458mg

Special Tips

It is wise to rub the turkey legs with olive oil before searing them. This will allow them to take on a much crispier texture and help avoid burning.

Turkey Meatballs

(Serves: 4 / **Prep Time:** 20 minutes / **Sous Vide Cooking Time:** 60 minutes)

Ingredients

- 1 lb. ground turkey
- 3 scallions, finely chopped
- 1 large egg, beaten
- 1 tablespoon seasoned breadcrumbs
- 1 teaspoon dried oregano
- Salt and pepper as needed
- ½ cup of pesto (plus 2 teaspoons extra)
- 2 oz. mozzarella, torn into ¼ oz. pieces
- 4 large dinner rolls

How To

1. Prepare your Sous Vide water bath using your immersion circulator, and increase the temperature to 145-degrees Fahrenheit
2. Add the turkey, egg, breadcrumbs, scallions and oregano in a medium-sized bowl

3. Mix well and season the mixture with salt and pepper
4. Give it a good mix again to incorporate everything
5. Form 8 balls, using the mixture, and put a light indent in each, using your thumb
6. Top the balls using ¼ teaspoon of pesto and ¼ ounce of mozzarella cheese
7. Press well to ensure the pesto and cheese has been engulfed by the meat
8. Shape the balls again
9. Place the balls in 2 resealable zip bags and seal them using the immersion method
10. Submerge underwater and cook for 60 minutes
11. Once cooked, remove the balls and pat dry using the kitchen towels
12. Take a non-stick skillet and put it over a medium heat and heat ½ cup of pesto
13. Add in the meatballs and stir well to coat them with the pesto
14. Place 2 meatballs in each of the dinner rolls and serve!

Nutrition Values (Per Serving)

- Calories: 771
- Carbohydrate: 72g
- Protein: 58g
- Fat: 29g
- Sugar: 9g
- Sodium: 629mg

Thai Green Curry Noodle Soup

(Serves: 2 / **Prep Time:** 45 minutes / **Sous Vide Cooking Time:** 90 minutes)

Ingredients

- 1 chicken breast, boneless and skinless
- Salt and pepper as needed
- 1 can (13.5 oz.) coconut milk
- 2 tablespoons Thai Green Curry Paste
- 1¾ cups chicken stock
- 1 cup enoki mushrooms
- 5 kaffir lime leaves, torn in half
- 2 tablespoons fish sauce
- 1½ tablespoons palm sugar
- ½ cup Thai basil leaves, roughly chopped
- 2 oz cooked egg noodle nests
- 1 cup cilantro, roughly chopped
- 1 cup bean sprouts
- 2 tablespoons fried noodles
- 2 red Thai chilis, roughly chopped

How To

1. Prepare your water bath using your Sous Vide immersion circulator, and raise the temperature to 140-degrees Fahrenheit
2. Take the chicken and season it generously with salt and pepper and place it in a medium-sized, resealable bag with 1 tablespoon of coconut milk
3. Seal it using the immersion method and submerge. Cook for 90 minutes

4. After 35 minutes, place a medium-sized saucepan over a medium heat
5. Add the green curry paste and half the coconut milk
6. Bring the mix to a simmer and cook for 5-10 minutes until the coconut milk starts to show a beady texture
7. Add the chicken stock and the rest of the coconut milk and bring the mixture to a simmer once again, keep cooking for about 15 minutes
8. Add the kaffir lime leaves, enoki mushrooms, palm sugar and fish sauce
9. Lower the heat to medium-low and simmer for about 10 minutes
10. Remove from the heat and season with palm sugar and fish sauce, stir in the basil
11. Once the chicken is cooked fully, transfer it to a cooking board. Let it cool for few minutes and then cut into slices
12. Serve the chicken with the curry sauce and a topping of cooked egg noodles
13. Garnish the chicken with some bean sprouts, cilantro, Thai chilies and fried noodles. Serve!

Nutrition Values (Per Serving)

- Calories: 237
- Carbohydrate: 21g
- Protein: 15g
- Fat: 11g
- Sugar: 5g
- Sodium: 567mg

Chicken Parmesan Balls

(Serves: 6 / **Prep Time:** 30 minutes / **Sous Vide Cooking Time:** 45 minutes)

Ingredients

- 1 lb. ground chicken
- 2 tablespoons onion, finely chopped
- ¼ teaspoon garlic powder
- Salt and pepper as needed
- 2 tablespoons seasoned breadcrumbs
- 1 egg
- 32 small, diced cubes of mozzarella cheese
- 1 tablespoon butter
- 3 tablespoons panko
- ½ cup tomato sauce
- ½ oz. grated parmesan cheese
- Chopped parsley for garnishing

How To

1. Prepare your Sous Vide water bath using your immersion circulator, and raise the temperature to 145-degrees Fahrenheit
2. Mix the chicken with onion, salt, garlic powder, pepper and seasoned bread crumbs in a bowl
3. Add the egg and mix well
4. Scoop out 32 balls
5. Top each ball with 1 cube of cheese and press the meat around the cheese

6. Put the balls in a zip bag and chill for 20 minutes
7. Seal the bag using the immersion method and cook for 45 minutes
8. Remove the balls from the bag
9. Melt butter over a medium-high heat and add the panko
10. Cook until golden brown. Warm the tomato sauce
11. Transfer the balls in a serving dish and top with tomato sauce, panko and cheese
12. Garnish with chopped parsley and serve by piercing them with a toothpick

Nutrition Values (Per Serving)

- Calories: 277
- Carbohydrate: 15g
- Protein: 16g
- Fat: 17g
- Sugar: 2g
- Sodium: 414mg

Chicken & Avocado Salad

(Serves: 2 / **Prep Time:** 5 minutes / **Sous Vide Cooking Time:** 75 minutes)

Ingredients

- 1 chicken breast
- 1 avocado, sliced
- 10 pieces of halved cherry tomatoes
- 2 cups chopped lettuce
- 2 tablespoons olive oil
- 1 tablespoon lemon juice
- 1 garlic clove, crushed
- Salt and pepper as needed
- 2 teaspoons honey

How To

1. Prepare your Sous Vide water bath, using your immersion circulator, and raise the temperature to 140-degrees Fahrenheit
2. Add the breast to a Sous Vide zip bag and seal using the immersion method, submerge and cook for 75 minutes
3. Season the breast with salt and pepper
4. Pan fry 1 tablespoon of olive oil for 30 seconds
5. Slice the breasts
6. Add the garlic, lemon juice, honey and olive oil in a small bowl
7. Add the lettuce, cherry tomatoes and avocado and toss
8. Top the salad with chicken and season with pepper and salt
9. Serve!

Nutrition Values (Per Serving)

- Calories: 520
- Carbohydrate: 13g
- Protein: 68g
- Fat: 22g
- Sugar: 5g
- Sodium: 214mg

Sweet Chili Chicken

(Serves: 2 / **Prep Time:** 30 minutes / **Sous Vide Cooking Time:** 120 minutes)

Ingredients

- 4 chicken thighs
- 2 tablespoons olive oil
- Salt and pepper as needed
- 1 garlic clove, crushed
- 3 tablespoons fish sauce
- ¼ cup lime juice
- 1 tablespoon palm sugar
- 3 tablespoons Thai basil, chopped
- 3 tablespoons cilantro, chopped
- 2 red chilies (deseeded), chopped
- 1 tablespoon sweet chili sauce

How To

1. Prepare your water bath using your Sous Vide immersion circulator, and increase the temperature to 150-degrees Fahrenheit
2. Cover the chicken thighs with cling film and chill them for a while
3. Place them in a zip bag along with the olive oil, salt and pepper, and seal using the immersion method
4. Cook for 2 hours
5. Once done, heat the olive oil in a pan and chop the chicken into 4-5 pieces
6. Dip them in the veggie oil and cook until crispy
7. Combine all the above dressing ingredients in a bowl and place to one side
8. Sprinkle with salt on top and serve with the sauce

Nutrition Values (Per Serving)

- Calories: 721
- Carbohydrate: 9g
- Protein: 46g
- Fat: 54g
- Sugar: 4g
- Sodium: 572mg

Lemon Grass Salad

(Serves: 2 / **Prep Time:** 20 minutes / **Sous Vide Cooking Time:** 75 minutes)

Ingredients

- 2 chicken breasts, skinless
- Salt and pepper as needed
- Vegetable oil
- 1 cup unsalted cashews
- 2 tablespoons palm sugar

- 4 red Thai chilis, thinly sliced
- 1 garlic clove, peeled
- 3 tablespoons fish sauce
- 2 teaspoons freshly squeezed lime juice
- 1 cup cilantro, roughly chopped
- 1 scallion, thinly sliced
- 1 stalk lemon grass, white part only slightly bruised and thinly sliced
- 1 piece 2-inch ginger, julienned

How To

1. Prepare your Sous Vide water bath using your immersion circulator, and increase the temperature to 140-degrees Fahrenheit
2. Take the chicken and season it with salt and pepper, place the chicken in a zip bag and seal using the immersion method and cook for 75 minutes
3. After 60 minutes, heat 1 inch of vegetable oil, in a medium-sized saucepan, to 350-degrees Fahrenheit over a medium-high heat
4. Add the cashews and golden fry them for 1 minute, dry them
5. Pound the palm sugar, garlic, and chili in a mortar and pestle
6. Add the fish sauce and lime juice
7. Once the timer has finished, remove the bag from the water bath and take out the chicken
8. Allow to cool, once the chicken has reached the room temperature, take a knife and cut the chicken in bite-sized pieces and put in a bowl
9. Add the dressings and toss
10. Add the cilantro, ginger, lemon grass, scallion, and fried cashews and mix well
11. Garnish with additional chilis and serve!

Nutrition Values (Per Serving)

- Calories: 470
- Carbohydrate: 18g
- Protein: 44g

- Fat: 26g
- Sugar: 7g
- Sodium: 231mg

Coconut Chicken

(Serves: 2 / **Prep Time:** 10 minutes / **Sous Vide Cooking Time:** 60 minutes)

Ingredients

- 2 chicken breasts
- 4 tablespoons coconut milk
- Salt and pepper as needed

For Sauce
- 4 tablespoons satay sauce
- 2 tablespoons coconut milk
- Dash of fish sauce

How To

1. Prepare your Sous Vide water bath using your immersion circulator, and raise the temperature to 140-degrees Fahrenheit
2. Add the chicken in a zip bag and add the salt, pepper and 4 tablespoons of milk
3. Seal using the immersion method and cook for 60 minutes
4. Once done, mix the sauce ingredients in a bowl and microwave for 30 seconds
5. Slice the chicken and arrange on serving platter
6. Pour the sauce on top!
7. Serve

Nutrition Values (Per Serving)

- Calories: 923
- Carbohydrate: 51g
- Protein: 71g
- Fat: 50g
- Sugar: 3g
- Sodium: 216mg

Chicken Saltimbocca

(Serves: 4 / **Prep Time:** 15 minutes / **Sous Vide Cooking Time**: 90 minutes)

Ingredients

- 4 small chicken breasts, boneless, skinless
- 8 sage leaves
- 4 pieces of thinly sliced prosciutto
- Freshly ground black pepper
- 1 tablespoon extra-virgin olive oil
- 2 oz. grated provolone

How To

1. Prepare your Sous Vide water bath using your immersion circulator, and increase the temperature to 145-degrees Fahrenheit
2. Transfer the chicken breast to a very clean flat surface and season with pepper and salt
3. Top each of the chicken breast with sage leaves and 1 slice of prosciutto
4. Place them in a zip bag and seal using the immersion method and cook for 90 minutes
5. Once cooked, remove the chicken from the bag and pat dry
6. Add some oil in a large skillet over a medium-high heat

7. Put the chicken and prosciutto and sear for 1 minute
8. Give the chicken pieces a flip and top each of the pieces with 1 tablespoon of provolone
9. Cover the skillet with lid and cook for 30 seconds to allow the cheese to melt
10. Add the chicken on a serving platter and garnish with sage leaves
11. Serve!

Nutrition Values (Per Serving)

- Calories: 299
- Carbohydrate: 5g
- Protein: 24g
- Fat: 20g
- Sugar: 0g
- Sodium: 403mg

Zucchini Mini Chicken Bites

(Serves: 2 / **Prep Time:** 30 minutes / **Sous Vide Cooking Time**: 75 minutes)

Ingredients

- 1 chicken breast, boneless, skinless, butterflied
- Salt and pepper as needed
- 3 tablespoons extra-virgin olive oil
- 1 tablespoon pesto
- 1 zucchini, sliced into ¼ inch pieces
- ¼ cup water
- 1 avocado
- 1 cup fresh basil leaves

How To

1. Prepare your Sous Vide water bath using your immersion circulator, and raise the temperature to 140-degrees Fahrenheit
2. Pound the chicken breast with mallet until it has an even thickness, season with pepper and salt and place in a zip bag
3. Add 1 tablespoon of oil and the pesto and seal using the immersion method and cook for 75 minutes
4. After 60 minutes, heat 1 tablespoon of olive oil in large skillet over a medium-high heat, and add the zucchini and water
5. Cook until the water has evaporated
6. Once cooked, carefully remove the bag from the water bath and take out the chicken
7. Heat the remaining oil over a medium/high heat. Allow it to shimmer
8. Add in the chicken and sear for 2 minutes per side
9. Transfer the chicken on a cutting board and allow it to cool for 5 minutes
10. Slice it into pieces, roughly the same size as the zucchini

11. Slice the avocado to the same size
12. Serve by stacking slices of avocado on top of the chicken and topping them with a slice of zucchini and a basil leaf
13. Secure with toothpicks and drizzle olive oil over and then serve!

Nutrition Values (Per Serving)

- Calories: 260
- Carbohydrate: 36g
- Protein: 11g
- Fat: 7g
- Sugar: 3g
- Sodium: 416mg

Singaporean Chicken Wings

(Serves: 2 / **Prep Time:** 15 minutes / **Sous Vide Cooking Time**: 120 minutes)

Ingredients

- ¾ teaspoon soy sauce
- ¾ teaspoon Chinese rice wine
- ¾ teaspoon honey
- ¼ teaspoon five-spice
- 2 whole chicken wings
- ½ inch fresh ginger
- 1 clove garlic, smashed
- Sliced scallions for serving

How To

1. Prepare your Sous Vide water bath using your immersion circulator, and raise the temperature to 160-degrees Fahrenheit
2. Add the soy sauce, rice wine, honey and five spice in a bowl and mix well
3. Place the chicken wings, garlic, ginger in a zip bag
4. Seal using the immersion method and cook for 120 minutes
5. Heat your broiler to high heat and line a broil-safe baking sheet with aluminum foil
6. Remove the wings and transfer to your broiling pan
7. Broil for 3-5 minutes
8. Then, arrange on a serving platter and sprinkle some sliced scallions over it
9. Serve!

Nutrition Values (Per Serving)

- Calories: 402
- Carbohydrate: 11g
- Protein: 21g
- Fat: 18g
- Sugar: 6g
- Sodium: 340mg

CHAPTER 3 | FISH & SHELLFISH

Slow Cooker Shellfish

(Serves: 2 / **Prep Time:** 30 minutes / **Sous Vide Cooking Time:** 60 minutes)

Ingredients

- 4 oz. canned snails
- ¼ cup dry white wine
- 1 diced celery stalk
- 1 diced carrot
- 1 quartered shallot
- 1 bay leaf
- 1 tablespoon black peppercorn (plus an additional teaspoon of ground black pepper)
- 1 tablespoon extra-virgin olive oil
- 8 tablespoons unsalted butter, room temperature
- 1 tablespoon minced fresh parsley
- 2 garlic cloves, minced
- 2 teaspoons kosher salt
- ¼ cup panko breadcrumbs
- Sliced up baguette

How To

1. Prepare your Sous-vide water bath to a temperature of 154-degrees Fahrenheit
2. Take a large-sized, heavy-duty resealable bag and add in the snails, shallots, celery, carrots, wine, peppercorns, olive oil, and bay leaf
3. Seal the bag using the immersion method, submerge it underwater and cook for about 60 minutes
4. Take a stand mixer and add the butter in
5. Add the parsley, salt, garlic, and ground pepper and mix gently until all the ingredients are finely mixed
6. Put the mixture to a plastic wrap and roll it into a small log
7. Compress the log, using the plastic wrap, and let it chill in the fridge
8. Once the snails are done, remove them from the bag and discard any cooking liquid alongside the vegetables
9. Set your broiler to high heat
10. Arrange your snails in a large-sized ramekin and slice the butter into thin rounds
11. Place the butter on top of your snails
12. Sprinkle some breadcrumbs over the butter and broil for about 3 minutes until the crumbs are done
13. Serve with some warmed baguette slices!

Nutrition Values (Per Serving)

- Calories: 252
- Carbohydrate: 2g
- Protein: 8g
- Fat: 24g
- Sugar: 0g
- Sodium: 125mg

Shrimp Salad

(Serves: 4 / **Prep Time:** 10 minutes / **Sous Vide Cooking Time:** 24 minutes)

Ingredients

- 1 chopped red onion
- Juice of 2 limes
- 1 teaspoon extra-virgin olive oil
- ¼ teaspoon sea salt
- ⅛ teaspoon white pepper
- 1 lb. (450 g) raw shrimp, peeled and de-veined
- 1 diced tomato
- 1 diced avocado
- 1 jalapeno, seeded and diced
- 1 tablespoon chopped cilantro

How To

1. Prepare your Sous-vide water bath to a temperature of 148-degrees Fahrenheit
2. Add the lime juice, red onion, sea salt, white pepper, extra virgin olive oil, white pepper and shrimp into your heavy-duty plastic bag
3. Seal the bag using the immersion method
4. Submerge the bag underwater and cook for 24 minutes
5. Remove and chill the plastic bag in an ice bath for about 10 minutes
6. Take a large-sized bowl and add the tomato, avocado, jalapeno and cilantro
7. Remove it from the bag and top it up with the salad.
8. Serve!

Nutrition Values (Per Serving)

- Calories: 148
- Carbohydrate: 7g
- Protein: 24g
- Fat: 2g
- Sugar: 3g
- Sodium: 548mg

Moroccan Red Snapper

(Serves: 4 / **Prep Time:** 10 minutes / **Sous Vide Cooking Time:** 30 minutes)

Ingredients

- 4 pieces cleaned red snapper
- 2 tablespoons butter
- Salt and pepper as needed

For Citrus Sauce

- 1 lemon
- 1 grapefruit

- 1 lime
- 3 oranges
- 2 tablespoons canola oil
- 1 yellow onion
- 1 diced zucchini
- 1 teaspoon saffron threads
- 1 teaspoon diced chili pepper
- 1 tablespoon sugar
- 3 cups fish stock
- 3 tablespoons chopped cilantro

How To

1. Prepare your Sous-vide water bath to a temperature of 132-degrees Fahrenheit
2. Season the snapper fillets with salt and pepper and transfer them to a heavy-duty Sous Vide zip bag. (use multiple bags if necessary)
3. Divide the butter equally between the bags if more than one bag is used. If not, add the whole amount of butter to the single bag
4. Seal using the immersion method and submerge underwater, cook for 30 minutes
5. While the fish is being cooked, start preparing your sauce by peeling the fruits and dicing up the flesh (make sure to remove the pith)
6. Take a large-sized pan and place it over medium-heat, add the oil and allow it to heat up
7. Add in the onion and zucchini and sauté for 2-3 minutes
8. Add the saffron, fruits, diced pepper and sugar and cook for 1 more minute
9. Add the fish stock and bring the mix to a boil, lower down the heat to low and simmer for 10 minutes
10. Remove the heat and stir in cilantro, keep it on the side
11. Take the fish out from the bag and transfer them to your serving platter
12. Spoon the fruity-saffron sauce over the top and serve

Nutrition Values (Per Serving)

- Calories: 285
- Carbohydrate: 21g
- Protein: 32g
- Fat: 5g
- Sugar: 3g
- Sodium: 602mg

Shrimp & Leek

(Serves: 4 / **Prep Time:** 20 minutes / **Sous Vide Cooking Time:** 60 minutes)

Ingredients

- 6 leeks
- 5 tablespoons extra-virgin olive oil
- Kosher salt as needed
- Freshly ground black pepper
- 1 small-sized shallot, minced
- 1 tablespoon champagne vinegar
- 1 teaspoon Dijon mustard
- 1/3 lb. cooked bay shrimp
- Chopped fresh parsley for garnishing

How To

1. Prepare your Sous-vide water bath to a temperature of 183-degrees Fahrenheit
2. Cut off the top of your leeks and discard them
3. Trim the root ends of each leek and wash them in cold water
4. Brush the leek with 1 tablespoon of olive oil
5. Season with salt and put the leeks in a large-sized zipper bag and seal it using the immersion method
6. Submerge the bag underwater and cook for about 1 hour
7. To make the vinaigrette, take a small-sized bowl and whisk the shallot, Dijon mustard, vinegar and ¼ cup of olive oil all together. Season with some salt and pepper.
8. Once cooked, remove the bag from the water bath and transfer it to an ice bath. Chill the leeks
9. Divide the leeks between four plates and season them with salt
10. Top the leeks with the bay shrimp and spoon on some vinaigrette
11. Sprinkle with fresh parsley and serve!

Nutrition Values (Per Serving)

- Calories: 148
- Carbohydrate: 7g
- Protein: 24g
- Fat: 2g
- Sugar: 3g
- Sodium: 758mg

Pumpkin Shrimp

(Serves: 6 / **Prep Time:** 10 minutes / **Sous Vide Cooking Time:** 15-35 minutes)

Ingredients

- 8 large raw shrimps, peeled and de-veined
- 1 tablespoon butter
- Salt and pepper as needed

For Soup

- 1 lb. pumpkin
- 4 tablespoons lime juice
- 2 yellow onions, chopped
- 1-2 small red chilies, finely chopped
- 1 stem of lemon grass, white part only, chopped
- 1 teaspoon shrimp paste
- 1 teaspoon sugar
- 1½ cups coconut milk
- 1 teaspoon tamarind paste
- 1 cup water
- ½ cup coconut cream
- 1 tablespoon fish sauce
- 2 tablespoons fresh Thai basil, chopped

How To

1. Prepare your Sous-vide water bath to a temperature of 122-degrees Fahrenheit
2. Add the shrimps into your Sous Vide bag with the butter
3. Sprinkle salt and pepper in and seal the bag using the immersion method and cook for 15-35 minutes
4. Peel the pumpkin and remove the seeds. Cut the flesh into 1-inch chunks
5. Add the onion, lemon grass, chili, shrimp paste, sugar and ½ the coconut milk into a food processor. Mix them well
6. Add the onion puree, remaining coconut milk, tamarind paste and water into a separate pot
7. Put the pumpkin to this pot and bring to a boil
8. Once the boiling point is reached, lower down the heat and simmer for 10 minutes
9. Remove the shrimps from the bag and add them to the soup
10. Add in the coconut cream, fish sauce, lime juice and basil, stir them well.
11. Serve!

Nutrition Values (Per Serving)

- Calories: 221
- Carbohydrate: 11g
- Protein: 17g
- Fat: 14g
- Sugar: 3g
- Sodium: 852mg

Special Tips

You may roast the pumpkin seeds in canola oil (at 300-degrees Fahrenheit) in an oven for about 10-20 minutes and use them as garnish for an extra flavor.

Miso Butter Cod

(Serves: 2 / **Prep Time:** 15 minutes / **Sous Vide Cooking Time:** 30 minutes)

Ingredients

- 1 large Atlantic Cod fillet
- 2 tablespoons miso paste
- 1½ tablespoons brown sugar
- 2 tablespoons soy sauce
- 2 tablespoons mirin
- 2 tablespoons butter
- Sesame seeds for garnishing

How To

1. Prepare your Sous-vide water bath to a temperature of 131-degrees Fahrenheit
2. Marinate the cod with the brown sugar, miso paste, mirin and soy sauce mixture

3. Transfer the fish to a heavy-duty sous vide zip bag and seal it using the immersion method
4. Cook for 30 minutes
5. Place a pan over the medium heat. Add in 1 tablespoon of butter
6. Sear the cod for 1 minute and pour the juices from the bag into the pan
7. Reduce until it thickened and add 1 tablespoon of butter on top and stir
8. Drizzle the sauce onto the cod and garnish with some sesame seeds
9. Serve over steamed rice!

Nutrition Values (Per Serving)

- Calories: 309
- Carbohydrate: 7g
- Protein: 38g
- Fat: 15g
- Sugar: 1g
- Sodium: 806mg

Dijon Cream Sauce with Salmon

(Serves: 2 / **Prep Time:** 15 minutes / **Sous Vide Cooking Time:** 45 minutes)

Ingredients

- 4 skinless salmon fillets
- 1 bunch of spinach
- ½ cup Dijon mustard
- 1 cup heavy cream
- 1 tablespoon lemon juice
- Salt and pepper as needed

How To

1. Prepare your Sous-vide water bath to a temperature of 115-degrees Fahrenheit
2. Season the salmon with salt
3. Transfer to a resealable bag and seal using the immersion method. Cook for 45 minutes
4. Take a pan and place it on a medium heat and add the spinach and cook until wilted
5. Add the lemon juice, pepper and salt, and keep cooking over a low heat
6. Take another saucepan and place it over medium heat
7. Add the heavy cream and Dijon mustard. Let it all boil a bit and then lower down the heat
8. Mix them well and season with salt and pepper
9. Take out the cooked salmon, drizzle the sauce on top, assemble the spinach on the side, and serve!

Nutrition Values (Per Serving)

- Calories: 204
- Carbohydrate: 7g
- Protein: 28g
- Fat: 8g
- Sugar: 3g
- Sodium: 489mg

Mahi-Mahi Corn Salad

(Serves: 4 / **Prep Time:** 20 minutes / **Sous Vide Cooking Time:** 15-35 minutes)

Ingredients
- 4 mahi-mahi portions
- ½ teaspoon paprika
- ½ teaspoon onion powder

- ½ teaspoon garlic powder
- ¼ teaspoon cayenne pepper
- Salt and pepper as needed

For the Salad
- 3 cups corn
- ½ pint cherry tomatoes, halved

- 1 red bell pepper, diced
- 2 tablespoons fresh basil, chopped

For dressing
- 2 tablespoons lime juice
- 1 teaspoon ancho chile powder

- 1 tablespoon olive oil
- Salt and pepper as needed

For garnishing
- Lime wedge
- 1 tablespoon fresh basil

How To
1. Prepare your Sous-vide water bath to a temperature of 122-degrees Fahrenheit
2. Season the mahi-mahi fillet with salt and pepper and put it in a sous vide zip bag. Whisk together the garlic powder, paprika, onion powder, and cayenne. Sprinkle the spice mix on top of the fish and seal the bag.
3. Transfer the bag to the water bath and cook for 15-35 minutes
4. Preheat the oven to 400-degrees Fahrenheit
5. Add the corn and red pepper on a baking tray. Drizzle the olive oil over the top with salt and pepper. Cook until the corn kernels are soft.
6. In a bowl, mix the cooked corn, roasted red peppers, tomatoes, and basil and whisk them well. In another bowl mix well the ingredients for the dressing and pour over the corn kernels.
7. Take the Mahi-mahi fillet out of the bag and pat dry. Sear over high-heat in a pan about 2 minutes per side.
8. For serving, take a large spoonful of the corn mix and place on the plates. Add the mahi-mahi fillet on top. Garnish with lime wedge and basil. Serve!

Nutrition Values (Per Serving)
- Calories: 412
- Carbohydrate: 24g
- Protein: 44g

- Fat: 6g
- Sugar: 18g
- Sodium: 385mg

Lobster Rolls

(Serves: 2 / **Prep Time:** 15 minutes / **Sous Vide Cooking Time:** 25 minutes)

Ingredients

- 2 lobster tails
- 1 tablespoon butter
- 2 green onions, chopped
- 3 tablespoons mayonnaise
- A pinch of salt
- A pinch of black pepper
- 2 teaspoons lemon juice
- Buttered Buns for serving

How To

1. Prepare your Sous-vide water bath to a temperature of 140-degrees Fahrenheit
2. Pour the water into a small pot and bring to a boil
3. Cut the lobster tails down the center from the top of the shell
4. Once the water has reached boiling point, submerge the lobsters and cook for 90 seconds
5. Remove them and soak in cold water for 5 minutes
6. Crack the shells and remove the tails from the shell
7. Add the shells in a bag and add the butter. Seal the bag using the immersion method, and cook for 25 minutes
8. Remove the tails from the water bath and pat them dry. Place them in a small bowl and chill for 30 minutes
9. Chop up the tail and mix with the mayonnaise, green onions, salt, pepper, and lime juice.
10. Serve with some toasted, buttered buns

Nutrition Values (Per Serving)

- Calories: 556
- Carbohydrate: 23g
- Protein: 79g
- Fat: 21g
- Sugar: 3g
- Sodium: 513mg

Dover Sole

(Serves: 2 / **Prep Time:** 5 minutes / **Sous Vide Cooking Time:** 30 minutes)

Ingredients

- 2 sole fillets
- Kosher salt as needed
- Freshly ground black pepper

- 1 garlic clove, minced
- 4 tablespoons unsalted butter
- 4 tablespoons dry white wine
- The zest of 1 lemon
- 2 tablespoons fresh lemon juice
- Fresh parsley for garnishing, chopped

How To

1. Prepare your Sous-vide water bath to a temperature of 134-degrees Fahrenheit
2. Season the sole with some pepper and salt
3. Divide the soles into their own medium-sized zip bags and divide the butter, lemon zest, wine, garlic and lemon juice between the bags
4. Seal the bags using the immersion method and cook for 30 minutes
5. Once done, remove the bags from the water and arrange them on a serving plate
6. Spoon some of your cooking liquid over the fish and garnish with parsley. Serve!

Nutrition Values (Per Serving)

- Calories: 595
- Carbohydrate: 27g
- Protein: 53g
- Fat: 28g
- Sugar: 8g
- Sodium: 370mg

Shrimp Cocktail Slider

(Serves: 2 / **Prep Time:** 30 minutes / **Sous Vide Cooking Time:** 15 minutes)

Ingredients

- 10 small-sized shrimps, peeled and de-veined
- Kosher salt and pepper as needed
- 4 tablespoons fresh dill, chopped
- 1 tablespoon unsalted butter
- 4 tablespoons mayonnaise
- 2 tablespoons red onions, minced
- 2 teaspoons freshly squeezed lemon juice
- 2 teaspoons ketchup
- Tabasco sauce
- 4 small-sized, oblong dinner rolls
- 8 small-sized leaves of butter lettuce
- ½ lemon, sliced into wedges

How To

1. Prepare your Sous-vide water bath to a temperature of 149-degrees Fahrenheit
2. Take a bowl and add the mayonnaise, red onion, lemon juice, ketchup and Tabasco sauce in it. Whisk them well to create the seasoning
3. Take the mixture and season it well with pepper and salt and divide the mixture and shrimps equally between two heavy-duty, resealable plastic bags
4. Add 1 tablespoon of dill and ½ tablespoon of butter to each of the bags
5. Seal the bags using the immersion method, submerge and cook for 15 minutes
6. Preheat your oven to 400-degrees Fahrenheit and warm the rolls for about 10 minutes
7. Remove them and slice in half lengthwise
8. Once done, remove the contents of the bag and strain over a medium bowl
9. Transfer the shrimps to the bowl with the dressing. Give it a nice toss
10. Take 2 lettuce leaves and place the shrimp mixture on top of the lettuce rolls
11. Serve with lemon

Nutrition Values (Per Serving)

- Calories: 375
- Carbohydrate: 15g
- Protein: 17g
- Fat: 28g
- Sugar: 8g
- Sodium: 443mg

Poached Salmon

(Serves: 2 / **Prep Time:** 20 minutes / **Sous Vide Cooking Time:** 25 minutes)

Ingredients

- 2 skinless, center-cut salmon fillets
- Kosher salt and black pepper as needed
- ¾ cup extra virgin olive oil
- 1 large-sized shallot, sliced into thin rings
- 12 whole Thai basil leaves, lightly bruised
- 1 teaspoon ginger, minced
- 3 Oz mixed greens* - optional
- 1 lemon

How To

1. Prepare your Sous-vide water bath to a temperature of 128-degrees Fahrenheit
2. Season the salmon with salt and pepper and add the fillets in a heavy-duty zipper bag. Add in the shallot slices, olive oil, ginger, mixed greens and basil leaves
3. Whisk well and seal the bag using the immersion method
4. Submerge the bag underwater and cook for about 25 minutes
5. Once done, transfer the greens from the bag to a serving platter

6. Take the salmon fillets and put them on top of your serving platter
7. Pass the rest of the mixture through a metal mesh and into a medium-sized bowl
8. Add some lemon juice to your olive oil
9. Mix well and drizzle the mixture on top of your salmon
10. Serve!

Nutrition Values (Per Serving)
- Calories: 298
- Carbohydrate: 0g
- Protein: 27g
- Fat: 18g
- Sugar: 0g
- Sodium: 425mg

(**Note: Mixed Greens*** - The blend may vary, but typically, a bag of packaged mixed greens contains the leaves of baby romaine and oak leaf lettuces, Swiss chard, mizuna, arugula, frisée, and radicchio.)

Pan Tomate Espelette Shrimp

(**Serves:** 2-4 / **Prep Time:** 15 minutes / **Sous Vide Cooking Time:** 25 minutes)

Ingredients
- 1 lb. shrimps, peeled and de-veined
- 1 tablespoon extra-virgin olive oil
- ¾ teaspoon Piment d'Espelette*
- Kosher salt as needed
- ½ high-quality loaf of bread cut up into 1½ inch slices
- 1 garlic clove, halved
- 2 beefsteak tomatoes, 1 sliced horizontally, the other sliced into wedges
- Flaky sea salt as needed

How To
1. Prepare your Sous-vide water bath to a temperature of 122-degrees Fahrenheit
2. Take a large-sized bowl and put the shrimps in it along with the olive oil, a pinch of kosher salt and the Piment d'Espelette
3. Whisk it well and transfer the mixture to a large-sized heavy-duty zip bag. Seal the bag using the immersion method
4. Submerge the bag underwater and cook for 25 minutes
5. Place a grill pan over a medium-high heat for 5 minutes before the shrimps are done
6. Carefully arrange the bread slices in a single layer in your pan and toast them on both sides

7. Once toasted, remove the bread and rub one side of the slices with the garlic clove
8. Rub the tomato halves over your toast as well and divide them between your serving plates
9. Once cooked, remove the bag and drain the liquid
10. Return the grill pan to a medium-high heat and add the shrimp a single layer
11. Sear for 10 seconds and divide the shrimps among the tomato bread
12. Drizzle the olive oil over your shrimps
13. Sprinkle some salt over and serve with the tomato wedges!

Nutrition Values (Per Serving)

- Calories: 341
- Carbohydrate: 25g
- Protein: 21g
- Fat: 6g
- Sugar: 3g
- Sodium: 517mg

(**Note: Piment d'Espelette*** - The Espelette pepper is a variety of species C. annuum that is cultivated in the French commune of Espelette, Pyrénées-Atlantiques, traditionally the northern territory of the Basque people.)

Crispy Skinned Salmon

(**Serves:** 2 / **Prep Time:** 45 minutes / **Sous Vide Cooking Time:** 8 minutes)

Ingredients

- 2 skin-on salmon fillets
- Salt and black pepper as needed
- 1 tablespoon extra-virgin olive oil
- 4½ tablespoons soy sauce
- 2 tablespoons minced fresh ginger
- 2 thinly sliced Thai Chilis
- 6 tablespoons sesame oil
- 4 ounces prepared Chinese egg noodles
- 6 oz. cooked broccolini
- 5 teaspoons sesame seeds for garnishing, toasted

How To

1. Prepare your Sous-vide water bath to a temperature of 149-degrees Fahrenheit
2. Skin the salmon and transfer them to a parchment paper-lined baking sheet. Season with salt and pepper
3. Take a sheet and lay it on top of the skin and place another baking sheet on top
4. Transfer to an oven and bake for 30 minutes
5. Season with salt and pepper and transfer the baked salmon to large-sized, resealable zipper bag

6. Seal the bag using the immersion method, submerge underwater and cook for 8 minutes
7. Take a small-sized bowl and add the ginger, chilis, 4 tablespoons of soy sauce, 4 tablespoons of sesame oil and whisk everything well to prepare the dipping sauce
8. Divide it all between two serving bowls
9. Toss the noodles and broccolini with 2 teaspoons of sesame oil and ½ teaspoon of soy sauce
10. Divide it between two serving plates as well
11. Once cooked, remove the contents of the bag and place one fillet on the bed of noodles
12. Garnish with some toasted sesame seeds and salmon skin
13. Serve the salmon alongside the sauce

Nutrition Values (Per Serving)

- Calories: 649
- Carbohydrate: 117g
- Protein: 31g
- Fat: 6g
- Sugar: 0g
- Sodium: 492mg

Scallop Curry

(Serves: 2/ **Prep Time:** 15 minutes / **Sous Vide Cooking Time:** 60 minutes)

Ingredients

- 2 tablespoons yellow curry powder
- 1 tablespoon tomato paste
- ½ cup coconut cream
- 1 teaspoon chili garlic sauce
- 1 teaspoon chicken base
- 1 tablespoon freshly squeeze lime juice
- 6 large-sized sea scallops
- Cooked basmati rice, as needed for serving
- Fresh cilantro, chopped

How To

1. Prepare your Sous-vide water bath to a temperature of 134-degrees Fahrenheit
2. Take a medium-sized bowl and add in the coconut cream, tomato paste, curry powder, lime juice, chicken base, and chili-garlic sauce and mix them well
3. Add the mixture to a heavy-duty resealable zipper bag and add the scallops as well
4. Seal the bag using the immersion method and submerge underwater
5. Cook for about 60 minutes
6. Once cooked, take the bag out from the water bath and transfer the contents to a serving bowl
7. Put the scallops on top of your basmati rice
8. Serve with a some chopped, fresh cilantro

Nutrition Values (Per Serving)

- Calories: 582
- Carbohydrate: 0g
- Protein: 21g
- Fat: 14g
- Sugar: 0g
- Sodium: 516mg

Crispy Frog Legs

(Serves: 2 / **Prep Time:** 15 minutes / **Sous Vide Cooking Time:** 45 minutes)

Ingredients

- 1 lb. frog legs
- Kosher salt and pepper as needed
- 2 tablespoons unsalted butter
- 1 minced garlic clove
- 1 teaspoon red pepper flakes
- 3 tablespoons finely chopped fresh parsley
- 2 tablespoon lemon juice

How To

1. Prepare your Sous-vide water bath to a temperature of 135-degrees Fahrenheit
2. Season the legs with salt and pepper
3. Take a large-sized, heavy-duty resealable zip bag and add the frog legs. Seal the bag using the immersion method
4. Submerge the bag underwater and cook for 45 minutes
5. Once cooked, take the bag out from the water bath and pat the legs dry using the kitchen towel
6. Take a non-stick skillet, place it over medium-high heat and melt the butter
7. The moment the butter starts to brown, add the frog legs along with the red pepper flakes, garlic and season with pepper and salt
8. Cook for about 2 minutes, flip it, and cook for another 2 minutes
9. Remove them from the heat and serve with lemon juice and parsley

Nutrition Values (Per Serving)

- Calories: 300
- Carbohydrate: 8g
- Protein: 20g
- Fat: 3g
- Sugar: 1g
- Sodium: 212mg

Tom Yum Goong Prawns

(Serves: 2 / **Prep Time:** 15 minutes / **Sous Vide Cooking Time:** 15 minutes)

Ingredients

- 12 large-sized, peeled, tail-on shrimp
- Kosher salt and pepper as needed
- 1 stalk of lemon grass with outer leaves removed and lightly smashed into slices of 1 inch
- 5 kaffir lime leaves, torn in half
- 1 piece of 2-inches galangal, thinly sliced
- 4 Thai Chilis, stalk removed, and smashed
- 4 oyster mushrooms, halved lengthwise
- 8 cherry tomatoes
- ½ white onion, sliced into ½ inch wedges
- 3 tablespoons fish sauce
- 1 teaspoon palm sugar
- 10 tablespoons coconut milk
- 3 tablespoons freshly squeezed lime juice
- 3 tablespoons Thai roasted chili paste
- ¼ cup cilantro, roughly chopped

How To

1. Prepare your Sous-vide water bath to a temperature of 149-degrees Fahrenheit
2. Lightly season your shrimps with pepper and salt
3. Take a heavy-duty resealable bag and put the shrimp in it
4. Seal the bag using the immersion method and submerge it underwater. Cook for about 15 minutes
5. Take a pot filled with boiling water and add the lemon grass, galangal, kaffir lime leaves, and the Thai chilis to the pot. Boil for 10 minutes to prepare the soup
6. Add the mushrooms, onion, and tomatoes, and keep boiling for another 2 minutes
7. Add the fish sauce alongside the sugar and bring the mixture to a boil, let it boil for 2 minutes
8. Remove the heat immediately and stir in the lime juice, coconut milk, cilantro and chili paste
9. Season with some fish sauce, lime juice or palm sugar
10. Remove the bag out from the water bath and remove the shrimp out, transfer them to your soup pot
11. Mix them well and serve!

Nutrition Values (Per Serving)

- Calories: 348
- Carbohydrate: 7g
- Protein: 24g
- Fat: 2g
- Sugar: 3g
- Sodium: 458mg

Salmon with Sweet Potato Puree

(Serves: 2 / **Prep Time:** 30 minutes / **Sous Vide Cooking Time:** 60 minutes)

Ingredients

- 2 pieces skin-on salmon fillets
- Olive oil
- 2 sprigs thyme
- 4 garlic cloves
- 3 pieces sweet potatoes
- ¼ cup coconut milk
- 1 bunch rainbow chard
- 1 small-sized grated ginger
- Soy sauce
- 1 bunch radish
- Sea salt

How To

1. Prepare your Sous-vide water bath to a temperature of 122-degrees Fahrenheit
2. Take a resealable zipper bag and add in the salmon, 2 garlic cloves, thyme, and olive oil.
3. Seal the bag using the immersion method, submerge underwater and cook for 1 hour
4. Wrap the potatoes in foil and roast them in the oven for 45 minutes at 375-degrees Fahrenheit
5. Cut the potatoes in half and then, carefully scoop out the flesh and put it in a blender with the coconut milk and blend them together. Season with pepper and salt
6. Steam the chard for 3 minutes
7. Take another pan and add the olive oil, minced garlic, grated ginger together with the chard and soy sauce. Sauté for a while
8. Cut the radish in half and drizzle the olive oil on top
9. Roast for 30 minutes at 375-degrees Fahrenheit
10. Then, sear the salmon in a hot pan with a pinch of salt
11. Assemble on your serving platter by placing the potato, chard and finally the salmon on top of everything
12. Scatter some roasted radish over and serve!

Nutrition Values (Per Serving)

- Calories: 579
- Carbohydrate: 3g
- Protein: 42g
- Fat: 33g
- Sugar: 1g
- Sodium: 493mg

Singaporean Prawn Noodle

(Serves: 2 / **Prep Time:** 10 minutes / **Sous Vide Cooking Time:** 15 minutes)

Ingredients
- 20 pieces small, tail-on shrimp
- 2 nests vermicelli noodle, cooked and drained
- 1 teaspoon Chinese white wine
- 1 teaspoon curry powder
- 1 tablespoon light soy sauce
- 1 green onion, thinly sliced
- 2 tablespoons vegetable oil

How To
1. Prepare your Sous-vide water bath to a temperature of 149-degrees Fahrenheit
2. Put the prawns in a resealable zip bag and seal using the immersion method
3. Cook for 15 minutes
4. Place a skillet over a medium heat
5. Add the vegetable oil, Chinese white wine, curry powder and soy sauce
6. Whisk well and add the noodles. Cook until everything is mixed
7. Add the prawns and toss
8. Top it up with some green onions. Serve!

Nutrition Values (Per Serving)
- Calories: 239
- Carbohydrate: 2g
- Protein: 16g
- Fat: 7g
- Sugar: 0g
- Sodium: 443mg

Sweet Mango Shrimp

(Serves: 4 / **Prep Time:** 10 minutes / **Sous Vide Cooking Time:** 15 minutes)

Ingredients
- 24 medium-sized shrimps, peeled and de-veined
- 4 pieces' mangoes, peeled and shredded, cut into thin strips
- 2 medium-sized shallots, thinly-sliced
- ¾ cup halved cherry tomatoes
- 2 tablespoons chopped, fresh Thai basil leaves
- ¼ cup toasted dry pan peanuts

For Thai Dressing
- ¼ cup freshly squeeze lime juice
- 6 tablespoons palm sugar
- 5 tablespoons fish sauce
- 4-8 pieces' garlic cloves
- 4-8 pieces small red chili

How To

1. Prepare your Sous-vide water bath to a temperature of 135-degrees Fahrenheit
2. Take a heavy-duty, large resealable zipper bag and layer the shrimp in a single layer inside
3. Seal the bag using the immersion method. Submerge under water and cook for 15 minutes
4. Put the lime juice, fish sauce, and palm sugar in a small bowl and mix well
5. Take a mortar and pestle and pound well the garlic
6. Add the chilis and keep pounding
7. Whisk well, then add the mixture to the dressing
8. Once the shrimps are ready, take them out
9. Transfer them to a large-sized bowl
10. Add the green mango strips, Thai basil, shallots, tomato halves and peanuts to the bowl
11. Top off with the dressing and serve!

Nutrition Values (Per Serving)

- Calories: 245
- Carbohydrate: 11g
- Protein: 19g
- Fat: 11g
- Sugar: 5g
- Sodium: 532mg

Shrimp Scampi

(Serves: 4 / **Prep Time:** 20 minutes / **Sous Vide Cooking Time:** 30 minutes)

Ingredients

- 4 tablespoons unsalted butter
- 2 tablespoons freshly squeeze lemon juice
- 2 cloves fresh garlic, minced
- 1 teaspoon fresh lemon zest
- 1 teaspoon kosher salt
- ½ teaspoon freshly ground black pepper
- 1 lb. jumbo shrimps, peeled and de-veined
- ½ cup of panko bread crumbs
- 1 tablespoon fresh parsley, minced

How To

1. Prepare your Sous-vide water bath to a temperature of 135-degrees Fahrenheit
2. Place a large-sized skillet over medium heat
3. Add 3 tablespoons of butter and melt in the skillet
4. Add the lemon juice, salt, pepper and zest along with the garlic
5. Remove the heat immediately and allow it to cool for about 5 minutes
6. Add the shrimps in a large-sized, resealable bag and add the butter mixture
7. Seal the bag using the immersion method, submerge underwater and cook for 30 minutes
8. In the meantime, melt more butter (1 tablespoon) into the pan and place it over a medium heat again
9. Add the bread crumbs when the butter stops foaming and toss them well. Remove from the heat
10. After cooking the shrimps for 25 minutes, prepare your broiler by heating it to high
11. When the timer goes off, divide the shrimps along with the cooking liquid, into 4 broiler-safe ramekins/dishes
12. Top up with crumbs
13. Broil for 2 minutes until a golden brown
14. Sprinkle with some parsley and Serve!

Nutrition Values (Per Serving)

- Calories: 293
- Carbohydrate: 4g
- Protein: 16g
- Fat: 24g
- Sugar: 0g
- Sodium: 513mg

Buttery Scallops

(Serves: 6 / **Prep Time:** 5 minutes / **Sous Vide Cooking Time:** 35 minutes)

Ingredients

- 4¼ oz. scallops
- 2 teaspoons brown butter
- Salt and pepper as needed

How To

1. Prepare your Sous-vide water bath to a temperature of 140-degrees Fahrenheit
2. Pat the scallops dry using kitchen towel
3. Add the scallops in a heavy-duty, resealable bag and add the brown butter, pepper and salt, and seal using the immersion method
4. Submerge and cook for 35 minutes
5. Once done, remove the bag and pat the scallops dry using the kitchen towel

6. Place a pan over a high heat
7. Add in a teaspoon of butter and allow it to heat up
8. Add the scallops and sear for about 30 seconds on each side
9. Serve over the brown butter

Nutrition Values (Per Serving)

- Calories: 334
- Carbohydrate: 10g
- Protein: 20g
- Fat: 24g
- Sugar: 2g
- Sodium: 310mg

Crab Mango Salad

(Serves: 2 / **Prep Time:** 20 minutes / **Sous Vide Cooking Time:** 45 minutes)

Ingredients

- 2 blue swimmer crabs
- 1 large-sized mango
- ¼ cup halved cherry tomatoes
- 1 cup rocket lettuce
- ¼ julienned red onion
- Salt and pepper as needed
- 2 tablespoons olive oil
- 1 tablespoon lime juice
- 1 tablespoon freshly squeezed orange juice
- 2 teaspoons honey

How To

1. Prepare your Sous-vide water bath to a temperature of 154-degrees Fahrenheit
2. Take a pot of water and let it boil
3. Add the crabs in and let them boil for 60 seconds
4. Chop the legs of the crabs, using pincers, and put them in a heavy-duty, resealable bag. Zip it up using the immersion method
5. Submerge underwater and cook for 45 minutes
6. Add the cooked crabs to an ice bath
7. Add all the dressing ingredients in a bowl. Mix them well
8. Take the crab meat out of the crab and transfer to your serving dish
9. Add the dressing to the crab meat and toss well to coat them
10. Serve!

Nutrition Values (Per Serving)

- Calories: 148
- Carbohydrate: 7g
- Protein: 24g
- Fat: 2g
- Sugar: 3g
- Sodium: 518mg

Swordfish Steak

(Serves: 2 / **Prep Time:** 15 minutes / **Sous Vide Cooking Time:** 30 minutes)

Ingredients
- 2 pieces (6 ounces) swordfish steaks
- 2 tablespoons extra virgin olive oil
- Zest and juice of 2 lemons
- 4 sprigs fresh thyme
- Kosher salt as needed
- Freshly ground black pepper

How To
1. Prepare your Sous-Vide water bath using your immersion circulator and raise the temperature to 130-degrees Fahrenheit
2. Season the sword fish with pepper and salt and add to a zip bag
3. Add the olive oil, lemon juice, zest, thyme and seal using the immersion method
4. Submerge underwater and cook for 30 minutes
5. Remove the bag from the water and take out the sword fish
6. Pat it dry using a kitchen towel
7. Make sure to reserve the cooking liquid
8. Heat up your grill to 600-700 degrees Fahrenheit and add the sword fish, sear 2 minutes per side
9. Place the dish to your serving plate and allow it to rest for about 5 minutes
10. Divide the Swordfish amongst two serving plates and drizzle the reserved cooking liquid. Serve!

Nutrition Values (Per Serving)
- Calories: 476
- Carbohydrate: 11g
- Protein: 32g
- Fat: 33g
- Sugar: 2g
- Sodium: 136mg

Special Tips
If you want the fish to have a brighter, shiny texture, you may spritz it with some lime before serving!

Salmon Soba Noodles

(Serves: 4 / **Prep Time:** 10 minutes / **Sous Vide Cooking Time:** 20 minutes)

Ingredients

For Salmon
- 6 oz. salmon fillets, skin-on
- Salt and pepper as needed
- 1 teaspoon sesame oil
- 1 cup extra-virgin oil
- 1 tablespoon fresh ginger, grated
- 2 tablespoons honey

For Sesame Soba
- 4 oz. dry soba noodles
- 1 tablespoon grape seed oil
- 2 garlic cloves, chopped
- ½ broccoli head
- 3 tablespoons tahini
- 1 teaspoon sesame oil
- 2 teaspoons extra-virgin olive oil
- ¼ juiced lime
- 1 sliced stalk green onion
- ¼ cup cilantro, roughly chopped
- 1 teaspoon toasted sesame seeds
- Lime wedges and sesame seeds for garnishing

How To

1. Prepare your Sous-vide water bath to a temperature of 123.8-degrees Fahrenheit. Season the fillets with salt and pepper.
2. Add the sesame oil, olive oil, ginger, and honey in a medium-size bowl. Whisk them well and transfer to a heavy-duty zipper bag
3. Add the fillets and toss to coat well. Seal the bag using the immersion method, submerge the bag and cook for 20 minutes
4. While it is being cooked, prepare your soba noodles by cooking according to the package label
5. Once done, place another skillet over a medium-high heat
6. Add the grape seed oil and allow it to heat up. Add the broccoli and garlic, and stir fry them for about 7-8 minutes
7. Take a small-sized mixing bowl and mix in your tahini, olive oil, sesame oil, lime juice, cilantro, green onions, and toasted sesame seeds
8. Once done, drain your cooked noodles and add them to the fried garlic and broccoli
9. Heat another skillet over a medium-high heat
10. Take one piece of Parchment paper and place it on the bottom of your skillet

11. Once cooked, take the salmon out from the bag and place it in the pan, skin side facing down. Sear for about 1 minute
12. Divide your soba noodles into 2 serving bowls. Garnish with some lime wedge and sesame seeds. Serve!

Nutrition Values (Per Serving)
- Calories: 346
- Carbohydrate: 54g
- Protein: 15g
- Fat: 10g
- Sugar: 6g
- Sodium: 1012mg

Sous Vide Lobster Rolls

(Serves: 2 / **Prep Time:** 10 minutes / **Sous Vide Cooking Time:** 45 minutes)

Ingredients
- 2 lobster tails, cut into ½ inch pieces
- 6 tablespoons unsalted butter
- 1 teaspoon sea salt
- 1 teaspoon chopped, fresh tarragon
- 1 teaspoon chopped chives
- ½ teaspoon garlic powder
- 1 teaspoon lemon zest
- 2 toasted hot dog buns for serving

How To
1. Prepare your Sous-vide water bath to a temperature of 122-degrees Fahrenheit
2. Add the salt, butter, lobster, garlic powder, tarragon, lemon zest, and chives in a heavy-duty, resealable zip bag and seal using the immersion method
3. Submerge and cook for 45 minutes
4. Once done, remove from the water bath and put the lobsters in a medium sized bowl
5. Pour in some of extra butter
6. Place the lobster pieces in the hot dog buns and serve with extra butter

Nutrition Values (Per Serving)
- Calories: 348
- Carbohydrate: 7g
- Protein: 24g
- Fat: 2g
- Sugar: 3g
- Sodium: 358mg

Salmon with Hollandaise Sauce

(Serves: 4 / **Prep Time:** 5 minutes / **Sous Vide Cooking Time:** 75 minutes)

Ingredients
- 2 salmon fillets
- Salt as needed

For Hollandaise Sauce
- 4 tablespoons butter
- 1 egg yolk
- 1 teaspoon lemon juice
- 1 teaspoon water
- ½ diced shallot
- A pinch of cayenne
- Salt as needed

How To
1. Prepare the salmon by rubbing it all over with salt
2. Allow the salted salmon to chill for 30 minutes
3. Prepare your Sous-vide water bath to a temperature of 148-degrees Fahrenheit
4. Place the sauce ingredients in a large-sized, resealable zipper bag. Seal the bag using the immersion method and cook for 45 minutes
5. Once the sauce is done, lower the temperature of the bath to the temperature required for the salmon
6. Add the salmon in another bag and seal it using the immersion method
7. Cook for 30 minutes underwater
8. Remove the sauce from the water bath and pour it into a blender
9. Blend it well until light yellow
10. Take the salmon out from the bath and pat them dry
11. Sear if needed and serve with the hollandaise sauce

Nutrition Values (Per Serving)
- Calories: 418
- Carbohydrate: 9g
- Protein: 33g
- Fat: 28g
- Sugar: 5g
- Sodium: 203mg

Sea Scallops & Sprinkled Sesame

(Serves: 4 / **Prep Time:** 15 minutes / **Sous Vide Cooking Time:** 30 minutes)

Ingredients
- 12 pieces' fresh sea scallops, side muscles removed
- Salt and ground black pepper as needed

- 2 tablespoons miso
- 2 tablespoons sake
- 2 tablespoons unsalted melted butter
- 1 tablespoon all-purpose flour
- 1 teaspoon cornstarch
- 1 tablespoon sesame oil
- Black and white sesame seeds for garnish

How To

1. Prepare your Sous-vide water bath to a temperature of 122-degrees Fahrenheit. Season the scallops with pepper and salt
2. Divide the scallops between two separate resealable zip bags and seal the bags using the immersion method. Submerge the bags and cook for 30 minutes
3. Add the miso, sake and remaining seasoning of black pepper in a bowl and mix well to prepare the miso seasoning
4. Once cooked, take the scallops out from the bag and pat dry
5. In another bowl, mix in melted butter, flour, cornstarch, and salt. Mix well
6. Brush the mixture all over the scallops
7. Pour some sesame oil into a large-sized skillet
8. Place the skillet over a high heat and wait until the oil shimmers. Add the scallops to the oil and sear both sides for 1 minute (30 secs each side)
9. Once done, move it to a serving plate and drizzle the miso dressing over the top. Garnish with the sesame seeds and serve!

Nutrition Values (Per Serving)

- Calories: 259
- Carbohydrate: 17g
- Protein: 13g
- Fat: 17g
- Sugar: 6g
- Sodium: 478mg

Monkfish Medallions

(**Serves:** 2 / **Prep Time:** 15 minutes / **Sous Vide Cooking Time:** 30 minutes)

Ingredients

- 1 monkfish steak
- Kosher salt as needed
- Ground black pepper as needed
- 4 tablespoons unsalted butter
- 1 tablespoon chopped fresh parsley

How To

1. Prepare your Sous-vide water bath to a temperature of 130-degrees Fahrenheit
2. Season the fish with pepper and salt
3. Add the fish in a large-sized resealable bag and seal it using the immersion method. Submerge underwater and cook for about 30 minutes
4. Once done, take the bag out and transfer the steak to a cutting board
5. Slice it into ½ inch thick medallions
6. Place a large-sized skillet over medium high heat
7. Add the butter and let it melt
8. Add the monkfish medallions and brown them for about 5 minutes until they turn golden brown
9. Remove the heat immediately and season it thoroughly with pepper and salt
10. Serve with the topping of parsley

Nutrition Values (Per Serving)

- Calories: 288
- Carbohydrate: 10g
- Protein: 18g
- Fat: 10g
- Sugar: 4g
- Sodium: 482mg

Smoked Prawn

(Serves: 2 / **Prep Time:** 10 minutes / **Sous Vide Cooking Time:** 15 minutes)

Ingredients

- 24 pieces of de-shelled small prawns
- 4 tablespoons extra-virgin olive oil
- Smoked salt
- Pepper as needed

How To

1. Take a large-sized pot of water and heat to a temperature of 149-degrees Fahrenheit using your Sous Vide immersion circulator
2. Add the prawns, olive oil, pepper and smoked salt in a heavy-duty plastic zipper bag
3. Seal it using the immersion method, and cook for 15 minutes
4. Once cooked, place the prawns in a hot pan and sear until they turn golden brown
5. Add some extra smoked salt to enhance the flavors.
6. Serve!

Nutrition Values (Per Serving)

- Calories: 560
- Carbohydrate: 86g
- Protein: 25g
- Fat: 12g
- Sugar: 11g
- Sodium: 390mg

Chilean Sea Bass

(Serves: 3 / **Prep Time:** 5 minutes / **Sous Vide Cooking Time:** 30 minutes)

Ingredients
- 1 lb. skinless Chilean sea bass
- 1 tablespoon extra-virgin olive oil
- Salt and pepper as needed

How To
1. Prepare your Sous-vide water bath to a temperature of 134-degrees Fahrenheit
2. Season the sea bass with salt and pepper
3. Add the bass in a heavy-duty, resealable zipper bag and add the olive oil
4. Seal using the immersion method. Submerge and cook underwater for 30 minutes
5. Remove the bag and place the fish on your serving platter
6. Serve!

Nutrition Values (Per Serving)
- Calories: 656
- Carbohydrate: 3g
- Protein: 84g
- Fat: 32g
- Sugar: 1g
- Sodium: 343mg

Salmon Rillettes

(Serves: 2 / **Prep Time:** 10 minutes / **Sous Vide Cooking Time:** 20 minutes)

Ingredients
- ½ lb. salmon fillets, skin and pin bones removed
- 1 teaspoon sea salt
- 6 tablespoons unsalted butter
- 2 shallots, peeled and minced
- 1 garlic clove, peeled and minced
- ½ oz. lemon juice

How To
1. Take a Sous Vide water bath and preheat it to a temperature of 130-degrees Fahrenheit using your immersion circulator
2. Add the salmon fillets, unsalted butter, sea salt, garlic cloves, shallots, and lemon juice in a heavy-duty, resealable bag and seal it using the immersion method

3. Submerge underwater and cook for 20 minutes
4. Take the salmon out from the bag and break into small portions
5. Divide the salmon between 8 crocks and season each of them with lemon butter sauce from the bag
6. Put the crocks in the fridge and chill for 2 hours
7. Serve as a spread with some bread slices

Nutrition Values (Per Serving)

- Calories: 277
- Carbohydrate: 0g
- Protein: 20g
- Fat: 21g
- Sugar: 0g
- Sodium: 411mg

Sous Vide Salmon Belly

(**Serves:** 4 / **Prep Time:** 5 minutes / **Sous Vide Cooking Time:** 30 minutes)

Ingredients

- ¼ cup maple syrup
- ¼ cup soy sauce
- 1 tablespoon Sriracha sauce*
- 1 lb. salmon belly, skin removed

How To

1. Prepare your Sous-vide water bath to a temperature of 130-degrees Fahrenheit
2. Add the maple syrup, Sriracha, and soy sauce into a medium-sized bowl and mix well
3. Place the bowl in a large-sized, heavy-duty zip bag and seal using the immersion method
4. Submerge the bag underwater and cook for 30 minutes
5. Once done, remove the bag and transfer to an ice-cold water bath
6. Allow it to cool down, remove the belly and serve!

Nutrition Values (Per Serving)

- Calories: 327
- Carbohydrate: 5g
- Protein: 7g
- Fat: 31g
- Sugar: 1g
- Sodium: 431mg

(**Note: Sriracha sauce*** - Sriracha is a type of hot sauce or chili sauce made from a paste of chili peppers, garlic, distilled vinegar, salt, and sugar.)

Baby Octopus Dish

(Serves: 4 / **Prep Time:** 10 minutes / **Sous Vide Cooking Time:** 50 minutes)

Ingredients
- 1 lb. baby octopus
- 1 tablespoon extra-virgin olive oil
- 1 tablespoon lemon juice, freshly squeezed
- Kosher salt and black pepper as needed

How To
1. Prepare your Sous-vide water bath to a temperature of 134-degrees Fahrenheit
2. Add the octopus in a heavy-duty resealable zipper bag
3. Seal the bag using the immersion method and cook underwater for 50 minutes
4. Once cooked, remove the octopus and pat it dry
5. Toss the cooked octopus with some olive oil and lemon juice and season it with salt and pepper
6. Serve!

Nutrition Values (Per Serving)
- Calories: 378
- Carbohydrate: 4g
- Protein: 25g
- Fat: 29g
- Sugar: 0g
- Sodium: 392mg

Special Tips
If you want a nice crispy chard, grill the cooked and seasoned octopus for 1 minute on each side.

Scallop Sashimi with Yuzu Vinaigrette

(Serves: 4/ **Prep Time:** 25 minutes + 20 minutes' chill time
/ **Sous Vide Cooking Time:** 30 minutes)

Ingredients
- 4-8 dry, large-sized sea scallops
- 2 tablespoons red grapefruit juice
- 1 tablespoon soy sauce
- 1 teaspoon lime juice
- 1 teaspoon finely minced, medium-hot red Chili

- 1 teaspoon Japanese sweet cooking wine
- 1 tablespoon extra-virgin olive oil
- 8 mint leaves
- 1 head Belgian endive, base trimmed up and halved lengthwise. The halves should then be cut lengthwise into ¼ inch wedges
- 1 avocado, pitted, peeled, halved and cut lengthwise into ½ inch thick slices
- 1 red grapefruit
- Sea salt as needed
- 2 shiso leaves for serving

How To

1. Prepare your Sous-vide water bath to a temperature of 122-degrees Fahrenheit
2. Add the scallops in a large-sized, resealable bag and seal it using the immersion method and cook for 30 minutes. Let the bags chill for 20 minutes in an ice bath
3. While they are chilling, take a bowl and mix together the grapefruit juice, Japanese cooking wine, soy sauce, lime juice, red chili and oil until they are finely blended
4. Taste your vinaigrette to ensure it has a nice tangy, salty flavor, sweet and spicy
5. Transfer your chilled scallops to a cutting board and discard any excess liquid
6. Slice the scallops horizontally into ¼ inch thick coins using a sharp knife.
7. Serve with 2 shiso leaves placed in the center of a chilled plate, and arrange your scallop coins alongside the Belgian endive wedges on top
8. Scatter some avocado slices and grapefruit around the scallops with a final drizzle of vinaigrette
9. Sprinkle some salt and serve!

Nutrition Values (Per Serving)

- Calories: 232
- Carbohydrate: 34g
- Protein: 13g

- Fat: 10g
- Sugar: 8g
- Sodium: 559mg

Salmon Egg Bites

(Serves: 6 / **Prep Time:** 5 minutes / **Sous Vide Cooking Time:** 60 minutes)

Ingredients

- 6 whole eggs
- ¼ cup crème fraiche
- ¼ cup cream cheese
- 4 spears asparagus
- 2 oz. smoked salmon

- 2 oz. chèvre
- ½ oz. minced shallot
- 2 teaspoons chopped, fresh dill
- Salt and pepper as needed

Tools Required:
- 6 x 4 oz. canning jars

How To

1. Prepare your Sous-vide water bath to a temperature of 170-degrees Fahrenheit
2. Add the eggs, cream fraiche, cream cheese and salt into a blender
3. Chop the asparagus into ½ cm chunks. Add them in a mixing bowl with the shallots
4. Chop the salmon into small portions and add them to your shallots
5. Whisk well with some minced dill
6. Whisk everything with a fork
7. Lay out the canning jars and add the egg mixture between them
8. Divide the salmon mix into six and put one portion in each jar
9. Add 1/6 chèvre into the jars and lock the lid to fingertip tightness
10. Put them into the water bath and cook for 1 hour
11. Once done, take out from the water bath.
12. Sprinkle some salt over and serve

Nutrition Values (Per Serving)

- Calories: 589
- Carbohydrate: 61g
- Protein: 28g
- Fat: 26g
- Sugar: 9g
- Sodium: 590mg

Rosemary Salmon Slab

(Serves: 4 / **Prep Time:** 5 minutes / **Sous Vide Cooking Time:** 30 minutes)

Ingredients

- 1 lb. wild salmon
- 2 tablespoons olive oil
- 1 tablespoon chopped rosemary
- Zest and juice of one lemon
- ¼ teaspoon garlic powder
- ¼ teaspoon black pepper
- 2 garlic cloves
- ⅛ teaspoon of sea salt

How To

1. Prepare your Sous-vide water bath to a temperature of 115-degrees Fahrenheit
2. Add the pepper, salt, rosemary, lemon juice, zest, and garlic powder into a small bowl
3. Whisk well until the whole mixture is emulsified
4. Place the salmon in a heavy-duty, resealable zip bag. Zip the bag and seal using the immersion method. Submerge and cook for 30 minutes
5. Slice the 2 garlic cloves into very thin slices
6. Once cooked, remove the bag from the bath and pour it onto your plate. Keep the juices
7. Put a frying pan over a medium high heat
8. Add 1 tablespoon of olive oil and heat. Add the garlic slices and sauté them
9. Remove and let them rest
10. Now add the salmon into the oil, and cook for 3 minutes
11. Remove and garnish with some garlic slices
12. Serve!

Nutrition Values (Per Serving)

- Calories: 438
- Carbohydrate: 4g
- Protein: 37g
- Fat: 30g
- Sugar: 2g
- Sodium: 458mg

CHAPTER 4 | BEEF, LAMB & OTHER RED MEATS

Teriyaki Beef Cubes

(Serves: 2 / **Prep Time:** 10 minutes / **Sous Vide Cooking Time:** 60 minutes)

Ingredients
- 2 fillet mignon steaks
- ½ cup teriyaki sauce (extra 6 tablespoons)
- 2 tablespoons soy sauce
- 2 teaspoons fresh chilis, chopped
- 1½ tablespoons sesame seeds, toasted
- Rice noodles
- 2 tablespoons sesame oil
- 1 tablespoon scallion for garnishing, finely chopped

How To
1. Prepare the Sous Vide water bath using your immersion circulator and raise the temperature to 134-degrees Fahrenheit
2. Slice the steaks into small portions and put them in a zipper bag
3. Add ½ a cup of teriyaki sauce to the bag. Seal using the immersion method, submerge and cook for 1 hour.
4. Add the soy sauce and chopped chilis in a small bowl
5. Add the sesame seeds in another bowl
6. After 50 minutes of cooking, start cooking the rice noodles according to the package's instructions
7. Once done, drain the noodles and put them on a serving platter
8. Take the bag out from the water and remove the beef. Discard the marinade
9. Take a large skillet and put it over a high heat. Add your sesame oil and allow the oil to heat up.
10. Add the beef and 6 tablespoons of teriyaki sauce, and cook for 5 seconds
11. Transfer the cooked beef to your serving platter and garnish with toasted sesame seeds and scallions
12. Serve with the prepped chili-soy dip

Nutrition Values (Per Serving)
- Calories: 445
- Carbohydrate: 15g
- Protein: 38g
- Fat: 26g
- Sugar: 7g
- Sodium: 597mg

Willy Cheesesteak

(Serves: 4 / **Prep Time:** 1 minutes / **Sous Vide Cooking Time:** 60 minutes)

Ingredients

- 1 red bell pepper, thinly sliced
- 1 yellow bell pepper, thinly sliced
- ½ white onion, thinly sliced
- 2 tablespoons extra-virgin olive oil
- Kosher salt and black pepper as needed
- 1 lb. cooked skirt steak, thinly sliced
- 4 soft hoagie rolls
- 8 slices of Provolone cheese

How To

1. Prepare the Sous Vide water bath using your immersion circulator and raise the temperature to 185-degrees Fahrenheit
2. Add the bell peppers, onion and olive oil in a heavy-duty zip bag
3. Season the mixture with salt and pepper
4. Seal the bag using the immersion method and submerge and cook for 1 hour.
5. At the 55-minute mark, put the cooked steak in another zip bag and submerge it
6. Allow both to cook for 5-minutes more and take them out
7. Preheat your oven to 400-degrees Fahrenheit
8. Slice the hoagie rolls in half and top them with cheese
9. Place them in the oven and bake for 2 minutes
10. Add the pepper, steak and onions, then serve!

Nutrition Values (Per Serving)

- Calories: 294
- Carbohydrate: 18g
- Protein: 13g
- Fat: 19g
- Sugar: 1g
- Sodium: 343mg

Fried Spinach & Tri Tip

(Serves: 2 / **Prep Time:** 5 minutes / **Sous Vide Cooking Time:** 2 hours)

Ingredients

- 1 piece tri tip roast
- Kosher salt and black pepper as needed
- 2 teaspoons garlic powder
- 2 teaspoons canola oil
- 1 pack baby spinach

How To

1. Prepare the Sous Vide water bath using your immersion circulator and raise the temperature to 134-degrees Fahrenheit
2. Season the steak with pepper, garlic powder and salt
3. Add the steak in a heavy-duty resealable bag and submerge. Allow it to cook for about 2 hours
4. Once cooked, remove the bag from the water bath.
5. Take a cast-iron skillet and place it over medium-high heat
6. After 2 minutes, put 1 teaspoon of canola oil in the skillet
7. Add the spinach and toss well
8. Pour the bag juices into the skillet and toss well. Keep cooking for 30 seconds
9. Transfer to a serving platter and slice the steak against the grain, into ¼ inch pieces
10. Transfer it to the platter with the spinach and serve!

Nutrition Values (Per Serving)

- Calories: 445
- Carbohydrate: 15g
- Protein: 38g
- Fat: 26g
- Sugar: 7g
- Sodium: 412mg

Prime Rib

(**Serves:** 12 / **Prep Time:** 45 minutes / **Sous Vide Cooking Time:** 6 hours)

Ingredients

- 3 lbs. bone-in beef ribeye roast
- Kosher salt as needed
- 1 tablespoon black peppercorn, coarsely ground
- 1 tablespoon green peppercorn, coarsely ground
- 1 tablespoon pink peppercorn, coarsely ground
- 1 tablespoon dried celery seeds
- 2 tablespoons dried garlic powder
- 4 sprigs rosemary
- 1-quart beef stock
- 2 egg whites

How To

1. Season the beef with kosher salt and chill for 12 hours
2. Prepare the Sous Vide water bath using your immersion circulator and raise the temperature to 132-degrees Fahrenheit

3. Add the beef in a zip bag and seal using the immersion method. Cook for 6 hours
4. Pre-heat the oven to 425-degrees Fahrenheit and remove the beef. Pat it dry
5. Mix the peppercorns, celery seeds, garlic powder and rosemary together in a bowl
6. Brush the top of your cooked roast with egg white and season with the mixture and salt
7. Put the roast on a baking rack and roast for 10-15 minutes. Allow it to rest for 10-15 minutes and carve
8. Pour the cooking liquid from the bag in a large saucepan, bring to a boil and simmer until the amount has halved.
9. Carve the roast and serve with the stock.

Nutrition Values (Per Serving)

- Calories: 504
- Carbohydrate: 4g
- Protein: 33g
- Fat: 40g
- Sugar: 0g
- Sodium: 1025mg

New York Strip Steak

(Serves: 1 / **Prep Time:** 5 minutes / **Sous Vide Cooking Time:** 60 minutes)

Ingredients

- New York Strip Steak
- Salt and pepper as needed
- Olive oil
- Steak seasoning as you prefer
- Rosemary and thyme

How To

1. Prepare the Sous Vide water bath using your immersion circulator and raise the temperature to 129-degrees Fahrenheit
2. Season the steak with pepper and salt and place the herbs on top
3. Add it in a zip bag and seal using the immersion method. Cook for 1 hour
4. Once done, remove from the bag and pat dry
5. Drizzle olive oil over and season
6. Grill for 1 minute (each side) at 400-degrees Fahrenheit
7. Slice and serve!

Nutrition Values (Per Serving)

- Calories: 757
- Carbohydrate: 1g
- Protein: 58g
- Fat: 56g
- Sugar: 0g
- Sodium: 489mg

Veal Marsala

(Serves: 4 / **Prep Time:** 15 minutes / **Sous Vide Cooking Time:** 90 minutes)

Ingredients

- 1 lb. veal cutlets
- 2 teaspoons garlic salt
- 2 cups thinly sliced Cremini mushrooms
- ½ cup heavy cream
- 1 shallot, thinly sliced
- 3 tablespoons Marsala
- 2 tablespoons unsalted butter
- 1 teaspoon freshly ground black pepper
- 2 sprigs fresh thyme
- 2 tablespoons chives for garnishing, finely

How To

1. Prepare the Sous Vide water bath using your immersion circulator and raise the temperature to 140-degrees Fahrenheit. Season the veal with garlic salt
2. Add the mushrooms, cream, marsala, pepper, shallot, butter, and thyme along with the seasoned veal, in a heavy-duty resealable zip bag and seal using the immersion method
3. Submerge underwater and cook for 90 minutes
4. Once cooked, remove it from the water bath and place the cutlets on a serving plate
5. Discard the thyme and remove the cooking liquid
6. Pour the mixture into a non-stick skillet and bring to a simmer over medium-high heat
7. Keep simmering for about 5 minutes
8. Lower down the heat to low and add the veal to your sauce. Cook well
9. Put the veal back on the serving plate and serve with rice
10. Garnish with chives and serve!

Nutrition Values (Per Serving)

- Calories: 472
- Carbohydrate: 1g
- Protein: 399g
- Fat: 26g
- Sugar: 3g
- Sodium: 471mg

Italian Sausage

(Serves: 4 / **Prep Time:** 15 minutes / **Sous Vide Cooking Time:** 60 minutes)

Ingredients

- 2½ cups seedless red grapes, stems removed
- 1 tablespoon fresh rosemary, chopped

- 2 tablespoons butter
- 4 sweet Italian sausages
- 2 tablespoons balsamic vinegar
- Salt and ground black pepper as required

How To

1. Prepare the Sous Vide water bath using your immersion circulator and raise the temperature to 165-degrees Fahrenheit
2. Add the butter, grapes, salt, pepper, rosemary and sausages in a resealable zip bag and whisk well
3. Seal using the immersion method and submerge underwater. Cook for 1 hour.
4. Once done, remove the sausage and transfer them to your serving platter
5. Place the grapes and any remaining liquid in a small-sized saucepan
6. Add the balsamic vinegar and simmer for 3 minutes over medium-high heat
7. Serve the sausages with the grapes

Nutrition Values (Per Serving)

- Calories: 340
- Carbohydrate: 10g
- Protein: 12g
- Fat: 24g
- Sugar: 2g
- Sodium: 533mg

Special Tips

If you prefer, you can sear the sausages or grill them for 3 minutes for a more "crispy" texture

Sirloin Steak with Smashed Yukon Potatoes

(Serves: 4 / **Prep Time:** 20 minutes / **Sous Vide Cooking Time:** 60 minutes)

Ingredients

- 4 sirloin steaks
- 2 lbs. baby Yukon potatoes, cubed
- ¼ cup steak seasoning
- Salt and pepper as needed
- 4 tablespoon butter
- Canola oil for searing

How To

1. Prepare the Sous Vide water bath using your immersion circulator and raise the temperature to 129-degrees Fahrenheit
2. Season the steaks. Seal the steaks in a zip bag using the immersion method and cook for 1 hour
3. Take the potatoes and cook them in boiling water for 15 minutes

4. Strain the potatoes into a large mixing bowl and add the butter. Mash using the back of your spoon until mixed well
5. Season with salt and pepper
6. Once cooked, take the steak out from the bag and pat it dry using a kitchen towel
7. Heat a heavy bottomed pan over medium-heat and add the oil. Sear the steak for 1 minute
8. Serve with the smashed potatoes

Nutrition Values (Per Serving)

- Calories: 473
- Carbohydrate: 32g
- Protein: 30g
- Fat: 27g
- Sugar: 5g
- Sodium: 546mg

Beef Wellington

(**Serves:** 4 / **Prep Time:** 60 minutes / **Sous Vide Cooking Time:** 120 minutes)

Ingredients

- 1 lb. beef tenderloin fillet
- Salt and pepper as needed
- 2 tablespoons Dijon mustard
- 1 sheet puff pastry, thawed
- 8 oz. cremini mushrooms
- 1 shallot, diced
- 3 cloves garlic, chopped
- 1 tablespoon unsalted butter
- 6 slices prosciutto

How To

1. Prepare the Sous Vide water bath using your immersion circulator and raise the temperature to 124-degrees Fahrenheit
2. Take the beef tenderloin and generously season it with pepper and salt
3. Place in a zip bag and seal using the immersion method. Cook for 2 hours
4. Chop the mushrooms in a food processor, put the shallots and garlic in a hot pan
5. Cook until tender, add the chopped mushrooms and cook until water has evaporated
6. Add 1 tablespoon of butter and cook
7. Once done, remove the beef from the bag and pat dry
8. Heat the oil in a cast iron pan until shimmering. Sear the beef on all sides for 30 seconds
9. Spread the Dijon mustard all over the tenderloin
10. Lay a plastic wrap on a surface and arrange your prosciutto slices horizontally. Spread the Duxelles* thinly over the prosciutto and place the tenderloin on top
11. Roll the tender loin in the plastic wrap tightly and chill for 20 minutes
12. Roll out your thawed pastry and brush with egg wash. Unwrap the tender loin and place in the pastry puff
13. Bake for 10 minutes in your oven at 475-degrees Fahrenheit, slice and serve!

Nutrition Values (Per Serving)

- Calories: 354
- Carbohydrate: 11g
- Protein: 25g
- Fat: 22g
- Sugar: 0.13g
- Sodium: 263mg

(Note: Duxelles* - In step 5 and 6, we cooked the mushrooms and other vegetables. That particular mixture is referred to as Duxelles.)

Short Rib Tacos

(Serves: 4 / **Prep Time:** 15 minutes / **Sous Vide Cooking Time:** 120 minutes)

Ingredients

- 2 lbs. short rib, thinly sliced
- ½ cup soy sauce
- 3 green onion stalks, sliced
- 1 tablespoon Sambal chili paste
- 6 cloves garlic, chopped
- 2 tablespoons brown sugar
- 1-inch ginger, peeled and grated
- 1 tablespoon sesame oil
- ½ a teaspoon red pepper powder
- 8 corn tortillas
- Kimchi for topping
- Sliced avocado

How To

1. Prepare the Sous Vide water bath using your immersion circulator and increase the temperature to 138-degrees Fahrenheit
2. Add the soy sauce, green onion, garlic, chili paste, brown sugar, ginger, red pepper powder and sesame oil in a saucepan and simmer until the sugar has dissolved
3. Allow to chill and put in a zipper bag, seal using the immersion method and cook for 2 hours
4. Add the marinade from the bag in a saucepan and reduce over medium heat until syrupy
5. Take the short ribs and transfer them to a baking sheet, place them under your broil and broil for 10 minutes
6. Dice the short ribs into ¼ inch cubes
7. Assemble the tacos with avocado, tortilla, and Kimchi and finish with sauce

Nutrition Values (Per Serving)

- Calories: 470
- Carbohydrate: 60g
- Protein: 24g
- Fat: 13g
- Sugar: 4g
- Sodium: 520mg

Hot Dogs

(Serves: 4 / **Prep Time:** 5 minutes / **Sous Vide Cooking Time:** 60 minutes)

Ingredients
- 8 hot dogs
- 8 hot dog buns
- Mustard
- Ketchup

How To
1. Prepare the Sous Vide water bath using your immersion circulator and raise the temperature to 140-degrees Fahrenheit
2. Seal the hot dogs in a zip bag using the immersion method
3. Submerge underwater and cook for 1 hour
4. Serve by placing the hot dogs in the buns and dressing them with mustard and ketchup

Nutrition Values (Per Serving)
- Calories: 230
- Carbohydrate: 3g
- Protein: 6g
- Fat: 10g
- Sugar: 2g
- Sodium: 43mg

Beef Burgers

(Serves: 4 / **Prep Time:** 15 minutes / **Sous Vide Cooking Time:** 60 minutes)

Ingredients
- 10 oz. ground beef
- 2 hamburger buns
- 2 slices American cheese
- Salt and pepper as needed
- Condiments for topping
- Butter for toasting

How To
1. Prepare the Sous Vide water bath using your immersion circulator and raise the temperature to 137-degrees Fahrenheit
2. Shape the beef into patties and season them with salt and pepper
3. Put in a zip bag and seal using the immersion method. Cook for 1 hour
4. Toast the buns in a warm cast iron pan and butter
5. Once the burgers are cooked, place them in the pan and sear for 30 seconds per side
6. Add the cheese on top and allow it to melt

7. Assemble the burger with topping and condiments
8. Serve!

Nutrition Values (Per Serving)

- Calories: 287
- Carbohydrate: 34g
- Protein: 11g
- Fat: 12g
- Sugar: 5g
- Sodium: 362mg

Italian Sausage Sandwich

(Serves: 4 / **Prep Time:** 15 minutes / **Sous Vide Cooking Time:** 180 minutes)

Ingredients

- 1 lb. Italian sausage
- 1 red bell pepper, seeded and cored
- 1 yellow bell pepper, also seeded and cored
- 1 large onion, thinly sliced
- 1 garlic clove, minced
- 1 cup chopped tomatoes, with juice
- 1 teaspoon dried oregano
- 1 teaspoon dried basil
- 1 teaspoon oil
- Salt and pepper as needed
- 4 pieces' bread loaves

How To

1. Prepare the Sous Vide water bath using your immersion circulator and raise the temperature to 140-degrees Fahrenheit
2. Take 2 separate resealable zip bags and divide your sausage into them
3. Do the same with garlic, basil, onion, peppers, tomato and oregano
4. Seal both bags, using the immersion method, and submerge underwater. Cook for 3 hours
5. Add the oil in a skillet and add in the sausage and fry for 1 minute per side
6. Push the sausages to one side and add the remaining contents of the bags to the skillet. Season with pepper and salt
7. Cook until the water has evaporated
8. Serve by making a sandwich of the sausage with bread loaves and the other contents

Nutrition Values (Per Serving)

- Calories: 192
- Carbohydrate: 15g
- Protein: 12g
- Fat: 10g
- Sugar: 2g
- Sodium: 504mg

Crispy Noodle & Beef

(Serves: 2 / **Prep Time:** 10 minutes / **Sous Vide Cooking Time:** 120 minutes)

Ingredients

- 2 rib eye steaks
- 1 nest noodles, boiled and drained
- 2 cups cooking oil
- 2 cups broccoli, boiled and drained
- 1 onion, sliced
- 2 cups warm chicken stock
- 2 tablespoons cornstarch
- 1 tablespoon fish sauce
- Salt and pepper as needed

How To

1. Prepare the Sous Vide water bath using your immersion circulator and raise the temperature to 134-degrees Fahrenheit
2. Place the steak in a zip bag and seal using the immersion method. Submerge and cook for 1-2 hours
3. Add the chicken stock, cornstarch and fish sauce in a bowl
4. Heat the oil and deep fry the noodles for about 5 minutes (half at a time)
5. Place them to one side
6. Fry the onion and add the broccoli, chicken stock, cornstarch and fish sauce
7. Cook for a few minutes until it thickens
8. Take the cooked steaks and pat them dry using a kitchen towel. Sear them for 1 minute using the same pan used to fry the noodles
9. Serve by assembling the noodles on the bottom, vegetables above, and steak over the whole dish
10. Season with extra pepper and salt

Nutrition Values (Per Serving)

- Calories: 576
- Carbohydrate: 28g
- Protein: 84g
- Fat: 7g
- Sugar: 2g
- Sodium: 103mg

Lamb Chops

(Serves: 2 / **Prep Time:** 15 minutes / **Sous Vide Cooking Time:** 120 minutes)

Ingredients

- 2 lamb loin chops
- Salt and pepper as needed

- 1 teaspoon spice blend
- 4 prunes
- 1 tablespoon honey
- 1 teaspoon extra-virgin olive oil

How To

1. Prepare the Sous Vide water bath using your immersion circulator and increase the temperature to 134-degrees Fahrenheit
2. Take the lamb chops and season them thoroughly with salt and pepper. Rub the lamb chops with the spice blend
3. Place the chops in a zip bag, add the prunes and honey, and seal using the immersion method
4. Submerge it underwater and cook for 2 hours
5. Once done, remove the lamb chops and save prunes and cooking liquid
6. Take out the cooked lamb chops and pat them dry using a kitchen towel
7. Place an iron skillet over medium heat for about 5 minutes
8. Add the olive oil and the lamb chops and sear for 30 seconds per side
9. Put on a serving plate and let it stay for 5 minutes
10. Drizzle some of the cooking liquid from the bag over the chops and serve with the prunes

Nutrition Values (Per Serving)

- Calories: 420
- Carbohydrate: 56g
- Protein: 25g
- Fat: 13g
- Sugar: 22g
- Sodium: 455mg

Teriyaki Skewered Lamb

(**Serves:** 2 / **Prep Time:** 10 minutes / **Sous Vide Cooking Time:** 180 minutes)

Ingredients

- 2 lamb backstop loin steaks, cut into 2-inch cubes
- 1 tablespoon soy sauce
- 1 tablespoon mirin
- 2 tablespoons sesame oil

How To

1. Prepare the Sous Vide water bath using your immersion circulator and raise the temperature to 140-degrees Fahrenheit
2. Add the lamb, soy and mirin in a zipper bag and seal using the immersion method

3. Cook for 3 hours
4. Once cooked, take the bag out from the water bath and take out the cooked lamb, pat them dry using kitchen towel
5. Thread onto skewers and discard the cooking liquid
6. Take a skillet and place it over medium-high heat, add the oil. Sear both sides and serve!

Nutrition Values (Per Serving)

- Calories: 419
- Carbohydrate: 26g
- Protein: 39g
- Fat: 17g
- Sugar: 2g
- Sodium: 405mg

Lamb Chops & Mint Pistachio

(Serves: 4 / **Prep Time:** 30 minutes / **Sous Vide Cooking Time:** 120 minutes)

Ingredients

- 2 full racks lamb sliced into chops
- Kosher salt and black pepper as needed
- 1 cup packed fresh mint leaves
- ½ cup unsalted pistachio nuts, shelled
- ½ cup packed fresh parsley
- ½ cup scallion, sliced
- 3 tablespoons lemon juice
- 2 cloves garlic, minced
- 6 tablespoons extra-virgin olive oil

How To

1. Prepare the Sous Vide water bath using your immersion circulator and raise the temperature to 125-degrees Fahrenheit
2. Season the lamb with salt and pepper
3. Put in a zip bag and seal using the immersion method. Cook for 2 hours
4. After 20 minutes, take the lamb out and set the grill to high
5. Add the mint, parsley, pistachios, scallions, garlic, and lemon juice in a food processor and form a paste
6. Drizzle 4 tablespoons of olive oil as you process, and keep going until you have a smooth paste
7. Season with salt and pepper
8. Brush your cooked lamb with 2 tablespoons of olive oil and grill for 1 minute per side
9. Serve the chops with pesto

Nutrition Values (Per Serving)

- Calories: 474
- Carbohydrate: 0g
- Protein: 18g

- Fat: 44g
- Sugar: 0g
- Sodium: 368mg

Lamb Rack with Dijon Mustard

(Serves: 4 / **Prep Time:** 5 minutes / **Sous Vide Cooking Time:** 60 minutes)

Ingredients

- 1 rack of lamb, trimmed
- 3 tablespoons honey
- 2 tablespoons Dijon mustard
- 1 teaspoon sherry vinegar
- ¼ teaspoon salt
- 2 tablespoons avocado oil (or any oil with a high smoke point)
- Mustard seeds and chopped green onion for garnishing

How To

1. Prepare the Sous Vide water bath using your immersion circulator and raise the temperature to 135-degrees Fahrenheit
2. Take a small-sized bowl and add all the listed ingredients (except lamb)
3. Mix well and place the trimmed lamb meat into a zip bag. Pour the sauce in and seal using the immersion method. Cook for 1 hour
4. Once done, take the bag out from the water bath and transfer the lamb to a serving plate, keep the juice on the side
5. Place a frying pan over medium-high heat, add 2 tablespoon of oil and allow it to heat up, and when it shimmers, add in the lamb and sear for 2 minutes per side
6. Slice it and drizzle the bag sauce over
7. Garnish with the mustard seeds and green onions
8. Enjoy!

Nutrition Values (Per Serving)

- Calories: 127
- Carbohydrate: 5g
- Protein: 13g

- Fat: 7g
- Sugar: 0g
- Sodium: 373mg

Quail Breast

(Serves: 4 / **Prep Time:** 15 minutes / **Sous Vide Cooking Time:** 120 minutes)

Ingredients
- 8 quail breasts, bone-in, skin-on
- Kosher salt and freshly ground black pepper
- 1 tablespoon extra-virgin olive oil

How To
1. Prepare the Sous Vide water bath using your immersion circulator and increase the temperature to 134-degrees Fahrenheit
2. Season the quail and place in a zip bag. Seal using the immersion method
3. Cook for 2 hours
4. Once done, remove the bag and take out the quail, pat it dry
5. Rub the cooked quail with oil
6. Take one cast iron skillet and heat it. Sear the breast for 1 minute per side
7. Transfer to a platter and serve

Nutrition Values (Per Serving)
- Calories: 320
- Carbohydrate: 28g
- Protein: 10g
- Fat: 3g
- Sugar: 2g
- Sodium: 170mg

Beef Bone Marrow

(Serves: 4 / **Prep Time:** 15 minutes / **Sous Vide Cooking Time:** 60 minutes)

Ingredients
- 2 pieces' large beef bone marrow, split lengthwise
- Kosher salt as needed
- Ground black pepper as needed

How To
1. Prepare the Sous Vide water bath using your immersion circulator and increase the temperature to 155-degrees Fahrenheit
2. Add the bones in a zip bag and seal using the immersion method
3. Submerge underwater and cook for 1 hour

4. Once done, remove the cooked bone marrow from the bag and transfer it to a baking sheet (make sure to keep the marrow side facing up)
5. Season with salt and pepper
6. Broil the bones for about 2 minutes until the marrow is golden brown
7. Serve!

Nutrition Values (Per Serving)

- Calories: 815
- Carbohydrate: 18g
- Protein: 67g

- Fat: 48g
- Sugar: 67g
- Sodium: 436mg

Dry Aged Steak

(Serves: 1 / **Prep Time:** 20 minutes / **Sous Vide Cooking Time:** 60 minutes)

Ingredients

- 1 dry-aged ribeye steak, boneless
- Salt and pepper as needed
- Lavender Greek seasoning
- 2 tablespoons chopped fresh parsley
- 2 tablespoons extra-virgin olive oil

- ½ teaspoon garlic, minced
- 1 lemon
- 1 tablespoon unsalted butter
- 1 cup mashed potatoes

How To

1. Prepare the Sous Vide water bath using your immersion circulator and raise the temperature to 137-degrees Fahrenheit
2. Season the steak with salt, pepper and lavender Greek seasoning
3. Place in a zip bag and seal using the immersion method. Submerge underwater and cook for 1 hour
4. After 55 minutes, prepare your Gremolata* by combining the parsley, garlic and olive oil in a small bowl
5. Add the juice of ½ the lemon and stir well
6. Season with pepper and salt
7. Once the meat is cooked, remove the steak and pat dry
8. Heat a cast iron skillet over medium high heat for 5 minutes. Add the butter and allow to melt
9. Transfer the steaks and sear both sides for 30 seconds
10. Transfer the steak to a platter and rest for 5 minutes
11. Serve with mashed potatoes and Gremolata

Nutrition Values (Per Serving)

- Calories: 496
- Carbohydrate: 44g
- Protein: 8g
- Fat: 27g
- Sugar: 17g
- Sodium: 494mg

(**Note: Germolata*** - The mixture of parsley, garlic and olive oil)

Bison Ribeye

(**Serves:** 2 / **Prep Time:** 15 minutes / **Sous Vide Cooking Time:** 180 minutes)

Ingredients

- 1 piece (16 oz.) bison Ribeye steak, bone-in
- Kosher salt as needed
- Freshly ground black pepper
- 1 tablespoon extra-virgin olive oil

How To

1. Prepare the Sous Vide water bath using your immersion circulator and increase the temperature to 134-degrees Fahrenheit
2. Take the steak and generously season both sides with salt and pepper
3. Place the steak in a medium-sized, resealable zip bag
4. Seal it, using immersion the method, and submerge it
5. Cook for 3 hours
6. Once cooked, take the steak out and pat it dry with kitchen towel
7. Place a cast-iron skillet over high heat, add in the oil
8. Put the steak in the skillet and sear for about 1 minute (both sides)
9. Allow to rest, slice and serve!

Nutrition Values (Per Serving)

- Calories: 455
- Carbohydrate: 19g
- Protein: 30g
- Fat: 29g
- Sugar: 9g
- Sodium: 519mg

Tzatziki Sauce & Meatball

(Serves: 2 / **Prep Time:** 30 minutes / **Sous Vide Cooking Time:** 120 minutes)

Ingredients

- 1 oz. ground lamb meat
- ¼ cup fresh parsley, chopped
- ¼ cup onion, minced
- ¼ cup toasted pine nuts, finely chopped
- 2 garlic cloves, minced
- Kosher salt as needed
- 2 teaspoons ground coriander
- ¼ teaspoon ground cinnamon
- 1 cup whole milk yogurt
- ½ cup diced cucumber
- 3 tablespoons fresh mint, chopped
- 1 teaspoon lemon juice
- ¼ teaspoon cayenne pepper
- Pitta bread

How To

1. Prepare the Sous Vide water bath using your immersion circulator and raise the temperature to 134-degrees Fahrenheit
2. Add the lamb, onion, pine nuts, 2 teaspoons of salt, garlic, cinnamon and coriander in a medium-sized bowl and mix well using your hand
3. Roll the lamb mix into 20 balls and divide them into two large, heavy-duty resealable zip bags
4. Seal them using the immersion method. Submerge underwater and cook for about 2 hours.
5. While they are cooking, put the yogurt, mint, cucumber, cayenne, lemon juice and 1 teaspoon of salt in a medium-sized bowl to prepare the Tzatziki sauce
6. Once done, remove the balls and broil them for 3-5 minutes over a foil-lined, broiler-safe baking sheet (with broiler set to high)
7. Serve the balls with your Tzatziki sauce along with some pitta bread

Nutrition Values (Per Serving)

- Calories: 251
- Carbohydrate: 20g
- Protein: 17g
- Fat: 12g
- Sugar: 3g
- Sodium: 545mg

Spicy Masala Lamb Racks

(Serves: 4/ **Prep Time:** 10 minutes / **Sous Vide Cooking Time:** 90 minutes)

Ingredients

- 1-1.5 lbs. frenched baby lamb racks
- 2 teaspoons Garam Masala spice blend

- ½ teaspoon salt
- ½ teaspoon pepper

How To

1. Prepare the Sous Vide water bath using your immersion circulator and raise the temperature to 135-degrees Fahrenheit
2. Season the lamb rack with pepper and salt on all sides
3. Rub the rack with Garam Masala
4. Place the rack in a heavy-duty resealable zip bag, making sure the bone side is facing up
5. Seal the bag using the immersion method, and cook for 90 minutes
6. Remove the meat and pat dry using kitchen towel
7. Sear with a blow torch
8. Slice the rack into lollipop shape and serve!

Nutrition Values (Per Serving)

- Calories: 335
- Carbohydrate: 3g
- Protein: 21g
- Fat: 26g
- Sugar: 0g
- Sodium: 2mg

Soy Garlic Tri Tip

(**Serves:** 4/ **Prep Time:** 5 minutes / **Sous Vide Cooking Time:** 120 minutes)

Ingredients

- 2 lbs. tri tip steak roast
- Salt and pepper as needed
- 2 tablespoons soy sauce
- 6 cloves garlic, pre-roasted, crushed

How To

1. Prepare the Sous Vide water bath and increase the temperature to 129-degrees Fahrenheit using your immersion circulator
2. Season both sides of the tri with salt and pepper
3. Place the tri-tip in a zip bag with the soy sauce and crushed garlic cloves
4. Seal using the immersion method. Submerge underwater and cook for 2 hours
5. Once done, remove the meat from the bag and allow it to rest for about 10 minutes until cooled
6. Put a cast-iron skillet over high heat
7. Sear the steak until golden brown, about 1 minute per side
8. Slice and serve with your favorite sauce.

Nutrition Values (Per Serving)

- Calories: 384
- Carbohydrate: 10g
- Protein: 31g
- Fat: 23g
- Sugar: 10g
- Sodium: 369mg

Lamb Rack with Fava Bean

(Serves: 2 / **Prep Time:** 30 minutes / **Sous Vide Cooking Time:** 120 minutes)

Ingredients

- 1 full rack of lamb
- Kosher salt and pepper as needed
- 2 sprigs fresh rosemary
- ¼ cup extra virgin-olive oil
- 2 cups of fresh fava beans, shelled, blanched and peeled
- 1 tablespoon freshly squeeze lemon juice
- 1 tablespoon fresh chives, minced
- 1 tablespoon fresh parsley, minced
- 1 tablespoon fresh mint
- 1 garlic clove, minced

How To

1. Prepare the Sous Vide water bath using your immersion circulator and increase the temperature to 125-degrees Fahrenheit
2. Take the lamb and generously season it with salt and pepper on both sides and transfer to a heavy duty zip bag
3. Seal using the immersion method and cook for 2 hours
4. Once done, remove the lamb and pat dry
5. Set the grill to high and brush up the lamb with 1 tablespoon of olive oil.
6. Grill over high heat for 3 minutes
7. Take the meat and transfer it to a cutting board, allow the meat to rest
8. Prepare the salad by mixing the fava beans, lemon juice, parsley, rosemary, chives, mint, garlic and 3 tablespoon of olive oil together
9. Season with salt and pepper
10. Carefully slice the lamb into chops and serve the chops with your fava beans

Nutrition Values (Per Serving)

- Calories: 331
- Carbohydrate: 8g
- Protein: 14g
- Fat: 28g
- Sugar: 4g
- Sodium: 296mg

Ribeye Cap

(Serves: 4 / **Prep Time:** 15 minutes / **Sous Vide Cooking Time:** 90 minutes)

Ingredients

- 1 lb. ribeye cap
- 2 tablespoons extra-virgin olive oil
- 4 tablespoons unsalted butter
- Kosher salt as needed
- Fresh ground black pepper

How To

1. Prepare the Sous Vide water bath using your immersion circulator and increase the temperature to 132-degrees Fahrenheit
2. Season the rib eye cap liberally with salt and put in a zip bag. Cook for 90 minutes
3. Once cooked, remove the ribeye cap from the bag and pat dry
4. Take a large-sized iron skillet and place it over medium-high heat and add the oil
5. Add the butter and steak and sear until dark golden brown on each side, giving 2 minutes per side. Make sure you keep basting with butter as you cook
6. Once the steak is cool enough, carefully slice the steak and season with a bit of pepper and salt
7. Serve!

Nutrition Values (Per Serving)

- Calories: 960
- Carbohydrate: 1g
- Protein: 87g
- Fat: 77g
- Sugar: 0g
- Sodium: 490mg

Indian Pickle Marinated Lamb Chop

(Serves: 2 / **Prep Time:** 2 minutes / **Sous Vide Cooking Time:** 120 minutes)

Ingredients

- 2 lamb loin chops
- 2 tablespoons Indian mixed pickle
- 2 teaspoons scallions, chopped

How To

1. Prepare the Sous Vide water bath using your immersion circulator and raise the temperature to 140-degrees Fahrenheit
2. Add the lamb chops and pickle in a zip bag and seal using the immersion method
3. Cook for 2 hours
4. Once done, remove the lamb from the bag and put on a serving plate. Discard the cooking liquid
5. Garnish with scallion and serve with some additional pickles resting on the side

Nutrition Values (Per Serving)

- Calories: 230
- Carbohydrate: 4g
- Protein: 10g
- Fat: 19g
- Sugar: 2g
- Sodium: 46mg

Lamb Backstrap

(Serves: 2 / **Prep Time:** 10 minutes / **Sous Vide Cooking Time:** 180 minutes)

Ingredients

- 2 lamb backstrap steaks
- 2 tablespoons extra-virgin olive oil
- Salt and black pepper as needed
- 2 tablespoons sesame oil
- 1 teaspoon sesame seeds
- Pinch of dried red pepper flakes

How To

1. Prepare the Sous Vide water bath using your immersion circulator and raise the temperature to 140-degrees Fahrenheit
2. Add the lamb and olive oil in a zip bag
3. Seal, using the immersion method and cook for 3 hours
4. Once cooked, remove the lamb and pat dry. Season with salt and pepper
5. Heat the sesame oil in a skillet over a medium-high heat until the oil shimmers
6. Place the lamb in and sear
7. Put the lamb on a cutting board and slice into bite sized portions
8. Serve with a garnish of sesame seeds and red flakes

Nutrition Values (Per Serving)

- Calories: 813
- Carbohydrate: 3g
- Protein: 42g
- Fat: 70g
- Sugar: 0g
- Sodium: 458mg

Lollipop Lamb Chops

(Serves: 4 / **Prep Time:** 10 minutes / **Sous Vide Cooking Time:** 60 minutes)

Ingredients

- 8 lollipop lamb chops
- 1 tablespoon olive oil
- ½ teaspoon Garam Masala
- ¼ teaspoon lemon pepper
- ½ tablespoon garlic powder
- Salt and pepper as needed
- ½ cup yogurt
- ¼ cup fresh cilantro, chopped
- 2 tablespoons mango chutney
- 1 tablespoon curry powder
- 1 tablespoon onion, finely chopped
- 1 tablespoon oil

How To

1. Prepare the Sous Vide water bath using your immersion circulator and increase the temperature to 140-degrees Fahrenheit
2. Lay chops on a cutting board and drizzle with olive oil
3. Sprinkle both sides with garam masala, lemon pepper, garlic powder, salt and pepper.
4. Place the chops in a zip bag and seal using the immersion method. Cook for 1 hour
5. While the lamb is underwater, start preparing the sauce by thoroughly mixing the yogurt, mango chutney, cilantro, curry powder, and onion in a bowl
6. Transfer to small dish
7. Once the chops are ready, remove from the bag and pat dry
8. Take a skillet and heat up 1 tablespoon of oil, over high heat, and add the chops when smoking hot
9. Sear the chops for 30 seconds per side and remove from the skillet. Drain quickly on a kitchen towel
10. Serve the chops by arranging them on a serving platter. Place the yogurt sauce on the side
11. Garnish with some chopped cilantro on top

Nutrition Values (Per Serving)

- Calories: 927
- Carbohydrate: 3g
- Protein: 35g
- Fat: 85g
- Sugar: 2g
- Sodium: 447mg

Harissa Lamb Kabob

(Serves: 4 / **Prep Time:** 30 minutes / **Sous Vide Cooking Time:** 120 minutes)

Ingredients

- 1 lb. leg lamb, boneless, cut into 1-inch pieces
- 2 tablespoons harissa
- 1 tablespoon extra-virgin olive oil
- 1 teaspoon kosher salt
- 1 teaspoon cumin
- 1 teaspoon coriander
- ½ teaspoon freshly ground black pepper
- Plain Greek yogurt
- Fresh mint leaves for serving

How To

1. Prepare the Sous Vide water bath using your immersion circulator and raise the temperature to 134-degrees Fahrenheit
2. Add all the listed ingredients except the mint and yogurt in a zip bag and mix well to coat the lamb
3. Seal using the immersion method, and cook for 2 hours
4. Once cooked, remove the lamb and pat dry with paper towels
5. Thread the pieces of lamb onto 4 wooden metal skewers
6. Grill them under a medium-high heat for 5 minutes
7. Place on a serving platter and rest for 5 minutes.
8. Serve with Greek yogurt and fresh mint

Nutrition Values (Per Serving)

- Calories: 582
- Carbohydrate: 58g
- Protein: 26g
- Fat: 26g
- Sugar: 5g
- Sodium: 69mg

Quail Legs

(Serves: 2 / **Prep Time:** 15 minutes / **Sous Vide Cooking Time:** 180 minutes)

Ingredients

- 8 quail legs, bone-in, skin-on
- Kosher salt as needed
- Fresh ground black pepper as needed
- 1 tablespoon extra-virgin olive oil

How To

1. Prepare the Sous Vide water bath using your immersion circulator and raise the temperature to 145-degrees Fahrenheit
2. Take the quail and season it carefully with pepper and salt, transfer the quail to a heavy duty zipper bag
3. Seal using the immersion method, and cook for 3 hours
4. Once done, remove the quail and pat dry with kitchen towels
5. Rub the quail with olive oil
6. Take an iron skillet and place it over high heat and allow it to heat for 5 minutes, then add the quail and sear until the skin turns golden brown (30 seconds per side)
7. Arrange on a platter and serve

Nutrition Values (Per Serving)

- Calories: 290
- Carbohydrate: 18g
- Protein: 27g
- Fat: 18g
- Sugar: 1g
- Sodium: 74mg

CHAPTER 5 | PORK

Pork Cheeks

(Serves: 4 / **Prep Time:** 30 minutes / **Sous Vide Cooking Time:** 5 hours)

Ingredients

- 1 lb. skinless pork cheeks
- Kosher salt, and black pepper, as needed
- 1 cup beef stock
- ½ cup tomato sauce
- 1 stalk celery, cut up into 1-inch dice
- 1 quartered shallot
- 3 sprigs fresh thyme
- 1 oz. whiskey
- Mashed potatoes

How To

1. Prepare the Sous Vide water bath using your immersion circulator and increase the temperature to 180-degrees Fahrenheit.
2. Take the cheeks and season it with salt and pepper and transfer them to a heavy-duty resealable zip bag.
3. Add in the stock, tomato sauce, shallot, whiskey, celery, and thyme to the bag.
4. Seal up the bag using the immersion method and submerge it underwater. Cook for 5 hours.
5. Once cooked, remove the bag and transfer it to a plate.
6. Strain the cooking liquid through a fine mesh strainer into a large saucepan. Discard any solid remains.
7. Bring the mixture to a simmer by placing it over medium-high heat.
8. Reduce the heat to medium-low and keep simmering for 20 minutes.
9. Lower down the heat to low levels and transfer the cheeks.
10. Simmer for 2-3 minutes.
11. Serve with the mashed potatoes.

Nutrition Values (Per Serving)

- Calories: 340
- Carbohydrate: 0g
- Protein: 41g
- Fat: 18g
- Sugar: 0g
- Sodium: 432mg

Pork Bacon –The Secret Canadian Recipe

(Serves: 4 / **Prep Time:** 7 minutes / **Sous Vide Cooking Time:** 6 hours)

Ingredients
- 8 slices Canadian bacon
- 1 teaspoon vegetable oil – optional
- Salt and pepper as needed

How To
1. Prepare the Sous Vide water bath using your immersion circulator and raise the temperature to 145-degrees Fahrenheit.
2. Take a resealable plastic zip bag and add the bacon in the bag.
3. Seal using the immersion method.
4. Submerge it underwater and cook for 6 hours.
5. Sprinkle with salt and pepper and serve!

Nutrition Values (Per Serving)
- Calories: 384
- Carbohydrate: 53g
- Protein: 16g
- Fat: 12g
- Sugar: 5g
- Sodium: 528mg

Special Tips
You may take a medium skillet and place it over medium heat with a bit of oil and sear the meat for a crispier texture.

Bacon Strips & Eggs

(Serves: 2 / **Prep Time:** 10 minutes / **Sous Vide Cooking Time:** 60 minutes)

Ingredients
- 4 egg yolks
- 2 slices British-style bacon rashers cut up into ½ inch by 3-inch slices
- 4 slices crisp toasted bread

How To
1. Prepare the Sous Vide water bath using your immersion circulator and raise the temperature to 143-degrees Fahrenheit.

2. Gently place each of your egg yolks in the resealable zipper bag and seal it using the immersion method.
3. Submerge it underwater and cook for about 1 hour.
4. In the meantime, fry your bacon slices until they are crisp.
5. Drain them on a kitchen towel.
6. Once the eggs are cooked, serve by carefully removing the yolks from the zip bag and placing it on top of the toast.
7. Top with the slices of bacon and serve!

Nutrition Values (Per Serving)
- Calories: 385
- Carbohydrate: 49g
- Protein: 16g
- Fat: 16g
- Sugar: 4g
- Sodium: 514mg

Pork Hoagies

(Serves: 4 / **Prep Time:** 15 minutes / **Sous Vide Cooking Time:** 12 hours)

Ingredients
- 1 lb. boneless pork shoulder chops
- 1 tablespoon dry rub + additional teaspoon for later use
- ¼ cup BBQ sauce
- 4 hoagie rolls
- 1 cup prepped fried pickles for topping

How To
1. Prepare the Sous Vide water bath using your immersion circulator and increase the temperature to 187-degrees Fahrenheit.
2. Slice up the pork into bite-sized portions and season with 1 tablespoon of dry rub.
3. Transfer the chops to a large resealable zipper bag and seal using the immersion method.
4. Cook for 12 hours.
5. Once cooked, remove the pork from the bag and shred it.
6. Season using the dry rub
7. Serve by topping the hoagie rolls with soft fried pickles and a drizzle of BBQ sauce.

Nutrition Values (Per Serving)
- Calories: 297
- Carbohydrate: 11g
- Protein: 37g
- Fat: 9g
- Sugar: 8g
- Sodium: 524mg

Special Tips

You can always go for store bought dry rubs; however, a good method to prepare dry rubs for pork shoulders might be to mix 1/3 teaspoon salt, 1/3 teaspoon ground black pepper, 1 teaspoon sugar, a bit of chili powder, cumin, paprika, onion powder all together into a fine blend.

Bacon Potato Mix

(Serves: 6 / **Prep Time:** 30 minutes / **Sous Vide Cooking Time:** 90 minutes)

Ingredients

- 1 ½ lb. Yukon potatoes, sliced up into ¾ inch pieces
- ½ cup chicken stock
- Salt and pepper, as needed
- 4 oz. thick bacon cut up into ¼ inch thick strips
- ½ cup onion, chopped
- 1/3 cup apple cider vinegar
- 4 thinly sliced scallions

How To

1. Prepare the Sous Vide water bath using your immersion circulator and increase the temperature to 185-degrees Fahrenheit.
2. Take a heavy duty resealable bag and add the potatoes alongside stock.
3. Season with some salt and seal it using the immersion method. Submerge and cook for about 1 and a ½ hour.
4. Place a large-sized skillet over medium-high heat.
5. Add the bacon and cook for 5-7 minutes.
6. Transfer it to a kitchen towel and dry it. Reserve the fat.
7. Return the heat to the skillet and add the onions. Cook for 1 minute.
8. Take a skillet and place it over medium heat, remove the bag from the water bath and pour the stock and potatoes from the bag into the skillet.
9. Add the cooked bacon and vinegar.
10. Bring the mixture to a simmer.
11. Add the scallions and season with a bit of pepper and salt.

Nutrition Values (Per Serving)

- Calories: 425
- Carbohydrate: 28g
- Protein: 17g
- Fat: 27g
- Sugar: 6g
- Sodium: 570mg

Molasses Pork Loin

(Serves: 6 / **Prep Time:** 15 minutes / **Sous Vide Cooking Time:** 240 minutes)

Ingredients

- 2 lbs. pork loin roast
- 1-piece bay leaf
- 3 oz. molasses
- ½ oz. soy sauce
- ½ oz. honey
- Juice of 2 lemons
- 2 strips lemon peel
- 4 chopped scallions
- ½ teaspoon garlic powder
- ¼ teaspoon Dijon mustard
- ¼ teaspoon ground ginger
- 1 oz. crushed corn chips
- Green onion for serving, sliced

How To

1. Prepare the Sous Vide water bath using your immersion circulator and raise the temperature to 142-degrees Fahrenheit.
2. Transfer the pork loin and bay leaf into a resealable zip bag.
3. Take a small bowl and mix the molasses, soy, lemon peel, honey, bay leaf, scallions, garlic powder, mustard, and ginger.
4. Ladle 1/3 of the mixture over the pork loin.
5. Seal using the immersion method. Cook for 4 hours.
6. Once cooked, take the pork out from the water bath and add the remaining glaze to a saucepan.
7. Boil all over high heat and cook until reduced to glaze.
8. Pour glaze over pork loin and toss crushed corn chips over all.
9. Serve with the sliced green onion

Nutrition Values (Per Serving)

- Calories: 163
- Carbohydrate: 28g
- Protein: 10g
- Fat: 2g
- Sugar: 20g
- Sodium: 134mg

Japanese Pork Cutlet

(Serves: 3 / **Prep Time:** 15 minutes / **Sous Vide Cooking Time:** 60 minutes)

Ingredients

- 3 pork loin chops
- Salt and pepper as needed

- 1 cup flour
- 2 whole eggs
- Panko crumbs as needed to coat the chops

How To

1. Prepare the Sous Vide water bath using your immersion circulator and raise the temperature to 140-degrees Fahrenheit.
2. Make tiny slits on the loin body and trim any excess fat. Season with salt and pepper.
3. Transfer to a resealable zip bag and seal using the immersion method. Submerge and cook for 1 hour.
4. Once cooked, remove the loin chops from the bag and pat them dry.
5. Dredge the loin in flour, egg and finally panko crumbs.
6. Heat up the oil to 450-degrees Fahrenheit and fry chops for 1 minute.
7. Put on a cooling rack and slice.
8. Serve on top of the steamed rice with vegetables.

Nutrition Values (Per Serving)

- Calories: 260
- Carbohydrate: 45g
- Protein: 8g
- Fat: 7g
- Sugar: 3g
- Sodium: 510mg

Apple Butter Pork Tenderloin

(Serves: 3 / **Prep Time:** 10 minutes / **Sous Vide Cooking Time:** 120 minutes)

Ingredients

- 1 pork tenderloin
- 1 jar apple butter
- Fresh rosemary sprigs
- Salt and pepper, as needed

How To

1. Prepare the Sous Vide water bath using your immersion circulator and raise the temperature to 145-degrees Fahrenheit.
2. Season the pork with salt and pepper.
3. Spread apple butter on pork.
4. Transfer to a resealable zip bag and add the rosemary sprigs.
5. Seal using the immersion method and cook for 2 hours.
6. Once done, remove the pork from the bag and pat dry.

7. Season with salt and pepper and apply apple butter generously.
8. Sear on hot grill.
9. Slice and serve!

Nutrition Values (Per Serving)

- Calories: 520
- Carbohydrate: 84g
- Protein: 12g
- Fat: 28g
- Sugar: 38g
- Sodium: 330mg

Pork Chop with Corn

(Serves: 3 / **Prep Time:** 15 minutes / **Sous Vide Cooking Time:** 60 minutes)

Ingredients

- 4 pieces' pork chop
- 1 small red bell pepper, diced
- 1 small yellow onion, diced
- 3 ears corn kernels
- ¼ cup cilantro, chopped
- Salt and pepper as needed
- Vegetable oil

How To

1. Prepare the Sous Vide water bath using your immersion circulator and raise the temperature to 140-degrees Fahrenheit.
2. Season the pork chop with salt.
3. Transfer to a resealable zip bag and seal using the immersion method. Cook for 1 hour.
4. Take a pan and put it over medium heat, add the oil and allow the oil to heat up
5. Add the onion, corn, and bell pepper.
6. Sauté for a while until barely browned.
7. Finish the corn mix with cilantro and set it aside.
8. Wipe the pan clean and place the pan over medium heat.
9. Add the oil and sear the pork chop for 1 minute per side.
10. Slice and serve with the salad.

Nutrition Values (Per Serving)

- Calories: 353
- Carbohydrate: 8g
- Protein: 41g
- Fat: 16g
- Sugar: 4g
- Sodium: 162mg

Mango Salsa & Pork

(Serves: 4 / **Prep Time:** 45 minutes / **Sous Vide Cooking Time:** 2 hours)

Ingredients

- ¼ cup light broth sugar
- 1 tablespoon ground allspice
- ½ teaspoon cayenne pepper
- ¼ teaspoon ground cinnamon
- ¼ teaspoon ground cloves
- Kosher salt and black pepper, as needed
- 2 lbs. pork tenderloin
- 2 tablespoons canola oil
- 2 pitted and peeled mangoes, finely diced
- ¼ cup fresh cilantro, chopped
- 1 red bell pepper, stemmed, seeded, and finely diced
- 3 tablespoons red onion, finely diced
- 2 tablespoons freshly squeezed lime juice
- 1 small jalapeno seeded and finely diced

How To

1. Prepare the Sous Vide water bath using your immersion circulator and raise the temperature to 135-degrees Fahrenheit.
2. Take a medium bowl and mix the sugar, allspice, cinnamon, cayenne, cloves, 2 teaspoons of salt, and 1 teaspoon of pepper.
3. Rub the mixture over the tenderloins.
4. Take a large-sized skillet and put it over medium heat, add the oil and once the oil simmers, transfer the pork and sear for 5 minutes, browning all sides.
5. Transfer to a plate and rest for 10 minutes.
6. Transfer the pork chop to a resealable zipper bag and seal using the immersion method. Cook for 2 hours.
7. Once cooked, take the bag out and allow it to rest for a while, take the chop out and slice it.
8. Prepare the salsa by mixing the mango, cilantro, bell pepper, onion, lime juice, and jalapeno in a mixing bowl.
9. Serve the sliced pork with salsa with a seasoning salt and pepper.

Nutrition Values (Per Serving)

- Calories: 217
- Carbohydrate: 11g
- Protein: 25g
- Fat: 8g
- Sugar: 8g
- Sodium: 112mg

Lemongrass Pork Chops

(Serves: 2 / **Prep Time:** 30 minutes / **Sous Vide Cooking Time:** 2 hours)

Ingredients

- 2 tablespoons coconut oil
- 1 stalk sliced lemon grass
- 1 tablespoon minced shallot
- 1 tablespoon soy sauce
- 1 tablespoon mirin
- 1 tablespoon rice wine vinegar
- 1 tablespoon light brown sugar
- 1 teaspoon minced fresh ginger
- 1 teaspoon fish sauce
- 1 teaspoon kosher salt
- 2 (10-ounce) bone-in pork rib chops
- 1 teaspoon minced garlic

How To

1. Prepare the Sous Vide water bath using your immersion circulator and raise the temperature to 140-degrees Fahrenheit.
2. Take a food processor and add 1 tablespoon of coconut oil, lemon grass, soy sauce, shallot, vinegar, mirin, brown sugar, garlic, fish sauce, ginger, and salt.
3. Process for 1 minute.
4. Place the pork chops into a resealable zip bag alongside soy-lemon grass mixture and seal using the immersion method. Cook for 2 hours.
5. Once cooked, remove the bag and take the pork chops out, pat them dry.
6. Heat a grill to high heat and sear the chops until well browned.
7. Allow it to rest for 2-3 minutes.
8. Serve!

Nutrition Values (Per Serving)

- Calories: 262
- Carbohydrate: 12g
- Protein: 26g
- Fat: 12g
- Sugar: 1.2g
- Sodium: 458mg

Pork & Zucchini Ribbons

(Serves: 2 / **Prep Time:** 20 minutes / **Sous Vide Cooking Time:** 3 hours)

Ingredients

- 2 (6-ounce) bone-in pork loin chops
- Salt and black pepper as needed
- 3 tablespoons extra-virgin olive oil
- 1 tablespoon freshly squeezed lemon juice

- 2 teaspoons red wine vinegar
- 2 teaspoons honey
- 2 tablespoons rice bran oil
- 2 medium zucchini, sliced into ribbons
- 2 tablespoons pine nuts, toasted up

How To

1. Prepare the Sous Vide water bath using your immersion circulator and raise the temperature to 140-degrees Fahrenheit.
2. Take the pork chops and season it with salt and pepper, transfer to a heavy duty zip bag and add 1 tablespoon of oil .
3. Seal using the immersion method and cook for 3 hours.
4. Prepare the dressing by whisking lemon juice, honey, vinegar, 2 tablespoons of olive oil and season with salt and pepper.
5. Once cooked, remove the bag from the water bath and discard the liquid.
6. Heat up rice bran oil in a large skillet over high heat and add the pork chops, sear until browned (1 minute per side)
7. Once done, transfer it to a cutting board and allow to rest for 5 minutes.
8. Take a medium bowl and add the zucchini ribbons with dressing
9. Thinly slice the pork chops and discard the bone.
10. Place the pork on top of the zucchini.
11. Top with pine nuts and serve!

Nutrition Values (Per Serving)

- Calories: 174
- Carbohydrate: 4g
- Protein: 19g

- Fat: 9g
- Sugar: 2g
- Sodium: 302mg

Herbed Pork Loin

(Serves: 4 / **Prep Time:** 20 minutes / **Sous Vide Cooking Time:** 2 hours)

Ingredients

- 1 (1 lb.) pork tenderloin, trimmed
- Salt and fresh ground pepper as needed
- 1 tablespoon chopped fresh basil + additional for serving
- 1 tablespoon chopped fresh parsley + additional for serving
- 1 tablespoon chopped fresh rosemary + additional for serving
- 2 tablespoons unsalted butter

How To

1. Prepare the Sous Vide water bath using your immersion circulator and raise the temperature to 134-degrees Fahrenheit. Season the tenderloin with pepper and salt
2. Rub herbs (a mixture of basil, parsley and rosemary) all over the tenderloin and transfer to a resalable zip bag
3. Add 1 tablespoon of butter
4. Seal using the immersion method. Submerge underwater and cook for 2 hours
5. Once cooked, remove the bag and remove the pork from the bag
6. Place a large-sized skillet over medium–high heat
7. Add the remaining butter and herb mixture and allow the butter to heat up
8. Add the pork and sear it well for 1-2 minutes each side, making sure to keep scooping the butter over the pork
9. Remove the heat and transfer the pork to a cutting board
10. Allow it to rest for 5 minutes and slice into medallions
11. Serve with extra herbs and a sprinkle of salt

Nutrition Values (Per Serving)

- Calories: 284
- Carbohydrate: 3g
- Protein: 33g

- Fat: 14g
- Sugar: 0g
- Sodium: 421mg

Red Pepper Salad & Pork Chop

(Serves: 4 / **Prep Time:** 15 minutes / **Sous Vide Cooking Time:** 1 hour)

Ingredients

- 4 pork chops
- 1 small red bell pepper, diced
- 1 small yellow onion, diced
- 2 cups frozen corn kernels
- ¼ cup cilantro, chopped
- Salt and pepper as needed
- Vegetable oil as needed

How To

1. Prepare the Sous Vide water bath using your immersion circulator and raise the temperature to 140-degrees Fahrenheit.
2. Season the pork carefully with salt

3. Transfer the pork to a resealable zip bag and seal using the immersion method. Submerge underwater and cook for 1 hour
4. Take a pan and put it over medium heat and add the oil, allow it to heat up
5. Add the onion, red pepper, corn and sauté for a while until they are slightly browned
6. Season with salt and pepper
7. Finish the corn mix with a garnish of chopped cilantro, keep it aside
8. Remove the pan from heat and wipe the oil
9. Place it back to medium-high heat
10. Put the oil and allow it to heat up
11. Transfer the cooked pork chops to the pan and sear each side for 1 minute
12. Serve the pork chops with the salad!

Nutrition Values (Per Serving)

- Calories: 657
- Carbohydrate: 49g
- Protein: 25g
- Fat: 41g
- Sugar: 25g
- Sodium: 489mg

Fragrant Nonya Pork Belly

(Serves: 7 / **Prep Time:** 10 minutes / **Sous Vide Cooking Time:** 7 hours)

Ingredients

- 1 lb. pork belly
- ¼ cup chopped shallots
- 3 sliced garlic cloves
- ½ tablespoon coriander seeds
- 2-star anise
- 4 large dried shiitake mushrooms
- 2 tablespoons coconut aminos
- 2 teaspoons brown sugar
- ½ teaspoon salt
- ¼ teaspoon ground white pepper

How To

1. Prepare the Sous Vide water bath using your immersion circulator and raise the temperature to 176-degrees Fahrenheit.
2. Chop up the pork belly into 1-inch cubes and transfer to a bowl.
3. Add the remaining ingredients and whisk them well.
4. Transfer to a resealable zip bag and seal using the immersion method.
5. Cook for 7 hours and remove the bag.
6. Transfer the solids to serving dish and discard the star anise.
7. Tip the cooking liquid to a small pan and reduce it over medium heat.
8. Pour the sauce over pork belly and serve!

Nutrition Values (Per Serving)

- Calories: 300
- Carbohydrate: 5g
- Protein: 4g
- Fat: 30g
- Sugar: 3g
- Sodium: 521mg

Special Tips

If you want more flavor, then use a mortar and pestle to crush the coriander seeds before adding them to the bag.

Italian Sausage & Autumn Grape

(Serves: 4 / **Prep Time:** 15 minutes / **Sous Vide Cooking Time:** 60 minutes)

Ingredients

- 2 ½ cups seedless purple grapes with stem removed
- 1 tablespoon chopped fresh rosemary
- 2 tablespoons butter
- 4 whole sweet Italian sausages
- 2 tablespoons balsamic vinegar
- Salt and ground black pepper, as needed

How To

1. Prepare the Sous Vide water bath using your immersion circulator and raise the temperature to 160-degrees Fahrenheit.
2. Take a plastic bag and add the grapes, rosemary, butter, and sausage in one layer.
3. Seal using the immersion method. Cook for 1 hour.
4. Remove the sausage to serving platter and pour the grapes and liquid in a saucepan.
5. Add the balsamic vinegar and simmer for 3 minutes over medium-high heat and season the mixture with salt and pepper.
6. Grill the sausage on medium-high heat for 3-4 minutes and serve with the grapes.

Nutrition Values (Per Serving)

- Calories: 341
- Carbohydrate: 11g
- Protein: 28g
- Fat: 21g
- Sugar: 6g
- Sodium: 602mg

Mushroom Mixed Pork Chops

(Serves: 2 / **Prep Time:** 5 minutes / **Sous Vide Cooking Time:** 55 minutes)

Ingredients
- 2 thick-cut bone-in pork chops
- Salt and fresh ground pepper, as needed
- 2 tablespoons unsalted butter, cold
- 4 oz. mixed wild mushrooms
- ¼ cup sherry
- ½ cup beef stock
- 1 tablespoon steak marinade
- Chopped garlic for garnish

How To
1. Prepare the Sous Vide water bath using your immersion circulator and raise the temperature to 140-degrees Fahrenheit.
2. Take the pork chop and season it thoroughly with salt and pepper and transfer to a resealable zip bag, seal using the immersion method and cook for 55 minutes.
3. Remove the pork chop and pat dry, discard cooking liquid.
4. Take a large skillet and put it over medium-high heat, add 1 tablespoon of butter and allow the butter to melt.
5. Add the pork chops and sear 1 minute per side and transfer to a platter.
6. Heat up the skillet once more and add the mushrooms, cook for 2-3 minutes.
7. Add the sherry and bring the mixture to a nice simmer, add the stock, and steak marinade and simmer until you have a thick sauce.
8. Remove the heat and swirl the remaining butter, season with salt and pepper and pour over the pork chops.
9. Garnish with chopped garlic and serve!

Nutrition Values (Per Serving)
- Calories: 392
- Carbohydrate: 20g
- Protein: 38g
- Fat: 17g
- Sugar: 12g
- Sodium: 119mg

Pork Cheek Tacos

(Serves: 8 / **Prep Time:** 20 minutes / **Sous Vide Cooking Time:** 12 hours)

Ingredients
- 2 lbs. skinless pork cheeks
- 1 tablespoon ancho chili powder

- 1 tablespoon kosher salt
- 1 tablespoon light brown sugar
- 2 teaspoons ground cumin
- 2 teaspoons garlic powder
- 1 teaspoon cayenne pepper
- 1 teaspoon freshly ground black pepper
- Corn tortillas
- Pickled red onion and fresh cilantro for serving

How To

1. Prepare the Sous Vide water bath using your immersion circulator and raise the temperature to 180-degrees Fahrenheit.
2. Add the pork cheeks, chili powder, salt, brown sugar, garlic powder, cumin, cayenne, and black pepper to a resealable zipper bag and seal using the immersion method.
3. Cook for 12 hours.
4. Once cooked, remove the bag and take the pork out, reserve the cooking liquid.
5. Take the pork and shred the pork into 1-inch pieces and transfer to a large bowl.
6. Stir in the cooking liquid and serve on tortillas with a topping of pickled red onion and fresh cilantro.

Nutrition Values (Per Serving)

- Calories: 475
- Carbohydrate: 20g
- Protein: 44g
- Fat: 26g
- Sugar: 10g
- Sodium: 576mg

Honey Mustard Pork

(Serves: 2 / **Prep Time:** 20 minutes / **Sous Vide Cooking Time:** 3 hours)

Ingredients

- 3 tablespoons extra-virgin olive oil
- 1 tablespoon + 2 teaspoons whole grain mustard
- 1 tablespoon + 1 teaspoon honey
- Salt and ground black pepper, as needed
- 2 pieces' bone-in pork loin chops
- 1 tablespoon freshly squeezed lemon juice
- 2 teaspoons red wine vinegar
- 2 tablespoons rice bran oil

- 2 cups mixed baby lettuce
- 2 tablespoons thinly sliced sundried tomatoes
- 2 teaspoons pine nuts, toasted

How To

1. Prepare the Sous Vide water bath using the immersion circulator and raise the temperature to 140-degrees Fahrenheit.
2. Take a small bowl and mix in 1 tablespoon olive oil, 1 tablespoon mustard, 1 tablespoon honey, and season with salt and pepper
3. Transfer to a resealable zip bag alongside the pork chop and toss well to coat it.
4. Seal using the immersion method and cook for 3 hours.
5. To prepare the dressing, add the lemon juice, vinegar, 2 tablespoons of olive oil, 2 teaspoons of mustard and the remaining honey in a bowl. Season with salt and pepper.
6. Remove the bag and remove the pork chop, discard the liquid.
7. Take a large skillet over high heat and add bran oil, heat it up and wait until it starts to smoke. Add the pork chops and sear for 30 seconds per side.
8. Rest for 5 minutes.
9. Take a medium bowl and add the lettuce, sun-dried tomatoes and pine nuts, toss well with 3 quarter of the dressing.
10. Take the pork chops and transfer them to your serving plate and top with the salad and dressing.
11. Serve!

Nutrition Values (Per Serving)

- Calories: 357
- Carbohydrate: 22g
- Protein: 47g
- Fat: 8g
- Sugar: 22g
- Sodium: 162mg

Pork Cheek Ragout

(Serves: 8 / **Prep Time:** 30 minutes / **Sous Vide Cooking Time:** 10 hours)

Ingredients

- 2 lbs. skinless pork cheeks
- 2 finely diced carrots
- ½ white onion, finely diced
- 1 cup canned tomato sauce
- 1 cup canned diced tomatoes
- 3 sprigs oregano

- 3 garlic cloves, crushed
- 1 teaspoon granulated sugar
- 2 pieces' bay leaves
- Kosher salt and black pepper, as needed
- Cooked pasta and fresh parsley for serving

How To

1. Prepare the Sous Vide water bath using your immersion circulator and raise the temperature to 180-degrees Fahrenheit.
2. Add the pork cheeks, carrots, onion, tomato sauce, diced tomatoes, garlic, oregano, sugar, bay leaves, 1 teaspoon of pepper, 1 tablespoon of salt to a heavy-duty re-sealable zip bag.
3. Seal using the immersion method. Cook for 10 hours.
4. Once done, remove the bag and then the pork, make sure to reserve the cooking liquid.
5. Shred using 2 forks into 1-inch pieces, transfer to large bowl and set it to the side.
6. Remove and discard the oregano from the cooking liquid, pour the contents to a food processor and pulse until the ingredients are uniformly chopped.
7. Take the sauce and season it well with pepper and salt, pour it over the pork toss to combine.
8. Toss the pasta with the mixture and serve with parsley!

Nutrition Values (Per Serving)

- Calories: 428
- Carbohydrate: 40g
- Protein: 26g
- Fat: 20g
- Sugar: 24g
- Sodium: 144mg

Pork Slices with Noodle Salad

(Serves: 2 / **Prep Time:** 20 minutes / **Sous Vide Cooking Time:** 12 hours)

Ingredients

- ½ pound boneless pork leg
- 1 tablespoon extra-virgin olive oil
- 1 tablespoon freshly squeezed lime juice
- 1 tablespoon fish sauce
- 1 tablespoon soy sauce
- 1 tablespoon rice vinegar
- 1 tablespoon palm sugar
- 2 vermicelli noodle nests

- ½ thinly sliced scallion
- 2 tablespoons roasted peanuts chopped up
- 2 tablespoons chopped fresh cilantro
- 2 tablespoons chopped fresh mint

How To

1. Prepare the Sous Vide water bath using your immersion circulator and raise the temperature to 176-degrees Fahrenheit.
2. Add the pork leg to a resealable zip bag alongside the olive oil.
3. Seal using the immersion method and cook for 12 hours.
4. Prepare your dressing by mixing the lime juice, soy sauce, fish sauce, rice vinegar, and palm sugar in a small-sized bowl, give the whole mixture a nice stir.
5. Once cooked, take the pork out from the water bath and allow it to cool.
6. Shred using forks into bite-sized pieces.
7. Bring a large pot of water and bring it to a boil over high heat, add the vermicelli noodle and cook for 2-3 minutes.
8. Transfer to a bowl and add the scallions, mint, cilantro, peanuts, dressing, and pork to the noodle and toss well.
9. Serve!

Nutrition Values (Per Serving)

- Calories: 411
- Carbohydrate: 62g
- Protein: 23g
- Fat: 11g
- Sugar: 12g
- Sodium: 561mg

Pork Chili Verde

(Serves: 8 / **Prep Time:** 40 minutes / **Sous Vide Cooking Time:** 24 hours)

Ingredients

- 2 lbs. boneless pork shoulder cut up into 1-inch pieces
- 1 tablespoon kosher salt
- 1 tablespoon ground cumin
- 1 teaspoon fresh ground black pepper
- 1 tablespoon extra-virgin olive oil
- 1 lb. tomatillos
- 3 poblano pepper, finely seeded and diced
- ½ white onion finely diced
- 1 jalapeno seeded and diced

- 3 garlic cloves, crushed
- 1 bunch roughly chopped cilantro
- 1 cup chicken broth
- ½ cup fresh squeezed lime juice
- 1 tablespoon Mexican oregano

How To

1. Prepare the Sous Vide water bath using your immersion circulator and raise the temperature to 150-degrees Fahrenheit.
2. Season the pork with salt, cumin, and pepper.
3. Take a large skillet and place it over medium-high heat, add the oil and allow it to heat up.
4. Add the pork and sear for 5-7 minutes.
5. Increase the heat back to medium-high and add the tomatillos, poblano pepper, onion, jalapeno, and garlic. Cook for 5 minutes until slightly charred.
6. Transfer the whole prepared mixture to a food processor and add the cilantro, lime juice, chicken broth, oregano, and process for 1 minute.
7. Transfer the sauce to a resealable zip bag alongside the pork and seal using the immersion method. Submerge it underwater and cook for 24 hours.
8. Once cooked, remove the bag and transfer the contents to a serving bowl. Sprinkle some salt and pepper and serve over rice.

Nutrition Values (Per Serving)

- Calories: 332
- Carbohydrate: 29g
- Protein: 15g
- Fat: 18g
- Sugar: 4g
- Sodium: 323mg

Garlic & Ginger Pork Kebobs

(Serves: 4 / **Prep Time:** 30 minutes / **Sous Vide Cooking Time:** 4 hours)

Ingredients

- 1 lb. boneless pork shoulder cut up into 1-inch pieces
- 1 tablespoon kosher salt
- 1 tablespoon minced salt
- 1 tablespoon minced fresh ginger
- 1 tablespoon garlic, minced
- 1 teaspoon cumin
- 1 teaspoon coriander
- 1 teaspoon garlic powder

- 1 teaspoon brown sugar
- 1 teaspoon fresh ground black pepper

How To

1. Prepare the Sous Vide water bath using your immersion circulator and raise the temperature to 150-degrees Fahrenheit.
2. Rub the pork with salt, garlic, ginger, cumin, coriander, garlic powder, pepper, and brown sugar, and transfer to a resealable bag.
3. Seal using the immersion method and cook for 4 hours.
4. Heat up the grill to medium-high heat and remove the pork from the bag once cooking is done, pierce it into skewers.
5. Grill for 3 minutes until browned all around
6. Serve!

Nutrition Values (Per Serving)

- Calories: 220
- Carbohydrate: 14g
- Protein: 13g
- Fat: 15g
- Sugar: 3g
- Sodium: 317mg

Cream-Poached Pork Loin

(**Serves:** 4 / **Prep Time:** 30 minutes / **Sous Vide Cooking Time:** 4 hours)

Ingredients

- 1 – 3 lbs. boneless pork loin roast
- Kosher salt and pepper as needed
- 2 thinly sliced onion
- ¼ cup cognac
- 1 cup whole milk
- 1 cup heavy cream

How To

1. Prepare the Sous Vide water bath using your immersion circulator and raise the temperature to 145-degrees Fahrenheit.
2. Season the pork with pepper and salt, take a large iron skillet and place it over medium-heat for 5 minutes.
3. Add the pork and sear for 15 minutes until all sides are browned.
4. Transfer to a platter, add the onion to the rendered fat (in the skillet) and cook for 5 minutes.

5. Add the cognac and bring to a simmer. Allow it to cool for 10 minutes.
6. Add the pork, onion, milk, and cream to a resealable zipper bag and seal using the immersion method. Submerge underwater and cook for 4 hours.
7. Once cooked, remove the bag from the water and take the pork out, transfer the pork to cutting board and cover it to keep it warm.
8. Pour the bag contents to a skillet and bring the mixture to a simmer over medium heat, keep cooking for 10 minutes and season with salt and pepper.
9. Slice the pork and serve with the cream sauce.

Nutrition Values (Per Serving)

- Calories: 1809
- Carbohydrate: 23g
- Protein: 109g
- Fat: 140g
- Sugar: 19g
- Sodium: 621mg

Hoisin Glazed Pork Tenderloin

(Serves: 3 / **Prep Time:** 20 minutes / **Sous Vide Cooking Time:** 3 hours)

Ingredients

- 1-piece pork tenderloin, trimmed
- 1 teaspoon kosher salt
- ½ teaspoon freshly ground black pepper
- 3 tablespoons hoisin sauce

How To

1. Prepare the Sous Vide water bath using your immersion circulator and raise the temperature to 145-degrees Fahrenheit.
2. Take the tenderloins and season it with pepper and salt and transfer to a resealable zip bag.
3. Seal using the immersion method and cook for 3 hours.
4. Remove the bag and then the pork, brush with hoisin sauce.
5. Heat up your grill to high grill and add the tenderloin, sear for 5 minutes until all sides are caramelized.
6. Allow it to rest and slice the tenderloin into medallions, serve!

Nutrition Values (Per Serving)

- Calories: 287
- Carbohydrate: 13g
- Protein: 33g
- Fat: 11g
- Sugar: 7g
- Sodium: 417mg

Smoked Sausage & Cabbage Potatoes

(Serves: 4 / **Prep Time:** 25 minutes / **Sous Vide Cooking Time:** 2 hours)

Ingredients

- ½ head green cabbage, cored and thinly sliced
- 1 Granny smith apple, peeled and cored, cut up into small dices
- 24 oz. red potatoes cut up into quarters and into ¼ inch thick wedges
- 1 small onion thinly sliced
- ¼ teaspoon celery salt
- 2 tablespoons cider vinegar
- 2 tablespoons packed brown sugar
- Salt and black pepper, as needed
- 1 pound precooked smoked pork sausage sliced up into 4 portions with each portion sliced into half lengthwise
- ½ cup chicken broth
- 2 tablespoons unsalted butter

How To

1. Prepare the Sous Vide water bath using your immersion circulator and raise the temperature to 185-degrees Fahrenheit.
2. Take a large bowl and add the cabbage, potatoes, onion, apple, cider vinegar, brown sugar, and celery salt. Season with salt and pepper
3. Divide the mixture and sausage among 2 resealable zip bags and add ¼ cup of chicken broth to each bags.
4. Seal using the immersion method and cook for 2 hours.
5. Take a skillet and place it over medium-high heat and add 1 tablespoon of butter, heat it up and add the bag contents to the skillet.
6. Bring it to a boil and reduce the heat, cook until the liquid evaporates. It should take about 5-6 minutes for the onion, potatoes, cabbage to be browned.
7. Transfer to a serving platter and repeat the process with the remaining cabbage- sausage mix.
8. Serve!

Nutrition Values (Per Serving)

- Calories: 510
- Carbohydrate: 39g
- Protein: 18g
- Fat: 32g
- Sugar: 10g
- Sodium: 496mg

Boneless Pork Ribs

(Serves: 4 / **Prep Time:** 30 minutes / **Sous Vide Cooking Time:** 8 hours)

Ingredients

- 1/3 cup unsweetened coconut milk
- 2 tablespoons peanut butter
- 2 tablespoons soy sauce
- 2 tablespoons light brown sugar
- 2 tablespoons dry white wine
- 2-inch fresh lemongrass
- 1 tablespoon Sriracha sauce
- 1 inch peeled fresh ginger
- 2 garlic cloves
- 2 teaspoons sesame oil
- 12 oz. boneless country style pork ribs
- Chopped up fresh cilantro and steamed basmati rice for serving

How To

1. Prepare the Sous Vide water bath using your immersion circulator and increase the temperature to 134-degrees Fahrenheit.
2. Add the coconut milk, peanut butter, soy sauce, brown sugar, wine, lemongrass, ginger, Sriracha sauce, sesame oil and garlic to a blender, blend until smooth.
3. Add the ribs to a resealable zip bag alongside the sauce and seal using the immersion method. Cook for 8 hours.
4. Once done, remove the bag and take the ribs out from the bag, transfer to plate.
5. Pour the bag contents to a large skillet and place it over medium-high heat, bring to a boil and lower heat to medium-low. Simmer for 10-15 minutes.
6. Then, add the ribs to the sauce and turn well to coat it.
7. Simmer for 5 minutes.
8. Garnish with fresh cilantro and serve with the rice!

Nutrition Values (Per Serving)

- Calories: 840
- Carbohydrate: 24g
- Protein: 53g
- Fat: 59g
- Sugar: 12g
- Sodium: 534mg

Coffee-Chili Pork Porterhouse

(Serves: 4 / **Prep Time:** 20 minutes / **Sous Vide Cooking Time:** 2 hours 30 minutes)

Ingredients

- 2 pieces bone-in pork porterhouse
- 1 tablespoon ancho chilis powder

- 1 tablespoon ground coffee
- 1 tablespoon light brown sugar
- 1 tablespoon garlic salt
- 1 tablespoon extra-virgin olive oil

How To

1. Prepare your Sous Vide water bath using your immersion circulator and increase the temperature to 145-degrees Fahrenheit.
2. Add the pork to a resealable bag and seal using the immersion method. Cook for 2 ½ hours.
3. Make your seasoning mixture by adding the chili powder, coffee, brown sugar, and garlic salt to a small bowl.
4. Remove the bag. Then take the pork out from the bag, pat it dry using kitchen towel.
5. Rub the chop with seasoning.
6. Take a cast iron skillet and put it over high heat and add the olive oil and sear the pork for 1-2 minutes per side.
7. Once done, transfer the pork to a cutting board and allow it to rest for 5 minutes, slice and serve!

Nutrition Values (Per Serving)

- Calories: 813
- Carbohydrate: 4g
- Protein: 56g
- Fat: 63g
- Sugar: 0g
- Sodium: 475mg

Balsamic Glazed Pork Rib Chop

(Serves: 2 / **Prep Time:** 20 minutes / **Sous Vide Cooking Time:** 180 minutes)

Ingredients

- 1-piece bone-in pork chop
- Kosher salt and black pepper, as needed
- 1 tablespoon extra-virgin olive oil
- 4 tablespoons aged balsamic vinegar

How To

1. Prepare your Sous Vide water bath using your immersion circulator and increase the temperature to 145-degrees Fahrenheit.
2. Take the pork and carefully season it with pepper and salt, transfer to a resealable zipper bag and seal using the immersion method.

3. Cook for 3 hours and remove the bag from the water bath and then the pork and pat it dry.
4. Take a sauté pan and place it over high heat for 5 minutes, add the olive oil and the pork chops.
5. Sear until browned on both sides.
6. Add 3 tablespoons of balsamic vinegar to the skillet and bring to a rapid simmer, keep simmer while spooning the vinegar over the chop. Keep repeating for 1 minute.
7. Once done, transfer the dish to your serving plate and serve it with the rest of the balsamic.

Nutrition Values (Per Serving)

- Calories: 529
- Carbohydrate: 45g
- Protein: 23g
- Fat: 29g
- Sugar: 13g
- Sodium: 155mg

Siu-Style Chinese Baby Back Ribs

(**Serves:** 6 / **Prep Time:** 30 minutes / **Sous Vide Cooking Time:** 4 hours)

Ingredients

- 1/3 cup hoisin sauce
- 1/3 cup dark soy sauce
- 1/3 cup granulated sugar
- 3 tablespoons honey
- 3 tablespoons sherry vinegar
- 1 tablespoon fermented bean paste
- 2 teaspoons sesame oil
- 2 crushed garlic cloves
- 1-inch piece fresh grated ginger
- 1 ½ teaspoon five spice powder
- ½ teaspoon salt
- ½ teaspoon white pepper
- ½ teaspoon fresh ground black pepper
- 3 lbs. baby back ribs with the membrane removed
- Cilantro leaves for garnishing

How To

1. Prepare the Sous Vide water bath using your immersion circulator and raise the temperature to 167-degrees Fahrenheit.
2. Take a large bowl and add the hoisin sauce, dark soy sauce, sugar, sherry vinegar, honey, bean paste, sesame oil, garlic, five spice powder, salt, ginger, white pepper, and black pepper.
3. Take a small-sized bowl and add 1/3 cup of the marinade, chill for later use.
4. Add the ribs to the remaining marinade and mix well to coat the ribs.

5. Divide the mixture among 3 large resealable bags and seal using the immersion method. Cook for 4 hours.
6. Heat up the grill to 400-degrees Fahrenheit and transfer the ribs to the grill, brush with the reserved marinade and cook for 3 minutes.
7. Flip them up and brush with more marinade, cook for another 3 minutes.
8. Transfer the dish to the cutting board and allow it to rest for 5 minutes, slice the rack into ribs and garnish with cilantro leaves. Serve!

Nutrition Values (Per Serving)

- Calories: 1041
- Carbohydrate: 33g
- Protein: 52g
- Fat: 77g
- Sugar: 26g
- Sodium: 567mg

CHAPTER 6 | VEGAN

Vegan Steel Cut Oats

(Serves: 2 / **Prep Time:** 5 minutes / **Sous-Vide Cooking Time:** 180 minutes)

Ingredients
- 2 cups water
- ½ cup steel cut oats
- ½ teaspoon salt
- Cinnamon and maple syrup for topping

How To
1. Prepare the Sous Vide water bath by using your immersion circulator and raise the temperature to 180 degrees Fahrenheit.
2. Take a heavy-duty resealable zipper bag and add all the listed ingredients except the cinnamon and maple syrup
3. Seal the bag using the immersion method and submerge underwater.
4. Cook for about 3 hours.
5. Once cooked, remove it and transfer the oats to your serving bowl.
6. Serve with a sprinkle of cinnamon and some maple syrup.

Nutrition Values (Per Serving)
- Calories: 141
- Carbohydrates: 19g
- Protein: 5g
- Fat: 6g
- Sugar: 6g
- Sodium: 87mg

Honey Drizzled Carrots

(Serves: 4 / **Prep Time:** 5 minutes / **Sous-Vide Cooking Time:** 75 minutes)

Ingredients
- 1-pound baby carrots
- 4 tablespoons vegan butter
- 1 tablespoon agave nectar
- 3 tablespoons honey
- ¼ teaspoon kosher salt
- ¼ teaspoon ground cardamom

How To

1. Prepare the Sous-vide water bath using your immersion circulator and increase the temperature to 185 degrees Fahrenheit
2. Add the carrots, honey, whole butter, kosher salt, and cardamom to a resealable bag
3. Seal using the immersion method. Cook for 75 minutes and once done, remove it from the water bath.
4. Strain the glaze by passing through a fine mesh.
5. Set it aside.
6. Take the carrots out from the bag and pour any excess glaze over them. Serve with a little bit of seasonings.

Nutrition Values (Per Serving)

- Calories: 174
- Carbohydrates: 42g
- Protein: 2g
- Fat: 1g
- Sugar: 31g
- Sodium: 180mg

Pickled Fennel

(Serves: 5 / **Prep Time:** 30 minutes / **Sous-Vide Cooking Time:** 30 minutes)

Ingredients

- 1 cup white wine vinegar
- 2 tablespoons beet sugar
- Juice and zest from 1 lemon
- 1 teaspoon kosher salt
- 2 medium bulb fennels, trimmed up and cut into ¼ inch thick slices

How To

1. Prepare the Sous Vide water bath using your immersion circulator and raise the temperature to 180-degrees Fahrenheit.
2. Take a large bowl and add the vinegar, sugar, lemon juice, salt, lemon zest, and whisk them well.
3. Transfer the mixture to your resealable zip bag.
4. Add the fennel and seal using the immersion method.
5. Submerge underwater and cook for 30 minutes.
6. Transfer to an ice bath and allow the mixture to reach the room temperature.
7. Serve!

Nutrition Values (Per Serving)

- Calories: 156
- Carbohydrates: 33g
- Protein: 5g
- Fat: 1g
- Sugar: 20g
- Sodium: 603mg

Lemon & Garlic Artichokes

(Serves: 4 / **Prep Time:** 30 minutes / **Sous-Vide Cooking Time:** 90 minutes)

Ingredients

- 4 tablespoons freshly squeezed lemon juice
- 12 pieces' baby artichokes
- 4 tablespoons vegan butter
- 2 fresh garlic cloves, minced
- 1 teaspoon fresh lemon zest
- Kosher salt, and black pepper, to taste
- Chopped up fresh parsley for garnishing

How To

1. Prepare the Sous Vide water bath using your immersion circulator and raise the temperature to 180-degrees Fahrenheit.
2. Take a large bowl and add the cold water and 2 tablespoons of lemon juice.
3. Peel and discard the outer tough layer of your artichoke and cut them into quarters.
4. Transfer to a cold water bath and let it sit for a while.
5. Take a large skillet and put it over medium high heat.
6. Add in the butter to the skillet and allow the butter to melt.
7. Add the garlic alongside 2 tablespoons of lemon juice and the zest.
8. Remove from heat and season with a bit of pepper and salt.
9. Allow it to cool for about 5 minutes.
10. Then, drain the artichokes from the cold water and place them in a large resealable bag. Add in the butter mixture as well.
11. Seal it up using the immersion method and submerge underwater for about 1 and a ½ hour.
12. Once cooked, transfer the artichokes to a bowl and serve with a garnish of parsley.

Nutrition Values (Per Serving)

- Calories: 408
- Carbohydrates: 49g
- Protein: 12g
- Fat: 20g
- Sugar: 5g
- Sodium: 549mg

Truffle Sunchokes

(Serves: 4 / **Prep Time:** 15 minutes / **Sous-Vide Cooking Time:** 90 minutes)

Ingredients
- 8 ounces peeled Sunchokes, sliced into ¼ inch thick pieces
- 3 tablespoons unsalted vegan butter
- 2 tablespoons agave nectar
- 1 teaspoon truffle oil
- Kosher salt, and black pepper, to taste

How To
1. Prepare the Sous Vide water bath using your immersion circulator and raise the temperature to 180-degrees Fahrenheit.
2. Take a heavy-duty resealable zip bag and add the butter, nectar, sunchokes, truffle oil and mix them well.
3. Sprinkle some salt and pepper, and then seal using the immersion method.
4. Submerge it underwater and cook for 1 ½ hour.
5. Once cooked, transfer the contents to a skillet.
6. Put the skillet over medium-high heat and cook for 5 minutes more until the liquid has evaporated.
7. Season with pepper and salt to adjust the flavor if needed
8. Serve!

Nutrition Values (Per Serving)
- Calories: 255
- Carbohydrates: 40g
- Protein: 5g
- Fat: 10g
- Sugar: 22g
- Sodium: 360mg

Spicy Giardiniera

(Serves: 8 / **Prep Time:** 30 minutes / **Sous-Vide Cooking Time:** 60 minutes)

Ingredients
- 2 cups white wine vinegar
- 1 cup water
- ½ cup beet sugar
- 3 tablespoons kosher salt
- 1 tablespoon whole black peppercorns

- 1 cup cauliflower, cut up into ½-inch pieces
- 1 stemmed and seeded bell pepper, cut up into ½-inch pieces
- 1 cup carrots, cut up into ½-inch pieces
- ½ thinly sliced white onion
- 2 seeded and stemmed Serrano peppers, cut up into ½-inch pieces

How To

1. Prepare the Sous-vide water bath using your immersion circulator and raise the temperature to 180-degrees Fahrenheit.
2. Take a large bowl and mix in vinegar, sugar, salt, water, and peppercorns.
3. Transfer the mixture to a large resealable zipper bag and add the cauliflower, onion, serrano peppers, vinegar mixture, bell pepper, and carrots.
4. Seal it up using the immersion method and submerge underwater, cook for about 1 hour.
5. Once cooked, take it out from the bag and serve

Nutrition Values (Per Serving)

- Calories: 245
- Carbohydrates: 42g
- Protein: 4g
- Fat: 7g
- Sugar: 30g
- Sodium: 640mg

Vegan Alfredo

(Serves: 6 / **Prep Time:** 15 minutes / **Sous-Vide Cooking Time:** 90 minutes)

Ingredients

- 4 cups chopped cauliflower
- 2 cups water
- 2/3 cup cashews
- 2 garlic cloves
- ½ teaspoon dried oregano
- ½ teaspoon dried basil
- ½ teaspoon dried rosemary
- 4 tablespoons nutritional yeast
- Salt, and pepper to taste

How To

1. Prepare the Sous-vide water bath using your immersion circulator and increase the temperature to 170-degrees Fahrenheit.
2. Take a heavy-duty resealable zip bag and add the cashews, cauliflower, oregano, water, garlic, rosemary, and basil.
3. Seal using the immersion method. Submerge underwater and cook for 90 minutes.
4. Transfer the cooked contents to a blender and puree.
5. Use the Alfredo over your favorite pasta.

Nutrition Values (Per Serving)

- Calories: 160
- Carbohydrates: 10g
- Protein: 8g
- Fat: 11g
- Sugar: 1g
- Sodium: 282mg

Mushroom & Truffle Oil

(Serves: 2 / **Prep Time:** 20 minutes / **Sous-Vide Cooking Time:** 60 minutes)

Ingredients

- 10 large button mushrooms
- 3 tablespoons truffle oil
- 3 tablespoons olive oil
- 1 tablespoon chopped fresh thyme
- 1 clove thinly sliced garlic
- Salt, and pepper to taste

How To

1. Prepare the Sous-vide water bath using your immersion circulator and raise the temperature to 185-degrees Fahrenheit.
2. Take a large bowl and add the truffle oil, mushrooms, olive oil, garlic, and thyme
3. Season with some pepper and salt.
4. Transfer the mushroom mixture to a large Sous-vide resealable zip bag and add the mixture to the bag.
5. Seal it up using the immersion method. Submerge underwater and cook for 1 hour.
6. Once cooked, drain the mushrooms and discard the cooking liquid.
7. Take a large skillet and put it over medium heat for 3 minutes.
8. Add the mushrooms and sear for about 1 minute to brown it.
9. Transfer the cooked mushroom to a serving plate and season with pepper and salt.
10. Top it up with thyme. Serve!

Nutrition Values (Per Serving)

- Calories: 440
- Carbohydrates: 28g
- Protein: 19g
- Fat: 28g
- Sugar: 6g
- Sodium: 314mg

White Cannellini Beans

(Serves: 5 / **Prep Time:** 15 minutes / **Sous-Vide Cooking Time:** 180 minutes)

Ingredients

- 1 cup cannellini beans (dried) soaked overnight in salty cold water
- 1 cup water
- ½ cup extra-virgin olive oil
- 1 peeled carrot, cut up into 1-inch dice
- 1 celery stalk, cut up into 1-inch dice
- 1 quartered shallot
- 4 crushed garlic cloves
- 2 fresh rosemary sprigs
- 2 bay leaves
- Kosher salt, and pepper to taste

How To

1. Prepare the Sous Vide water bath using your Sous-vide immersion circulator and raise the temperature to 190-degrees Fahrenheit.
2. Drain the soaked beans and rinse them.
3. Transfer to a heavy duty resealable zip bag and add the olive oil, celery, water, carrot, shallot, garlic, rosemary, and bay leaves.
4. Season with pepper and salt.
5. Seal using the immersion method and cook for 3 hours.
6. Once cooked, remove the beans and check for seasoning.
7. Discard the rosemary and serve!

Nutrition Values (Per Serving)

- Calories: 578
- Carbohydrates: 77g
- Protein: 31g
- Fat: 18g
- Sugar: 5g
- Sodium: 519mg

Special Tips

If you feel that the beans are a bit hard, then Sous-vide cook them for 1 hour more (with rosemary) to ensure that they have a tender texture.

Tofu Delight

(Serves: 8 / **Prep Time:** 20 minutes / **Sous-Vide Cooking Time:** 60 minutes)

Ingredients
- 1 cup vegetable broth
- 2 tablespoons tomato paste
- 1 tablespoon grated ginger
- 1 tablespoon rice wine
- 1 tablespoon rice wine vinegar
- 1 tablespoon agave nectar
- 2 teaspoons Sriracha sauce
- 3 minced garlic cloves
- 2 boxes cubed tofu

How To
1. Prepare your Sous Vide water bath using your immersion circulator and raise the temperature to 185-degrees Fahrenheit.
2. Take a medium bowl and add all the listed ingredients except the tofu.
3. Mix well.
4. Transfer the mixture to a heavy-duty resealable zipper bag and top with the tofu.
5. Seal it up using the immersion method. Cook for 1 hour.
6. Pour the contents into a serving bowl
7. Serve!

Nutrition Values (Per Serving)
- Calories: 186
- Carbohydrates: 28g
- Protein: 10g
- Fat: 6g
- Sugar: 15g
- Sodium: 13mg

White Beans

(Serves: 8 / **Prep Time:** 15 minutes / **Sous-Vide Cooking Time:** 3-4 hours)

Ingredients
- 1 cup dried and soaked navy beans
- 1 cup water
- ½ cup extra-virgin olive oil
- 1 peeled carrot, cut up into 1-inch dices

- 1 stalk celery, cut up into 1-inch dices
- 1 quartered shallot
- 4 cloves crushed garlic
- 2 sprigs fresh rosemary
- 2 pieces' bay leaves
- Kosher salt, to taste
- Freshly ground black pepper, to taste

How To

1. Prepare your Sous-vide water bath using your immersion circulator and raise the temperature to 190-degrees Fahrenheit.
2. Carefully drain and rinse your beans and add them alongside the rest of the ingredients to a heavy-duty zip bag.
3. Seal using the immersion method and submerge it underwater. Cook for about 3 hours.
4. Once cooked, taste the beans.
5. If they are firm, then cook for another 1 hour and pour them in a serving bowl.
6. Serve!

Nutrition Values (Per Serving)

- Calories: 210
- Carbohydrates: 36g
- Protein: 14g
- Fat: 2g
- Sugar: 2g
- Sodium: 224mg

Radishes with "Vegan" Butter

(Serves: 4 / **Prep Time:** 5 minutes / **Sous-Vide Cooking Time:** 45 minutes)

Ingredients

- 1 pound radishes, cut up in half lengthwise
- 3 tablespoons vegan butter
- ½ teaspoon sea salt

How To

1. Prepare your Sous Vide water bath using your immersion circulator and raise the temperature to 190-degrees Fahrenheit.

2. Add your radish halves, butter, and salt in a resealable zipper bag and seal it up using the immersion method.
3. Submerge underwater and cook for 45 minutes.
4. Once cooked, strain the liquid and discard.
5. Serve the radishes in a bowl!

Nutrition Values (Per Serving)
- Calories: 134
- Carbohydrates: 30g
- Protein: 1g
- Fat: 0g
- Sugar: 28g
- Sodium: 517mg

Sous-vide Rhubarb

(Serves: 4 / **Prep Time:** 15 minutes / **Sous-Vide Cooking Time:** 40 minutes)

Ingredients
- 2 cups rhubarb
- 1 tablespoon Grand Marnier
- 1 teaspoon beet sugar
- ½ teaspoon kosher salt
- ½ a teaspoon freshly ground black pepper

How To
1. Prepare the Sous-vide water bath to a temperature of 140-degrees Fahrenheit using your immersion circulator.
2. Take a large heavy-duty resealable zip bag and add all the listed ingredients. Whisk everything well.
3. Seal the bag using the immersion method/water displacement method.
4. Place it under your preheated water and cook for about 40 minutes.
5. Once cooked, take the bag out from the water bath, take the contents out and place it on a serving plate.
6. Serve warm!

Nutrition Values (Per Serving)

- Calories: 111
- Carbohydrates: 27g
- Protein: 1g
- Fat: 0g
- Sugar: 23g
- Sodium: 24mg

Chinese Black Bean Sauce

(Serves: 4 / **Prep Time:** 25 minutes / **Sous-Vide Cooking Time:** 90 minutes)

Ingredients

- 4 cups halved green beans
- 3 minced garlic cloves
- 2 teaspoons rice wine vinegar
- 1½ tablespoons prepared black bean sauce
- 1 tablespoon olive oil

How To

1. Prepare the Sous-vide water bath using your immersion circulator and raise the temperature to 170-degrees Fahrenheit.
2. Add all the listed ingredients into a large mixing bowl alongside the green beans. Coat everything evenly.
3. Take a heavy-duty zip bag and add the mixture.
4. Zip the bag using the immersion method and submerge it underwater.
5. Cook for about 1 hour and 30 minutes.
6. Once cooked, take it out and serve immediately!

Nutrition Values (Per Serving)

- Calories: 375
- Carbohydrates: 14g
- Protein: 12g
- Fat: 12g
- Sugar: 5g
- Sodium: 485mg

Chipotle & Black Beans

(Serves: 6 / **Prep Time:** 25 minutes / **Sous-Vide Cooking Time:** 6 hours)

Ingredients

- 1 cup dry black beans
- 2 2/3 cup water
- 1/3 cup freshly squeezed orange juice
- 2 tablespoons orange zest
- 1 teaspoon salt
- 1 teaspoon cumin
- ½ teaspoon chipotle chili powder

How To

1. Prepare the Sous-vide water bath using your immersion circulator and raise the temperature to 193-degrees Fahrenheit.
2. Take a heavy-duty resealable plastic bag and add the listed ingredients into the bag.
3. Submerge it underwater and cook for 6 hours.
4. Once cooked, take the bag out from the water bath.
5. Pour the contents into a nice sauté pan and place it over medium heat.
6. Simmer until the amount has been reduced.
7. Once your desired texture is achieved, remove from the heat and serve!

Nutrition Values (Per Serving)

- Calories: 466
- Carbohydrates: 15g
- Protein: 20g
- Fat: 37g
- Sugar: 3g
- Sodium: 546mg

Pickled Mixed Veggies

(Serves: 4 / **Prep Time:** 10 minutes / **Sous-Vide Cooking Time:** 40 minutes)

Ingredients

- 12 oz. beets, cut up into ½-inch slices
- ½ Serrano pepper, seeds removed
- 1 garlic clove, diced
- 2/3 cup white vinegar
- 2/3 cup filtered water
- 2 tablespoons pickling spice

How To

1. Prepare the Sous-vide water bath using your immersion circulator and raise the temperature to 190-degrees Fahrenheit.
2. Take 4-6 ounces' mason jar and add the Serrano pepper, beets, and garlic cloves

3. Take a medium stock pot and add the pickling spice, filtered water, white vinegar, and bring the mixture to a boil
4. Remove the stock and strain the mix over the beets in the jar.
5. Fill them up.
6. Seal it loosely and submerge it underwater. Cook for 40 minutes.
7. Allow the jars to cool and serve!

Nutrition Values (Per Serving)

- Calories: 174
- Carbohydrates: 34g
- Protein: 4g
- Fat: 2g
- Sugar: 19g
- Sodium: 610mg

Root Vegetables Mix

(Serves: 4 / **Prep Time:** 15 minutes / **Sous-Vide Cooking Time:** 180 minutes)

Ingredients

- 1 peeled turnip, cut up into 1-inch pieces
- 1 peeled rutabaga, cut up into 1-inch pieces
- 8 pieces petite carrots peeled up and cut into 1-inch pieces
- 1 peeled parsnip, cut up into 1-inch pieces
- ½ red onion, cut up into 1-inch pieces and peeled
- 4 pieces' garlic, crushed
- 4 sprigs fresh rosemary
- 2 tablespoons extra-virgin olive oil
- Kosher salt, and black pepper to taste
- 2 tablespoons unsalted vegan butter

How To

1. Prepare the Sous-vide water bath using your immersion circulator and raise the temperature to 185-degrees Fahrenheit.
2. Take two large heavy-duty resealable zipper bags and divide the vegetables and the rosemary between the bags.
3. Add 1 tablespoon of oil to the bag and season with some salt and pepper.
4. Seal the bags using the immersion method. Submerge underwater and cook for 3 hours
5. Take a skillet and place it over high heat and add in the oil.
6. Once done, add the contents of your bag to the skillet. Cook the mixture for about 5-6 minutes until the liquid comes to a syrupy consistency.
7. Add the butter to your veggies and toss them well.

8. Keep cooking for another 5 minutes until they are nicely browned.
9. Serve!

Nutrition Values (Per Serving)

- Calories: 268
- Carbohydrates: 43g
- Protein: 6g
- Fat: 10g
- Sugar: 16g
- Sodium: 612mg

Pickled Carrots

(Serves: 1 / **Prep Time:** 30 minutes / **Sous-Vide Cooking Time:** 90 minutes)

Ingredients

- 1 cup white wine vinegar
- ½ cup beet sugar
- 3 tablespoons kosher salt
- 1 teaspoon black peppercorns
- 1/3 cup ice cold water
- 10-12 pieces' petite carrots, peeled with the stems trimmed
- 4 sprigs fresh thyme
- 2 peeled garlic cloves

How To

1. Prepare the Sous-vide water bath using your immersion circulator and raise the temperature to 190-degrees Fahrenheit.
2. Take a medium-sized saucepan and add the vinegar, salt, sugar, and peppercorns and place it over medium heat.
3. Then, let the mixture reach the boiling point and keep stirring until the sugar has dissolved alongside the salt
4. Remove the heat and add the cold water.
5. Allow the mixture to cool down to room temperature.
6. Take a resealable bag and add the thyme, carrots, and garlic alongside the brine solution and seal it up using the immersion method.
7. Submerge underwater and cook for 90 minutes.
8. Once cooked, remove the bag from the water bath and place into an ice bath.
9. Carefully take the carrots out from the bag and serve !

Nutrition Values (Per Serving)

- Calories: 127
- Carbohydrates: 24g
- Protein: 2g
- Fat: 1g
- Sugar: 16g
- Sodium: 54mg

Sous Vide Garlic Tomatoes

(Serves: 4 / **Prep Time:** 10 minutes / **Sous-Vide Cooking Time:** 45 minutes)

Ingredients

- 4 pieces cored and diced tomatoes
- 2 tablespoons extra-virgin olive oil
- 3 minced garlic cloves
- 1 teaspoon dried oregano
- 1 teaspoon fine sea salt

How To

1. Prepare the Sous-vide water bath using your immersion circulator and raise the temperature to 145-degrees Fahrenheit.
2. Add all the listed ingredients to the resealable bag and seal using the immersion method.
3. Submerge underwater and let it cook for 45 minutes.
4. Once cooked, transfer the tomatoes to a serving plate.
5. Serve with some vegan French bread slices.

Nutrition Values (Per Serving)

- Calories: 289
- Carbohydrates: 44g
- Protein: 11g
- Fat: 8g
- Sugar: 2g
- Sodium: 326mg

Sweet Curried Winter Squash

(Serves: 6 / **Prep Time:** 20 minutes / **Sous-Vide Cooking Time:** 90 minutes)

Ingredients

- 1 medium winter squash
- 2 tablespoons unsalted vegan butter
- 1 to 2 tablespoons Thai curry paste
- ½ teaspoon kosher salt
- Fresh cilantro for serving
- Lime wedges for serving

How To

1. Prepare the Sous-vide water bath using your immersion circulator and raise the temperature to 185-degrees Fahrenheit.
2. Slice up the squash into half lengthwise and scoop out the seeds alongside the inner membrane. Keep the seeds for later use.

3. Slice the squash into wedges of about 1 ½-inch thickness.
4. Take a large heavy-duty bag resealable zip bags and add the squash wedges, curry paste, butter and salt and seal it using the immersion method.
5. Submerge it underwater and let it cook for 1 ½ hour.
6. Once cooked, remove the bag from water and give it a slight squeeze until it is soft.
7. If it is not soft, then add to the water once again and cook for 40 minutes more.
8. Transfer the cooked dish to a serving plate and drizzle with a bit of curry butter sauce from the bag.
9. Top your squash with a bit of cilantro, lime wedges and serve!

Nutrition Values (Per Serving)

- Calories: 185
- Carbohydrates: 27g
- Protein: 2g
- Fat: 9g
- Sugar: 5g
- Sodium: 422mg

Balsamic Mushroom & Herbs

(**Serves:** 4 / **Prep Time:** 15 minutes / **Sous-Vide Cooking Time:** 60 minutes)

Ingredients

- 1 pound cremini mushrooms with the stems removed
- 1 tablespoon extra-virgin olive oil
- 1 tablespoon apple balsamic vinegar
- 1 minced garlic clove
- 1 teaspoon kosher salt
- 1 teaspoon freshly ground black pepper
- 1 teaspoon minced fresh thyme

How To

1. Prepare the Sous-vide water bath using your immersion circulator and raise the temperature to 138-degrees Fahrenheit.
2. Add the listed ingredients to your resealable zip bag.
3. Seal using the immersion method and let it cook for 1 hour.
4. Once cooked, transfer the contents to a platter and serve!

Nutrition Values (Per Serving)

- Calories: 405
- Carbohydrates: 51g
- Protein: 12g
- Fat: 18g
- Sugar: 16g
- Sodium: 526mg

Currant & Braised Cabbage

(Serves: 4 / **Prep Time:** 15 minutes / **Sous-Vide Cooking Time:** 120 minutes)

Ingredients

- 1 ½ pounds red cabbage
- ¼ cup currants
- 1 thinly sliced shallot
- 3 thinly sliced garlic clove
- 1 tablespoon apple balsamic vinegar
- 1 tablespoon unsalted butter
- ½ a teaspoon kosher salt

How To

1. Prepare the Sous-vide water bath using your immersion circulator and raise the temperature to 185-degrees Fahrenheit.
2. Take the cabbage and slice the cabbage into quarters, make sure to discard the core.
3. Chop them up into 1 ½-inch pieces.
4. Take 2 heavy-duty resealable zipper bags and divide the cabbages between the two bags.
5. Divide as well the remaining ingredients equally between the bags
6. Seal using the immersion method. Submerge underwater and cook for 2 hours.
7. Once done, remove the bag and transfer to a bowl.
8. Add the cooking juices and season with a bit of salt and vinegar.
9. Serve!

Nutrition Values (Per Serving)

- Calories: 172
- Carbohydrates: 6g
- Protein: 7g
- Fat: 14g
- Sugar: 3g
- Sodium: 342mg

Sous-vide Pennies

(Serves: 4 / **Prep Time:** 15 minutes / **Sous-Vide Cooking Time:** 180 minutes)

Ingredients

- 1 pound carrots, peeled up and sliced into ¼ inch thick rounds
- 1/4 cup dried apricots, thinly sliced up
- ¼ cup freshly squeezed orange juice
- 2 tablespoons freshly squeezed lemon juice
- 1 tablespoon unsalted vegan butter
- 2 teaspoons beet sugar

- ½ a teaspoon kosher salt
- ¼ teaspoon orange zest
- ¼ teaspoon freshly ground black pepper
- 1/8 teaspoon ground cinnamon

How To

1. Prepare the Sous-vide water bath using your immersion circulator and raise the temperature to 183-degrees Fahrenheit.
2. Add the listed ingredients to your resealable zip bag and seal using the immersion method. Submerge underwater and cook for 3 hours.
3. Transfer the carrots to a serving platter with cooking liquid and season with salt and pepper.
4. Garnish with the additional lemon juice and serve!

Nutrition Values (Per Serving)

- Calories: 256
- Carbohydrates: 35g
- Protein: 2g
- Fat: 12g
- Sugar: 23g
- Sodium: 117mg

Pomme Purée

(**Serves:** 4 / **Prep Time:** 10 minutes / **Sous-vide Cooking Time:** 30 minutes)

Ingredients

- 1½ lb. potatoes, peeled
- 15-ounce vegan butter
- 8-ounce coconut milk
- A pinch of salt
- White pepper as needed

How To

1. Prepare your Sous-vide water bath using your immersion circulator and raise the temperature to 194-degrees Fahrenheit.
2. Slice the potatoes to 1 cm thick slices
3. Take your heavy-duty resealable zipper bag and add the potatoes, coconut milk, vegan butter and salt
4. Submerge underwater and let it cook for 30 minutes
5. Strain the mixture through a metal mesh/sieve and allow the butter mixture to pour into a bowl
6. Puree the potatoes by blending them or mashing them using a spoon
7. Pour the puree into the butter bowl
8. Season with pepper and serve!

Nutrition Values (Per Serving)

- Calories: 56
- Carbohydrates: 2g
- Protein: 1g
- Fat: 5g
- Sugar: 0g
- Sodium: 56mg

Sous-vide Golden Beets

(Serves: 2 / **Prep Time:** 20 minutes / **Sous-Vide Cooking Time:** 90 minutes)

Ingredients

- 1 lb. golden beets, cut up into ¼ inch thick slices
- 1 cup freshly squeezed orange juice
- ¼ cup freshly squeezed lemon juice
- 4 tablespoons unsalted vegan butter
- 1 tablespoon agave nectar
- 1 teaspoon freshly ground black peppercorns
- 1 teaspoon kosher salt

How To

1. Prepare the Sous-vide water bath using your immersion circulator and raise the temperature to 180-degrees Fahrenheit.
2. Add the listed ingredients to a resealable zip bag and seal using the immersion method. Cook for 1 ½ hours
3. Once done, remove the bag and take the beets out and set them aside.
4. Pour the cooking liquid into a saucepan and bring it to a simmer over medium-high heat.
5. Keep simmering until the liquid is lowered by half.
6. Remove from the heat and stir in beets.
7. Serve!

Nutrition Values (Per Serving)

- Calories: 169
- Carbohydrates: 7g
- Protein: 1g
- Fat: 16g
- Sugar: 4g
- Sodium: 112mg

Fingerling Cooked Potatoes

(Serves: 3 / **Prep Time:** 10 minutes / **Sous-Vide Cooking Time:** 45 minutes)

Ingredients
- 8 ounces fingerling potatoes
- Salt, and pepper to taste
- 1 tablespoon unsalted vegan butter
- 1 sprig rosemary

How To
1. Prepare the Sous-vide water bath using your immersion circulator and raise the temperature to 178-degrees Fahrenheit.
2. Take the potatoes and season it with salt and pepper and transfer them to a resealable zip bag.
3. Seal using the immersion method and submerge it underwater and cook for 45 minutes.
4. Once cooked, remove the bag and potatoes.
5. Cut the potatoes in half (lengthwise).
6. Take a large skillet and put it over medium-high heat.
7. Add the butter and allow it to melt, add the rosemary and potatoes.
8. Cook for 3 minutes and transfer to a plate.
9. Serve by seasoning it with a bit of salt if needed

Nutrition Values (Per Serving)
- Calories: 141
- Carbohydrates: 19g
- Protein: 5g
- Fat: 6g
- Sugar: 6g
- Sodium: 87mg

Daikon Radishes

(Serves: 4 / **Prep Time:** 10 minutes / **Sous-Vide Cooking Time:** 30 minutes)

Ingredients
- ½ cup white winger vinegar
- 3 tablespoons beet sugar
- 2 teaspoons kosher salt
- 1 large size Daikon radish, trimmed and sliced up

How To

1. Prepare the Sous-vide water bath using your immersion circulator and raise the temperature to 180-degrees Fahrenheit.
2. Take a large bowl and mix in vinegar, salt, and beet sugar.
3. Transfer to a Sous-vide zip bag and seal using the immersion method.
4. Submerge underwater and cook for 30 minutes
5. Once cooked, remove the bag and transfer to an ice bath.
6. Serve!

Nutrition Values (Per Serving)

- Calories: 141
- Carbohydrates: 19g
- Protein: 5g
- Fat: 6g
- Sugar: 6g
- Sodium: 87mg

Green Beans in Tomato Sauce

(Serves: 4 / **Prep Time:** 10 minutes / **Sous-Vide Cooking Time:** 180 minutes)

Ingredients

- 1 lb. trimmed green beans
- 1 can whole crushed tomatoes
- 1 thinly sliced onion
- 3 garlic clove, peeled and thinly sliced
- Kosher salt, to taste
- Extra-virgin olive oil

How To

1. Prepare the Sous-vide water bath using your immersion circulator and raise the temperature to 183-degrees Fahrenheit
2. Take a large heavy-duty resealable zip bag and add the tomatoes, green beans, garlic, and onion
3. Seal using the immersion method. Submerge underwater and let it cook for 3 hours.
4. Once cooked, transfer the contents of the bag to a large bowl.
5. Serve with a seasoning of salt and a drizzle of olive oil.

Nutrition Values (Per Serving)

- Calories: 277
- Carbohydrates: 6g
- Protein: 20g
- Fat: 19g
- Sugar: 2g
- Sodium: 470mg

French Fries

(Serves: 10 / **Prep Time:** 20 minutes / **Sous-Vide Cooking Time:** 25 minutes)

Ingredients
- 2 quarts' water
- 2 tablespoons kosher salt
- 1 teaspoon beet sugar
- 1 teaspoon baking powder
- 2 ½ pounds russet potatoes, cut up into French fry shapes

Tools Needed:
- Air Fryer

How To
1. Prepare the Sous-vide water bath using your immersion circulator and raise the temperature to 194-degrees Fahrenheit.
2. Take a large bowl and add the water, sugar, kosher salt, and baking powder.
3. Give everything a nice mix until everything dissolves.
4. Add the sliced up potatoes to the mixture and transfer it to a heavy-duty resealable zipper bag.
5. Seal using the immersion method. Submerge underwater and let it cook for 25 minutes.
6. Once done, remove the bag and pre-heat your Air Fryer to a temperature of 260-degrees Fahrenheit.
7. Let the fries cool for 20 minutes and Air Fry them for 8 minutes.
8. Transfer them to a freezer and let them chill for 60 minutes.
9. Preheat your fryer to 735-degrees Fahrenheit and cook them again for 2 minutes.
10. Serve!

Nutrition Values (Per Serving)
- Calories: 336
- Carbohydrates: 67g
- Protein: 8g
- Fat: 5g
- Sugar: 2g
- Sodium: 677mg

Moroccan Chickpeas

(Serves: 4 / **Prep Time:** 10 minutes / **Sous-Vide Cooking Time:** 180 minutes)

Ingredients
- 1 cup chickpeas, soaked overnight in cold salty water
- 3 cups water

- 2 tablespoons extra-virgin olive oil
- 1 teaspoon kosher salt
- ½ teaspoon ground cumin
- ½ teaspoon ground coriander
- ¼ teaspoon ground cinnamon
- 1/8 teaspoon ground cloves
- 1/8 teaspoon cayenne pepper
- Fresh cilantro for garnishing, chopped
- Harissa, to taste

How To

1. Prepare the Sous-vide water bath using your immersion circulator and increase the temperature to 190-degrees Fahrenheit.
2. Then, drain the soaked chickpeas and transfer them to a resealable bag with the soaking water
3. Add in the cumin, salt, olive oil, cloves, cinnamon, coriander, and cayenne pepper.
4. Seal using the immersion method. Submerge underwater and let it cook for 3 hours.
5. Drain the chickpeas from the liquid and transfer them to a bowl.
6. Season with a bit of salt.
7. Take a small bowl and add the olive oil and harissa.
8. Drizzle the mixture over the chickpeas.
9. Serve with a garnish of cilantro.

Nutrition Values (Per Serving)

- Calories: 171
- Carbohydrates: 29g
- Protein: 7g
- Fat: 5g
- Sugar: 4g
- Sodium: 24mg

Pickle in A Jar

(Serves: 6/ **Prep Time:** 30 minutes / **Sous-Vide Cooking Time:** 15 minutes)

Ingredients

- 1 cup white wine vinegar
- ½ cup beet sugar
- 2 teaspoons kosher salt
- 1 tablespoon pickling spice
- 2 English cucumbers sliced up into ¼ inch thick slices
- ½ white onion, thinly sliced

How To

1. Prepare the Sous-vide water bath using your immersion circulator and raise the temperature to 180-degrees Fahrenheit.
2. Take a large bowl and add the vinegar, sugar, salt, pickling spice and whisk them well.
3. Transfer to a heavy-duty resealable zipper bag alongside the cucumber and sliced onions and seal using the immersion method.
4. Submerge underwater and let it cook for 15 minutes.
5. Transfer the bag to an ice bath
6. Pour the mixture into a 4-6 ounce mason jar
7. Serve or store!

Nutrition Values (Per Serving)

- Calories: 117
- Carbohydrates: 27g
- Protein: 1g
- Fat: 1g
- Sugar: 19g
- Sodium: 304mg

Sous Vide Tomato Sauce

(Serves: 4 / **Prep Time:** 15 minutes / **Sous-Vide Cooking Time:** 15 minutes)

Ingredients

- 4 cups cored and halved fresh tomatoes
- ½ onion, chopped
- ¼ cup fresh basil
- 2 garlic cloves, minced
- Salt to taste
- Freshly ground black pepper, to taste
- 5 tablespoons extra-virgin olive oil

How To

1. Prepare the Sous Vide water bath using your immersion circulator and raise the temperature to 176-degrees Fahrenheit.
2. Take a heavy-duty large resealable zip bag and add in the tomatoes, ¼ cup basil, garlic, onion, and oil. Seal using the immersion method.
3. Submerge it underwater and let it cook for 15 minutes.
4. Once cooked, transfer the contents to a blender and puree for about 1 minute.
5. Add a bit of salt and pepper and serve.

Nutrition Values (Per Serving)

- Calories: 117
- Carbohydrates: 26g
- Protein: 5g
- Fat: 1g
- Sugar: 14g
- Sodium: 470mg

Southern Sweet Potatoes & Pecans

(Serves: 2 / **Prep Time:** 45 minutes / **Sous-Vide Cooking Time:** 180 minutes)

Ingredients

- 1 lb. sweet potatoes sliced up into ¼ inch thick rounds
- ½ teaspoon kosher salt
- ¼ cup pecans
- 1 tablespoon coconut oil

How To

1. Prepare the Sous Vide water bath using your immersion circulator and raise the temperature to 145-degrees Fahrenheit.
2. Add the potatoes and salt to your resealable bag and seal using the immersion method
3. Transfer the bag to the water bath and let it cook for 3 hours.
4. Toast the pecans in a dry skillet over medium heat.
5. Once done, transfer the pecans to a cutting board and chop them up.
6. Preheat your oven to 375-degrees Fahrenheit and line a rimmed baking sheet with parchment paper.
7. Once the potatoes are cooked, move them to a bowl and toss with the coconut oil.
8. Then, spread the potatoes on the baking sheet and bake for 20-30 minutes, making sure to flip them once.
9. Transfer to serving platter and serve with a sprinkle of toasted pecans.

Nutrition Values (Per Serving)

- Calories: 195
- Carbohydrates: 30g
- Protein: 6g
- Fat: 6g
- Sugar: 9g
- Sodium: 346mg

CHAPTER 7 | DESSERT

Vanilla Pudding

(Serves: 6 / **Prep Time:** 15 minutes / **Sous Vide Cooking Time:** 45 minutes)

Ingredients
- 1 cup whole milk
- 1 cup heavy cream
- ½ cup ultrafine sugar
- 3 large eggs (2 additional egg yolks)
- 3 tablespoons cornstarch
- 1 tablespoon vanilla extract
- A pinch of kosher salt
- Strawberries for garnishing

How To
1. Prepare the Sous Vide water bath using your immersion circulator and raise the temperature to 180-degrees Fahrenheit.
2. Then, take a blender and add all the listed ingredients except the garnishing, puree for 30-40 seconds until you have a frothy texture
3. Place the mixture to a resealable zip bag and seal it using the immersion method.
4. Submerge underwater and let it cook for 45 minutes.
5. Shake the bag about halfway through to prevent the formation of clumps.
6. Once done, remove the bag, and transfer it to the blender once again.
7. Purée again until it gets smooth.
8. Then, transfer it to a bowl and allow it to chill.
9. Serve with a garnish of strawberries or your favorite topping.

Nutrition Values (Per Serving)
- Calories: 148
- Carbohydrate: 21g
- Protein: 5g
- Fat: 5g
- Sugar: 15g
- Sodium: 106mg

Lemon & Blueberry Crème Brulée

(Serves: 6/ **Prep Time:** 10 minutes / **Sous Vide Cooking Time:** 45 minutes)

Ingredients
- 6 large egg yolks
- 1 1/3 cup superfine sugar
- 3 cups heavy whipping cream
- Zest of 2 lemons
- 4 tablespoons freshly squeezed lemon juice
- 1 teaspoon vanilla extract
- 1 cup fresh blueberries

How To

1. Set up your Sous Vide immersion circulator to a temperature of 195-degrees Fahrenheit and prepare your water bath
2. Take an electric mixer and mix in egg yolks and sugar until you have a creamy mixture. Set it aside.
3. Take a medium-sized saucepan and place it over medium heat, add the cream and heat it.
4. Add the lemon zest, juice, vanilla and simmer for 4-5 minute over low heat.
5. Remove the cream mixture from heat and allow it to cool. Once cooled, transfer a small amount into egg mixture and mix well.
6. Add in the remaining cream mixture to the egg and stir.
7. Divide the blueberries among six mini mason jars and pour the egg cream mixture evenly over the six jars filled with blueberries.
8. Tightly seal the lid and submerge underwater, cook for 45 minutes.
9. Remove the jars from the water and chill for 5 hours.
10. Caramelize a layer of sugar on top using a blowtorch and serve!

Nutrition Values (Per Serving)

- Calories: 298
- Carbohydrate: 43g
- Protein: 11g
- Fat: 10g
- Sugar: 36g
- Sodium: 58mg

Butter & Sea Salt Radish

(Serves: 4 / **Prep Time:** 15 minutes / **Sous Vide Cooking Time:** 45 minutes)

Ingredients

- 1 lb. halved radishes
- 3 tablespoons unsalted butter
- 1 teaspoon sea salt
- ½ teaspoon freshly ground black pepper

How To

1. Prepare your Sous Vide water bath using your immersion circulator and raise the temperature to 180-degrees Fahrenheit.
2. Take a medium-sized resealable bag and add all the listed ingredients to the bag
3. Seal it using the immersion method and let it cook underwater for about 45 minutes.
4. Once cooked, remove the bag and transfer the contents to a platter.
5. Serve!

Nutrition Values (Per Serving)

- Calories: 302
- Carbohydrate: 43g
- Protein: 9g
- Fat: 12g
- Sugar: 4g
- Sodium: 352mg

Banana & Peanut Butter Frozen Bites

(Serves: 6/ **Prep Time:** 0 minutes / **Sous Vide Cooking Time:** 30 minutes)

Ingredients

- 3 bananas
- 3 tablespoons peanut butter
- 3 tablespoons dark chocolate chips

How To

1. Set up your Sous Vide immersion circulator to a temperature of 140-degrees Fahrenheit and prepare your water bath.
2. Slice the bananas into ½ inch slices and add to a resealable bag.
3. Add the peanut butter and dark chocolate chips and seal using the immersion method.
4. Submerge underwater and let it cook for 30 minutes.
5. Stir the contents and chill in popsicle molds
6. Pop out of the molds and serve!

Nutrition Values (Per Serving)

- Calories: 296
- Carbohydrate: 31g
- Protein: 7g
- Fat: 18g
- Sugar: 26g
- Sodium: 10mg

Pumpkin Pie Jars

(Serves: 6 / **Prep Time:** 10 minutes / **Sous Vide Cooking Time:** 60 minutes)

Ingredients

- 1 large can pumpkin pie filling
- 1 egg + 3 egg yolks
- 2 tablespoons flour

- ½ teaspoon kosher salt
- 1 tablespoon pumpkin pie spice
- 1 can evaporated milk
- ½ cup white sugar
- ½ cup brown sugar
- Whipped cream and candied nuts for garnishing

How To

1. Set up your Sous Vide immersion circulator to a temperature of 175-degrees Fahrenheit and prepare your water bath.
2. Add 1 large can of pumpkin pie filling, 2 tablespoons of flour, ½ teaspoon of kosher salt, 1 tablespoon of pumpkin pie spice, 1 egg and 3 egg yolks alongside 1 can of evaporated milk.
3. Whisk them well.
4. Pour the mixture into 6.4-ounce jars and seal them tightly.
5. Submerge underwater and cook for 1 hour.
6. Once done, remove the jars and chill for 8 hours.
7. Garnish with whipped cream and candied nuts.
8. Serve!

Nutrition Values (Per Serving)

- Calories: 269
- Carbohydrate: 24g
- Protein: 5g
- Fat: 17g
- Sugar: 3g
- Sodium: 145mg

Pumpkin Crème Brulée

(Serves: 5 / **Prep Time:** 10 minutes / **Sous Vide Cooking Time:** 60 minutes)

Ingredients

- 1 cup milk
- 1 cup heavy whipping cream
- 3 whole eggs
- 3 egg yolks
- ½ cup pumpkin puree
- ¼ cup maple syrup
- ½ teaspoon pumpkin spice
- A pinch of kosher salt
- Granulated sugar

How To

1. Set up your Sous Vide immersion circulator to a temperature of 167-degrees Fahrenheit and prepare your water bath.

2. Take a large bowl and add the milk, heavy cream, 3 whole eggs, 3 egg yolks, ½ cup of pumpkin puree, ¼ cup of maple syrup, ½ teaspoon of pumpkin spice and a pinch of kosher salt.
3. Whisk them well and keep whisking until it is combined and smooth.
4. Pour the mixture into 6.4-ounce mason jars.
5. Place the lid loosely and cook for 1 hour underwater. Allow them to chill.
6. Spread a thin layer of sugar on top of the custard and caramelize with a blowtorch.
7. Serve!

Nutrition Values (Per Serving)

- Calories: 148
- Carbohydrate: 21g
- Protein: 5g
- Fat: 5g
- Sugar: 15g
- Sodium: 106mg

Amaretto Crème Brulée

(Serves: 12 / **Prep Time:** 30 minutes / **Sous Vide Cooking Time:** 60 minutes)

Ingredients

- 12 egg yolks
- ¾ cup sugar
- ½ teaspoon salt
- 2 ounces Amaretto
- 1-quart heavy cream

How To

1. Set up your Sous Vide immersion circulator to a temperature of 181-degrees Fahrenheit and prepare your water bath.
2. Add the salt, and egg yolks to a bowl and mix them well.
3. Add the Amaretto liqueur to egg mixture and combine them well.
4. Add in the heavy cream and whisk.
5. Then, strain the whole mixture into a bowl through a metal mesh strainer.
6. Allow the mixture to rest. Then fill up the 4-ounce mason jars, making sure that there is ½ inch space at the top
7. Gently tighten the lid and submerge underwater. Cook for 1 hour.
8. Chill in your fridge for 2 hours and sprinkle sugar on top.
9. Broil or caramelize the sugar using a blowtorch and serve!

Nutrition Values (Per Serving)

- Calories: 457
- Carbohydrate: 35g
- Protein: 6g
- Fat: 31g
- Sugar: 33g
- Sodium: 41mg

Cheesecake

(Serves: 6 / **Prep Time:** 10 minutes / **Sous Vide Cooking Time:** 90 minutes)

Ingredients

- 12 oz. cream cheese at room temperature
- ½ cup sugar
- ¼ cup creole cream cheese
- 2 eggs
- Zest of 1 lemon
- ½ tablespoon vanilla extract

How To

1. Set up your Sous Vide immersion circulator to a temperature of 176-degrees Fahrenheit and prepare your water bath.
2. Take a bowl and add both cream cheeses, and sugar and whisk them well
3. Gradually add the eggs one by one and keep beating until well combined.
4. Add the zest and vanilla and mix well.
5. Pour the cheesecake mixture into 6 different jars of 6 ounces and distribute evenly
6. Seal the jars with a lid.
7. Place the jars underwater and let them cook for 90 minutes.
8. Once done, remove from the water bath and chill until they are cooled
9. Serve chilled with a topping of fresh fruit compote.

Nutrition Values (Per Serving)

- Calories: 615
- Carbohydrate: 56g
- Protein: 8g
- Fat: 41g
- Sugar: 40g
- Sodium: 418mg

Peach Cobbler

(Serves: 6/ **Prep Time:** 15 minutes / **Sous Vide Cooking Time:** 180 minutes)

Ingredients

- 1 cup self-rising flour
- 1 cup granulated sugar
- 1 cup whole milk
- 1 teaspoon vanilla extract
- 8 tablespoons unsalted melted butter
- 2 cups roughly chopped peaches

How To

1. Set up your Sous Vide immersion circulator to a temperature of 195-degrees Fahrenheit and prepare your water bath.

2. Prepare 6 half-pint canning jars by greasing the jars with melted butter
3. Mix the flour and sugar in a large bowl. Then mix in milk and vanilla.
4. Stir in butter and peaches.
5. Divide the batter between jars and wipe sides, seal gently
6. Submerge underwater and cook for 3 hours.
7. Transfer the jars to a cooling rack, allow them to cool and serve!

Nutrition Values (Per Serving)

- Calories: 524
- Carbohydrate: 85g
- Protein: 6g
- Fat: 19g
- Sugar: 60g
- Sodium: 262mg

Banana Bread

(Serves: 9 / **Prep Time:** 30 minutes / **Sous Vide Cooking Time:** 210 minutes)

Ingredients

- ½ cup butter
- ½ cup brown sugar
- ½ cup white sugar
- 2 eggs
- 1 teaspoon vanilla
- 1 teaspoon salt
- 3 tablespoons milk
- 3 very ripe mashed bananas
- ½ teaspoon baking soda
- 2 cups all-purpose flour

How To

1. Set up your Sous Vide immersion circulator to a temperature of 190-degrees Fahrenheit and prepare your water bath.
2. Put the butter, white and brown sugar to a warm skillet and mix them well.
3. Remove the heat and allow the mixture to cool, add the egg, vanilla, milk, and sugar.
4. Stir well until the sugar has dissolved.
5. Put the bananas, flour, baking soda, and salt and whisk them well.
6. Transfer the mixture into 4-ounce mason jars and gently tighten the lid.
7. Cook for 3 and a ½ hours underwater.
8. Open the lid and enjoy!

Nutrition Values (Per Serving)

- Calories: 243
- Carbohydrate: 34g
- Protein: 6g
- Fat: 9g
- Sugar: 7g
- Sodium: 179mg

Blueberry Clafoutis

(Serves: 4 / **Prep Time:** 5 minutes / **Sous Vide Cooking Time:** 60 minutes)

Ingredients

- 1 egg
- ¼ cup heavy cream
- ¼ cup almond flour
- 1 tablespoon sugar
- 2 teaspoons coconut flour
- ¼ teaspoon baking powder
- ¼ teaspoon vanilla extract
- ½ cup fresh blueberries
- Granulated sugar for topping

How To

1. Set up your Sous Vide immersion circulator to a temperature of 185-degrees Fahrenheit and prepare your water bath.
2. Add all the listed ingredients except the blueberries to small mixing bowl and mix well.
3. Grease the mason jars with cooking spray and divide the batter among the jars
4. Top each jar with 2 tablespoons of blueberries and lightly seal them.
5. Cook for 1 hour underwater.
6. Once done, remove from the water bath and sprinkle a bit of sugar on top and serve!

Nutrition Values (Per Serving)

- Calories: 234
- Carbohydrate: 32g
- Protein: 4g
- Fat: 11g
- Sugar: 23g
- Sodium: 36mg

Coconut Congee & Cinnamon Sugar

(Serves: 6 / **Prep Time:** 45 minutes / **Sous Vide Cooking Time:** 90 minutes)

Ingredients

- 1 cup short grain rice
- 4 cups water
- 4 cups coconut milk
- 1 cup cinnamon sugar
- 1 tablespoon pumpkin pie spice
- A pinch of kosher salt

How To

1. Set up your Sous Vide immersion circulator to a temperature of 190-degrees Fahrenheit and prepare your water bath.
2. Add the rice, water, coconut milk, sugar and pumpkin pie spice to a resealable bag and seal them using the immersion method.

3. Cook for 1½ hours underwater.
4. Remove the congee (The Sous Vide rice) and season with salt
5. Serve!

Nutrition Values (Per Serving)

- Calories: 264
- Carbohydrate: 24g
- Protein: 15g

- Fat: 12g
- Sugar: 1g
- Sodium: 461mg

Salted Caramel Ice Cream

(Serves: 6 / **Prep Time:** 60 minutes / **Sous Vide Cooking Time:** 30 minutes)

Ingredients

- 1 ½ cup sugar
- 1 ¾ cups heavy cream
- 1 teaspoon sea salt
- 1 cup whole milk
- 5 egg yolks
- 1 teaspoon vanilla bean paste
- Pinch of kosher salt

Tools Required

- Ice Cream Maker

How To

1. Set up your Sous Vide immersion circulator to a temperature of 180-degrees Fahrenheit and prepare your water bath.
2. Heat up 1 cup of sugar in a large-sized nonstick saucepan, making sure to keep stirring it until it begins to melt.
3. Swirl until the sugar has melted and is slightly browned.
4. Whisk in 1 cup of heavy cream and cook until the mixture is smooth.
5. Stir in salt and remove the heat and allow the mixture to cool down.
6. Take a food processor and add the egg yolks, vanilla, 3/4 cup of cream, ½ cup of sugar, milk and purée for 30 seconds.
7. Transfer the mixture to a resealable zip bag and seal using the immersion method.
8. Cook for 30 minutes underwater.
9. Stir caramel* into the bag and allow it to chill overnight.
10. Allow the mixture to cool. Churn the mixture in ice cream maker
11. Freeze and serve!

Nutrition Values (Per Serving)

- Calories: 1013
- Carbohydrate: 94g
- Protein: 12g
- Fat: 68g
- Sugar: 94g
- Sodium: 526mg

(**Note: Caramel*** - we are talking about the melted sugar combination that we earlier set aside at step 2 and 3.)

Sweet Corn Gelato

(**Serves:** 6 / **Prep Time:** 60 minutes / **Sous Vide Cooking Time:** 30 minutes)

Ingredients

- 4 ears shucked corn
- 3 cups whole milk
- 1 cup heavy cream
- 1 cup granulated sugar
- 1 teaspoon kosher salt
- 6 large egg yolks
- ¼ cup crème fraiche

How To

1. Set up your Sous Vide immersion circulator to a temperature of 180-degrees Fahrenheit and prepare your water bath.
2. Take the corn cobs and slice off the kernels, transfer to a saucepan.
3. Add the milk, cream, salt, and sugar.
4. Lower down the heat and allow the mixture to simmer, remove the heat, allow it to steep for 30 seconds.
5. Strain the mixture out and discard corn and cobs.
6. Add the corn-infused milk and egg to the blender and purée for 30 seconds until it gets a frothy texture.
7. Transfer the whole mixture to a resealable bag and seal using the immersion method. Cook for 30 minutes.
8. Chill the bag in ice bath. Once the mixture is cool, mix in crème fraiche and churn the mixture in an ice cream maker.
9. Freeze and serve!

Nutrition Values (Per Serving)

- Calories: 801
- Carbohydrate: 102g
- Protein: 16g
- Fat: 39g
- Sugar: 92g
- Sodium: 474mg

Raspberry Mousse

(Serves: 8 / **Prep Time:** 15 minutes / **Sous Vide Cooking Time:** 45 minutes)

Ingredients

- 1 lb. raspberries
- ¼ cup ultrafine sugar
- 3 tablespoons fresh squeezed lemon juice
- ½ teaspoon kosher salt
- ¼ teaspoon ground cinnamon
- 1 cup heavy cream
- 1 teaspoon vanilla extract

How To

1. Set up your Sous Vide immersion circulator to a temperature of 180-degrees Fahrenheit and prepare your water bath.
2. Add the raspberries, sugar, salt, lemon juice and cinnamon to a resealable bag and seal using the immersion method. Cook for 45 minutes.
3. Once done, take the bag out from the water bath and pour the contents into a blender.
4. Purée until it gets smooth.
5. Take a large mixing bowl and mix in cream, vanilla until stiff peaks form.
6. Fold in raspberry purée and mix.
7. Divide among 8 serving bowls, chill and serve!

Nutrition Values (Per Serving)

- Calories: 394
- Carbohydrate: 30g
- Protein: 3g
- Fat: 30g
- Sugar: 21g
- Sodium: 87mg

Strawberry Mousse

(Serves: 8 / **Prep Time:** 45 minutes / **Sous Vide Cooking Time:** 45 minutes)

Ingredients

- 1 lb. strawberries, stemmed and halved
- ¼ cup packed light brown sugar
- 3 tablespoons freshly squeezed lemon juice
- ½ teaspoon kosher salt
- ¼ teaspoon ground cinnamon
- 1 cup heavy cream
- 1 teaspoon vanilla extract
- 1 cup crème fraiche

How To

1. Set up your Sous Vide immersion circulator to a temperature of 180-degrees Fahrenheit and prepare your water bath.

2. Add the strawberries, brown sugar, lemon juice, salt, and cinnamon to a large resealable zipper bag.
3. Seal using the immersion method and cook for 45 minutes.
4. Once done, remove the bag and pour the contents to a food processor.
5. Purée for a few seconds until you have a smooth mixture
6. Take a large chilled mixing bowl and add the heavy cream and vanilla, whisk well until stiff peaks form.
7. Fold in strawberry purée and crème fraiche.
8. Whisk them well and divide it among 8 serving bowls.
9. Serve chilled!

Nutrition Values (Per Serving)

- Calories: 265
- Carbohydrate: 22g
- Protein: 4g
- Fat: 17g
- Sugar: 21g
- Sodium: 206mg

Blueberry & Lemon Compote

(Serves: 8 / **Prep Time:** 15 minutes / **Sous Vide Cooking Time:** 60 minutes)

Ingredients

- ½ cup ultrafine sugar
- 1 tablespoon freshly squeezed lemon juice
- 1 tablespoon lemon zest
- 1 tablespoon cornstarch
- 1 lb. blueberries

How To

1. Set up your Sous Vide immersion circulator to a temperature of 180-degrees Fahrenheit and prepare your water bath.
2. Take a medium-sized bowl and mix in sugar, lemon juice, lemon zest, and cornstarch.
3. Add the blueberries and toss well to coat them.
4. Transfer the mixture to a resealable zip bag and seal using the immersion method.
5. Cook for 60 minutes.
6. Once done, remove the bag and transfer the contents to a serving dish.
7. Serve warm!

Nutrition Values (Per Serving)

- Calories: 182
- Carbohydrate: 47g
- Protein: 1g
- Fat: 1g
- Sugar: 40g
- Sodium: 3mg

Chocolate & Ricotta Mousse

(Serves: 8 / **Prep Time:** 30 minutes / **Sous Vide Cooking Time:** 60 minutes)

Ingredients

- 2 quarts' whole milk
- 6 tablespoons white wine vinegar
- 4 oz. semisweet chocolate chips
- ¼ cup powdered sugar
- Grand Marnier liquor
- 1 tablespoon orange zest
- 2 oz. ricotta

How To

1. Set up your Sous Vide immersion circulator to a temperature of 172-degrees Fahrenheit and prepare your water bath.
2. Put the milk and vinegar to a resealable zip bag.
3. Seal using the immersion method and cook for 1 hour.
4. Once done, remove the bag and skim the curds from top and transfer to a strainer lined with cheesecloth. Discard any remaining liquid.
5. Let it sit and drain the curd for about 10 minutes. Then chill for 1 hour.
6. Prepare your double broiler by setting a bowl over a small saucepan filled with 1 inch of water
7. Bring the water to a low simmer over medium heat.
8. Add the chocolate chips to a bowl of the double boiler and cook until it has melted.
9. Transfer to a food processor.
10. Add the sugar, orange zest, grand mariner, ricotta, and then process until smooth
11. Transfer to individual bowls and serve!

Nutrition Values (Per Serving)

- Calories: 472
- Carbohydrate: 37g
- Protein: 6g
- Fat: 35g
- Sugar: 34g
- Sodium: 103mg

Brioche Bread Pudding

(Serves: 4 / **Prep Time:** 30 minutes / **Sous Vide Cooking Time:** 120 minutes)

Ingredients

- 1 cup whole milk
- 1 cup heavy cream
- ½ cup granulated sugar
- ¼ cup maple syrup

- 2 tablespoons orange juice
- 1 tablespoon orange zest
- 1 teaspoon vanilla bean paste
- ½ teaspoon kosher salt
- 4 cups brioche, cut up into 1 inch cubes

How To

1. Set up your Sous Vide immersion circulator to a temperature of 170-degrees Fahrenheit and prepare your water bath.
2. Take a large bowl and add the milk, heavy cream, sugar, maple syrup, orange zest, juice, vanilla bean paste, and salt.
3. Mix well and add the brioche. Toss well
4. Divide the mixture among 4 mason jars of 4-ounces size and gently seal them using the finger-tip method
5. Cook for 2 hours underwater.
6. Heat up your broiler and place the jars in the broiler.
7. Brown for 2-3 minutes (with lids removed) and serve.

Nutrition Values (Per Serving)

- Calories: 246
- Carbohydrate: 19g
- Protein: 7g
- Fat: 16g
- Sugar: 3g
- Sodium: 164mg

Spiced Coconut Ice Cream

(Serves: 4 / **Prep Time:** 60 minutes / **Sous Vide Cooking Time:** 30 minutes)

Ingredients

- 1 can (13 oz.) full-fat coconut milk
- ¾ cup sugar
- ½ teaspoon kosher salt
- 2 teaspoons vanilla extract
- ½ teaspoon ground cinnamon
- ¼ teaspoon nutmeg
- ¼ teaspoon coriander
- 4 large egg yolks

Tools required

- Ice Cream Maker

How To

1. Set up your Sous Vide immersion circulator to a temperature of 180-degrees Fahrenheit and prepare your water bath.

2. Take a medium-sized saucepan and add the coconut milk, salt, sugar, cinnamon, vanilla, nutmeg, coriander and bring it to a simmer.
3. Once done, remove the heat and allow it to steep for 30 minutes.
4. Transfer to a blender and purée the mixture alongside the egg yolks for 30 seconds
5. Transfer the mixture to a resealable zip bag and seal using the immersion method.
6. Cook for 30 minutes, making sure to agitate the bag from time to time.
7. Chill the bag in an ice bath and churn the mixture in an ice cream maker.
8. Freeze and serve!

Nutrition Values (Per Serving)
- Calories: 693
- Carbohydrate: 36g
- Protein: 9g
- Fat: 60g
- Sugar: 32g
- Sodium: 183mg

Rhubarb Mousse

(Serves: 6 / **Prep Time:** 30 minutes / **Sous Vide Cooking Time:** 60 minutes)

Ingredients
- 1 oz. trimmed rhubarb cut up into 1-inch pieces
- ½ cup packed light brown sugar
- 1/3 cup freshly squeezed orange juice
- 1 tablespoon Grand Marnier
- ½ teaspoon kosher salt
- ¼ teaspoon ground cinnamon
- 2 large-sized eggs, separated
- ½ cup heavy cream
- 1 teaspoon vanilla extract

How To
1. Set up your Sous Vide immersion circulator to a temperature of 180-degrees Fahrenheit and prepare your water bath.
2. Put the rhubarb, ¼ cup of brown sugar, orange juice, salt, Grand Marnier, and cinnamon to a resealable zip bag.
3. Seal using the immersion method. Cook for 1 hour.
4. Once cooked, remove the bag from the water bath and pour the contents to a blender.
5. Then, transfer the rhubarb mixture to a large saucepan and place it over medium heat.
6. Mix in egg yolks and ¼ cup of brown sugar.
7. Cook for 3 minutes until the mixture is thick.

8. Once cooked, transfer the contents to a large bowl and allow it to cool.
9. Take another bowl and mix in egg whites until stiff peaks forms.
10. Fold the egg whites into rhubarb mixture and then stir to combine.
11. Take another bowl and mix in the cream and vanilla, mix until stiff peak forms.
12. Fold cream into rhubarb egg mixture and combine.
13. Spoon into serving cups, chill and serve!

Nutrition Values (Per Serving)

- Calories: 605
- Carbohydrate: 54g
- Protein: 6g
- Fat: 39g
- Sugar: 48g
- Sodium: 54mg

Chocolate Pots De Crème

(Serves: 12 / **Prep Time:** 45 minutes / **Sous Vide Cooking Time:** 45 minutes)

Ingredients

- 1 cup fruit-forward red wine
- ½ cup granulated sugar
- 12 oz. semisweet chocolate chips
- 8 ounces unsweetened dark chocolate, finely chopped up
- 1 cup whole milk
- ½ cup heavy cream
- 8 large egg yolks
- A pinch of kosher salt

How To

1. Set up your Sous Vide immersion circulator to a temperature of 180-degrees Fahrenheit and prepare your water bath.
2. Take a medium-sized saucepan and place it over medium-high heat.
3. Add the wine and sugar and bring the mixture to a boil, reduce heat to medium-low and simmer for 20 minutes. Remove and allow it to cool for 10 minutes.
4. Transfer to a food processor and add the chocolate chips, unsweetened dark chocolate, milk, cream, salt, and egg yolks. Blend well until smooth.
5. Then, transfer the mixture to a resealable bag and seal using the immersion method, cook for 45 minutes.
6. Once cooked, remove the bag and transfer the contents to a food processor.
7. Blend for 2 minutes.
8. Divide the mixture among 12 ramekins and cover them with plastic wrap.
9. Chill for 4 hours and serve!

Nutrition Values (Per Serving)

- Calories: 793
- Carbohydrate: 56g
- Protein: 13g
- Fat: 62g
- Sugar: 51g
- Sodium: 494mg

Champagne Zabaglione

(**Serves:** 6 / **Prep Time:** 15 minutes / **Sous Vide Cooking Time:** 45 minutes)

Ingredients

- 1 cup heavy cream
- ½ cup champagne
- ½ cup ultrafine sugar
- 4 large egg yolks
- 1 teaspoon vanilla extract
- A pinch of kosher salt

How To

1. Set up your Sous Vide immersion circulator to a temperature of 180-degrees Fahrenheit and prepare your water bath.
2. Add all the listed ingredients to a blender and purée for 30 seconds.
3. Transfer to a resealable zip bag and seal using the immersion method.
4. Cook for 45 minutes and once done, transfer the bag to an ice bath.
5. Serve immediately!

Nutrition Values (Per Serving)

- Calories: 375
- Carbohydrate: 28g
- Protein: 4g
- Fat: 27g
- Sugar: 27g
- Sodium: 62mg

Orange Curd

(**Serves:** 6 / **Prep Time:** 15 minutes / **Sous Vide Cooking Time:** 45 minutes)

Ingredients

- 1 cup ultrafine sugar
- 8 tablespoons unsalted butter, melted
- 6 egg yolks
- ¼ cup freshly squeezed orange juice
- A pinch of kosher salt

How To

1. Set up your Sous Vide immersion circulator to a temperature of 180-degrees Fahrenheit and prepare your water bath.
2. Add the listed ingredients to a blender and pulse the mixture for 20 seconds
3. Transfer to a resealable bag and seal using the immersion method.
4. Submerge it underwater and cook for 45 minutes. Keep agitating the bag from time to time.
5. Once cooked, remove the bag from the water bath and transfer to an ice bath.
6. Chill for 2 hours and serve!

Nutrition Values (Per Serving)

- Calories: 422
- Carbohydrate: 54g
- Protein: 5g
- Fat: 22g
- Sugar: 52g
- Sodium: 43mg

Rice & Cardamom Pudding

(Serves: 8 / **Prep Time:** 15 minutes / **Sous Vide Cooking Time:** 120 minutes)

Ingredients

- ½ cup raisins
- ½ cup dark rum
- 5 tablespoons unsalted butter
- 1/3 cup light brown sugar
- 4 cups cooked wild rice blend
- 1 cup whole milk
- 1 cup heavy cream
- 3 strips lemon peel
- 3 crushed cardamom pods, crushed and wrapped in cheese cloth
- 1 teaspoon vanilla extract
- Cinnamon

How To

1. Set up your Sous Vide immersion circulator to a temperature of 181-degrees Fahrenheit and prepare your water bath.
2. Put the raisins and rum into a small microwave bowl and heat for 1 minute.
3. Allow it to cool and remove the raisins using slotted spoon.
4. Take a medium non-stick skillet and place it over medium-high heat.
5. Add the butter and then brown sugar and heat it up.
6. Stir until it has melted and simmer for 5 minutes.
7. Add the cooked rice, milk, cream, lemon peel, cardamom and vanilla to butter mixture and bring the mixture to a boil.
8. Lower down the heat to low and simmer for about 2 minutes.

9. Remove from the heat and stir in raisins, spoon the mixture into resealable zip bag and seal using the immersion method.
10. Cook for 2 hours underwater.
11. Once cooked, take the bag out from the water bath and pour the mixture into a large bowl. Stir well and discard cardamom pod bundle alongside the lemon peels.
12. Sprinkle cinnamon and serve!

Nutrition Values (Per Serving)

- Calories: 362
- Carbohydrate: 50g
- Protein: 12g
- Fat: 13g
- Sugar: 38g
- Sodium: 132mg

Lemon Curd

(**Serves:** 3 / **Prep Time:** 8 hours 10 minutes / **Sous Vide Cooking Time:** 45 minutes)

Ingredients

- 6 tablespoons unsalted butter, melted and cooled
- 4 lemon juice
- 6 large egg yolks at room temperature
- 1 cup granulated sugar

How To

1. Set up your Sous Vide immersion circulator to a temperature of 179-degrees Fahrenheit and prepare your water bath.
2. Mix the sugar, butter, and lemon juice in a bowl.
3. Keep mixing until the sugar has dissolved and then add the egg yolks, mix them well.
4. Transfer the egg mixture to a resealable bag and seal using the immersion method.
5. Cook for 45 minutes underwater.
6. Transfer the bag to an ice bag and shake well.
7. Once the curd is cool, chill overnight.
8. Then, pour the curd into a bowl and whisk.
9. Serve and use as needed.

Nutrition Values (Per Serving)

- Calories: 178
- Carbohydrate: 15g
- Protein: 4g
- Fat: 12g
- Sugar: 13g
- Sodium: 31mg

Kiwi & Vanilla Fresh Mint

(Serves: 2 / **Prep Time:** 10 minutes / **Sous Vide Cooking Time:** 20 minutes)

Ingredients

- 2 peeled and sliced kiwis
- 2 tablespoons granulated sugar
- 1 tablespoon freshly squeezed lemon juice
- 2 generous tablespoons yogurt/ vanilla ice cream
- Fresh mint leaves for garnishing

How To

1. Set up your Sous Vide immersion circulator to a temperature of 176-degrees Fahrenheit and prepare your water bath.
2. Take a medium bowl and add the kiwi slices, sugar, lemon juice and stir.
3. Transfer the mixture to a resealable zipper bag and seal using the immersion method.
4. Cook for 20 minutes and remove the bag from the water bath.
5. Divide the mixture between 2 serving plates.
6. Scoop yogurt/ vanilla ice cream onto the plate next to your kiwi and garnish with some mint leaves.
7. Serve!

Nutrition Values (Per Serving)

- Calories: 148
- Carbohydrate: 21g
- Protein: 5g
- Fat: 5g
- Sugar: 15g
- Sodium: 106mg

Cinnamon Spiced Apples

(Serves: 4 / **Prep Time:** 20 minutes / **Sous Vide Cooking Time:** 120 minutes)

Ingredients

- 4 tart peeled apples
- 1 lemon juice
- 3 tablespoons unsalted butter
- 2 tablespoons light brown sugar
- 2 whole fresh dates pitted
- 2 tablespoons raisins
- 1 tablespoon ground cinnamon
- ¼ teaspoon fine sea salt
- ¼ teaspoon grated nutmeg
- 1/9 teaspoon vanilla extract
- Freshly whipped ice cream

How To

1. Set up your Sous Vide immersion circulator to a temperature of 183-degrees Fahrenheit and prepare your water bath.
2. Core the apples and toss the apples with lemon juice.
3. Take a medium bowl and add the butter, brown sugar, dates, raisins, cinnamon, salt, vanilla, and nutmeg.
4. Take a fork and mash the mixture into a chunky paste.
5. Divide the mixture and fill the apple cores.
6. Transfer the apple to a resealable zipper bag and seal using the immersion method. Cook for 2 hours.
7. Remove the bags from the water bath. Take the apples out from the bag and place them on serving plates.
8. Serve apples with whipped cream/ice cream.

Nutrition Values (Per Serving)

- Calories: 259
- Carbohydrate: 30g
- Protein: 0g
- Fat: 0g
- Sugar: 24g
- Sodium: 11mg

Vanilla & Butter Pears

(Serves: 2 / **Prep Time:** 10 minutes / **Sous Vide Cooking Time:** 30 minutes)

Ingredients

- 2 peeled ripe pears
- 1 vanilla bean
- 2 tablespoons dark brown sugar
- 1/8 teaspoon flaky sea salt
- 1 tablespoon unsalted butter
- Vanilla ice cream for serving

How To

1. Set up your Sous Vide immersion circulator to a temperature of 175-degrees Fahrenheit and prepare your water bath.
2. Slice the pears in half lengthwise.
3. Scoop out the core using a spoon, divide the pear halves between two resealable bags.
4. Then, cut/slice the vanilla bean in half and use the back of the spoon to scrape its seeds into a small bowl.
5. Add the brown sugar and salt.
6. Then, rub the vanilla bean seed into sugar using your fingers and combine.
7. Divide the mixture between the resealable bags and add 1 tablespoon of butter and one half of your vanilla pod into each bag.

8. Seal using the immersion method. Cook for 30 minutes.
9. Remove the bag from the water bath. Take the pears out from the bag and then transfer to serving bowls.
10. Drizzle the butter sauce from the bag over the pears and serve with vanilla ice cream.

Nutrition Values (Per Serving)

- Calories: 441
- Carbohydrate: 109g
- Protein: 1g
- Fat: 1g
- Sugar: 90g
- Sodium: 10mg

Lemon Raspberry Ricotta Cheesecake

(**Serves:** 12 / **Prep Time:** 8 hours 30 minutes / **Sous Vide Cooking Time:** 120 minutes)

Ingredients

- 9 oz. ricotta cheese
- 1 cup granulated sugar
- 7 oz. soft cream cheese
- ½ cup full-fat Greek yogurt
- ½ cup heavy cream
- 2 large eggs + 1 large egg yolk
- Finely grated zest one lemon + 2 tablespoons freshly squeezed juice
- 2 tablespoons all-purpose flour
- ¼ teaspoon vanilla extract
- Fine sea salt
- 1 ½ cup graham crackers
- 1/3 cup unsalted butter
- 2 pints' fresh raspberries

How To

1. Set up your Sous Vide immersion circulator to a temperature of 170-degrees Fahrenheit and prepare your water bath.
2. Preheat your oven to 375-degrees Fahrenheit.
3. Take a large bowl and mix in ricotta cheese, 2/3 cup of sugar, cream cheese, Greek yogurt, heavy cream, egg yolks, eggs, lemon zest, juice, 1 tablespoon of flour, vanilla, and ½ a teaspoon of salt.
4. Transfer to a resealable bag and seal using the immersion method. Cook for 2 hours.
5. Make the crust by taking another medium bowl and add the graham cracker crumbs, butter, 1/3 cup of sugar, pinch of salt and 1 tablespoon of flour.
6. Whisk well until fully combined and press the mixture into the bottom of a 9-inch springform pan.
7. Bake in your oven until the crust is browned, should take about 7-10 minutes.
8. Once cooked, remove the bag from the water bath and pat it dry.

9. Cut off one corner of the resealable bag. Pipe contents of bag carefully into the baked crust.
10. Press raspberries onto the surface and chill for 8 hours before serving.

Nutrition Values (Per Serving)

- Calories: 252
- Carbohydrate: 27g
- Protein: 4g
- Fat: 15g
- Sugar: 16g
- Sodium: 208mg

Doce De Banana

(**Serves:** 4 / **Prep Time:** 10 minutes / **Sous Vide Cooking Time:** 40 minutes)

Ingredients

- 5 small ripe bananas, firm but ripe, peeled and cut up into chunks
- 1 cup brown sugar
- 2 cinnamon sticks
- 6 whole cloves
- Whipped cream for serving
- Vanilla ice-cream for serving

How To

1. Set up your Sous Vide immersion circulator to a temperature of 176-degrees Fahrenheit and prepare your water bath.
2. Put the bananas, brown sugar, cinnamon sticks, and cloves to a resealable bag.
3. Seal using the immersion method and cook for 30-40 minutes.
4. Remove the bag and allow the contents to cool.
5. Open the bag and remove the cinnamon sticks and cloves.
6. Serve warm in a bowl with a topping of whipped cream and vanilla ice cream.

Nutrition Values (Per Serving)

- Calories: 310
- Carbohydrate: 80g
- Protein: 1g
- Fat: 0g
- Sugar: 65g
- Sodium: 9mg

Maple Raisin Rice Pudding

(Serves: 4 / **Prep Time:** 10 minutes / **Sous Vide Cooking Time:** 120 minutes)

Ingredients

- 3 cups skim milk
- 2 tablespoons butter
- 2 cups Arborio rice
- ½ cup maple syrup
- 2 teaspoons ground cinnamon
- ½ teaspoon ground ginger
- Ground cinnamon/cinnamon sugar for serving

How To

1. Set up your Sous Vide immersion circulator to a temperature of 140-degrees Fahrenheit and prepare your water bath.
2. Add all the listed ingredients except for the cinnamon to your resealable bag and stir well.
3. Seal using the immersion method. Submerge underwater and cook for 2 hours.
4. Once done, remove from the water bath and stir the ingredients.
5. Transfer the pudding to serving bowls.
6. Sprinkle cinnamon over the bowls and serve warm.

Nutrition Values (Per Serving)

- Calories: 300
- Carbohydrate: 49g
- Protein: 6g
- Fat: 8g
- Sugar: 18g
- Sodium: 140mg

Lavender Poached Honey Peaches

(Serves: 4 / **Prep Time:** 10 minutes / **Sous Vide Cooking Time:** 20 minutes)

Ingredients

- 2 halved and pitted peaches
- 1 tablespoon dried lavender buds
- ¼ cup water
- ¼ cup honey

For Whipped Mascarpone Cheese

- 1/3 cup mascarpone cheese
- ½ cup coconut cream
- 1 tablespoon maple syrup
- Just a drop lavender extract

How To

1. Set up your Sous Vide immersion circulator to a temperature of 185-degrees Fahrenheit and prepare your water bath.

2. Add the peaches and the remaining ingredients (except the whipped Mascarpone) to a resealable bag and seal using the immersion method.
3. Submerge underwater and cook for 20 minutes.
4. Once cooked, transfer the bag to an ice bath and place it in your fridge and allow it to chill for 1 hour
5. Take a medium-sized bowl and add the coconut cream and mascarpone cheese, mix well until a soft peak forms
6. Add the syrup and lavender to the bowl and keep whipping until you see the stable peaks
7. Serve the peach with a dollop of the whipped mascarpone and a drizzle of the bag liquid
8. Garnish with dried lavender and serve!

Nutrition Values (Per Serving)
- Calories: 656
- Carbohydrate: 162g
- Protein: 13g
- Fat: 3g
- Sugar: 147g
- Sodium: 8mg

Citrus Yogurt

(Serves: 4 / **Prep Time:** 15 minutes / **Sous Vide Cooking Time:** 180 minutes)

Ingredients
- ½ cup yogurt
- ½ tablespoon orange zest
- ½ tablespoon lemon zest
- ½ tablespoon lime zest
- 4 cups full cream milk

How To
1. Set up your Sous Vide immersion circulator to a temperature of 113-degrees Fahrenheit and prepare your water bath.
2. Heat the milk on stove top to a temperature of 180-degrees Fahrenheit.
3. Transfer to an ice bath and allow it to cool down to 110-degrees Fahrenheit.
4. Stir in yogurt.
5. Fold in the citrus zest.
6. Pour the mixture into 4-ounce canning jars and lightly close the lid.
7. Submerge underwater and cook for 3 hours.
8. Remove the jars and serve immediately!

Nutrition Values (Per Serving)
- Calories: 175
- Carbohydrate: 35g
- Protein: 6g
- Fat: 2g
- Sugar: 32g
- Sodium: 66mg

Sweet Candied Potatoes

(Serves: 8 / **Prep Time:** 45 minutes / **Sous Vide Cooking Time:** 120 minutes)

Ingredients

- 2 lbs. sweet potatoes, peeled up and cut into ¼ slices
- ½ cup unsalted butter
- ¼ cup maple syrup
- 2 oranges, juice and zest
- 1 teaspoon kosher salt
- 1 cup chopped walnuts
- 1 cinnamon stick
- ¼ cup brown sugar

How To

1. Set up your Sous Vide immersion circulator to a temperature of 155-degrees Fahrenheit and prepare your water bath.
2. Take a resealable bag and add the sweet potatoes and ¼ cup of butter.
3. Seal using the immersion method and cook for 2 hours.
4. Preheat your oven to 350-degrees Fahrenheit.
5. Remove the potatoes from the bag and pat dry.
6. Arrange the potatoes evenly in a baking dish.
7. Take a medium saucepan and bring ¼ cup of butter, brown sugar, maple syrup, orange zest, juice, walnuts, salt, and cinnamon stick to a boil.
8. Remove from heat and pour over sweet potatoes, discard the cinnamon stick
9. Bake for 30 minutes and serve warm!

Nutrition Values (Per Serving)

- Calories: 320
- Carbohydrate: 67g
- Protein: 3g
- Fat: 5g
- Sugar: 34g
- Sodium: 215mg

Mocha Pot De Crème

(Serves: 8 / **Prep Time:** 15 minutes / **Sous Vide Cooking Time:** 30 minutes)

Ingredients

- 1/3 cup espresso
- ¾ cup milk
- 1 cup heavy cream
- 6 oz. chopped chocolate
- 1/3 cup sugar
- ¼ teaspoon fine salt
- Whipped cream
- Cinnamon powder
- 4 large egg yolks

How To

1. Set up your Sous Vide immersion circulator to a temperature of 180-degrees Fahrenheit and prepare your water bath.
2. Take a medium-sized saucepan and heat it up over medium heat.
3. Add the heavy cream, espresso, milk and bring to a boil.
4. Once done, turn-off the heat and stir in chocolate. Then, cook once again over medium heat and occasionally stir for 15 minutes.
5. Take a medium bowl and add in the egg yolks, salt, and sugar. Stir well and add the chocolate crème mixture.
6. Once mixed together, cool the mixture for 10-15 minutes.
7. Add the contents to a resealable zipper bag and seal using the immersion method.
8. Cook for 30 minutes.
9. Spoon the mixture into small ramekins and garnish with cinnamon powder or whipped cream.
10. Chill for 2 hours and serve!

Nutrition Values (Per Serving)

- Calories: 218
- Carbohydrate: 45g
- Protein: 6g
- Fat: 3g
- Sugar: 42g
- Sodium: 98mg

Baked Ricotta

(**Serves:** 6 / **Prep Time:** 50 minutes / **Sous Vide Cooking Time:** 60 minutes)

Ingredients

- 2 quarts whole milk
- 6 tablespoons white wine vinegar
- 2 large eggs
- 2 tablespoons extra virgin olive oil
- 1 ½ teaspoon smoked salt
- 1 teaspoon fresh ground smoked black pepper

How To

1. Set up your Sous Vide immersion circulator to a temperature of 172-degrees Fahrenheit and prepare your water bath.
2. Add the milk and vinegar to a resealable zip bag.
3. Seal using the immersion method and cook for 1 hour.

4. Preheat your oven to 350-degrees Fahrenheit.
5. Remove the bag and skim the curd off the top.
6. Then, pass the mixture through a strainer lined with a cheesecloth and discard any remaining liquid.
7. Drain the curd for 10 minutes.
8. Transfer drained curds to food processor alongside the eggs, salt, olive oil, and pepper.
9. Process for 20 seconds.
10. Divide the ricotta mixture between 6 oven proof ramekins and bake for 30 minutes until golden brown.
11. Serve!

Nutrition Values (Per Serving)

- Calories: 145
- Carbohydrate: 3g
- Protein: 10g
- Fat: 10g
- Sugar: 0g
- Sodium: 342mg

CHAPTER 8 | COCKTAILS AND INFUSIONS

Lavender Syrup

(Serves: 4 / **Prep Time:** 5 minutes / **Sous Vide Cooking Time:** 60 minutes)

Ingredients
- 1 cup water
- 1 cup sugar
- 1 tablespoon culinary grade dried lavender

How To
1. Prepare your Sous Vide water bath using your immersion circulator and raise the temperature to 135-degrees Fahrenheit.
2. Take a heavy-duty resealable zipper bag and add the water, lavender, and sugar.
3. Seal it using the immersion method.
4. Submerge it underwater and cook for about 1 hour.
5. Once done, let it cool down to room temperature and strain through a metal mesh.
6. Serve chilled!

Nutrition Values (Per Serving)
- Calories: 112
- Carbohydrate: 101g
- Protein: 0g
- Fat: 0g
- Sugar: 218g
- Sodium: 2mg

Thyme Liqueur

(Serves: 12 / **Prep Time:** 15 minutes / **Sous Vide Cooking Time:** 90 minutes)

Ingredients
- Zest of 8 large oranges
- 4 sprigs fresh thyme
- 1 cup ultrafine sugar
- 1 cup water
- 1 cup vodka

How To
1. Prepare your Sous Vide water bath using your immersion circulator and raise the temperature to 180-degrees Fahrenheit.

2. Add all the listed ingredients to a heavy-duty resealable zip bag and seal using the immersion method.
3. Cook for 90 minutes.
4. Strain the mixture and serve chilled!

Nutrition Values (Per Serving)

- Calories: 507
- Carbohydrate: 110g
- Protein: 2g
- Fat: 8g
- Sugar: 105g
- Sodium: 15mg

Pineapple Rum

(Serves: 12 / **Prep Time:** 15 minutes / **Sous Vide Cooking Time:** 120 minutes)

Ingredients

- 1 peeled and cored pineapple cut into 1-inch pieces
- 1 bottle dark rum
- 1 cup granulated sugar

How To

1. Prepare your Sous Vide water bath using your immersion circulator and raise the temperature to 135-degrees Fahrenheit.
2. Take a resealable zipper bag and add the pineapple, rum, sugar, and seal using the immersion method.
3. Submerge underwater and cook for about 2 hours.
4. Once done, strain the mixture through a metal mesh strainer into a medium bowl.
5. Chill overnight and serve!

Nutrition Values (Per Serving)

- Calories: 442
- Carbohydrate: 45g
- Protein: 1g
- Fat: 0g
- Sugar: 54g
- Sodium: 8mg

Vodka Lemon Meyer

(Serves: 6 / **Prep Time:** 15 minutes / **Sous Vide Cooking Time:** 120 minutes)

Ingredients
- 1 cup vodka
- 1 cup granulated sugar
- 1 cup freshly squeezed Meyer lemon
- Zest of 3 Meyer lemons

How To
1. Prepare your Sous Vide water bath using your immersion circulator and raise the temperature to 135-degrees Fahrenheit.
2. Take a resealable zip bag and add all the listed ingredients.
3. Seal the bag using the immersion method. Submerge and cook for about 2 hours.
4. Once done, strain the mixture through a fine metal mesh strainer into a medium bowl.
5. Chill the mixture overnight and serve!

Nutrition Values (Per Serving)
- Calories: 354
- Carbohydrate: 48g
- Protein: 0g
- Fat: 0g
- Sugar: 47g
- Sodium: 6mg

Rosemary & Lemon Vodka

(Serves: 5 / **Prep Time:** 10 minutes / **Sous Vide Cooking Time:** 180 minutes)

Ingredients
- 1 bottle vodka
- Zest of 6 large lemons
- 5 sprigs fresh rosemary

How To
1. Prepare your Sous Vide water bath using your immersion circulator and raise the temperature to 145-degrees Fahrenheit.
2. Take a heavy-duty resealable zip bag and add all the listed ingredients.
3. Seal using the immersion method and cook for 3 hours.
4. Once done, transfer the contents through a strainer and allow it to cool.
5. Serve!

Nutrition Values (Per Serving)

- Calories: 247
- Carbohydrate: 23g
- Protein: 2g
- Fat: 16g
- Sugar: 21g
- Sodium: 82mg

Bloody Mary Vodka

(Serves: 20 / **Prep Time:** 20 minutes / **Sous Vide Cooking Time:** 180 minutes)

Ingredients

- 1 bottle vodka
- 6 quartered roma tomatoes
- 1 Anaheim pepper, stemmed and seeds removed, sliced into ½ inch pieces
- ¼ onion, peeled and sliced into ½-inch pieces
- 6 whole garlic cloves, peeled
- 1 thinly sliced jalapeno pepper
- 1 tablespoon whole black peppercorns
- Zest of 3 large limes

How To

1. Prepare your Sous Vide water bath using your immersion circulator and raise the temperature to 145-degrees Fahrenheit.
2. Add all the listed ingredients to your resealable zipper bag.
3. Seal using the immersion method.
4. Cook for about 3 hours and transfer the contents through a mesh strainer.
5. Serve!

Nutrition Values (Per Serving)

- Calories: 437
- Carbohydrate: 77g
- Protein: 10g
- Fat: 4g
- Sugar: 44g
- Sodium: 460mg

Coffee Liquor

(Serves: 20 / **Prep Time:** 10 minutes / **Sous Vide Cooking Time:** 180 minutes)

Ingredients

- 1 bottle vodka
- 32 oz. strong black coffee
- 2 cups granulated sugar
- ½ cup coffee beans
- 2 split vanilla beans

How To

1. Prepare your Sous Vide water bath using your immersion circulator and raise the temperature to 145-degrees Fahrenheit.
2. Take a heavy-duty large resealable zip bag and add all the listed ingredients.
3. Seal the bag using the immersion method.
4. Cook for about 3 hours underwater.
5. Once done, transfer the contents through a fine mesh strainer and let it cool.
6. Serve!

Nutrition Values (Per Serving)

- Calories: 216
- Carbohydrate: 25g
- Protein: 5g
- Fat: 12g
- Sugar: 23g
- Sodium: 92mg

Honey Ginger Shrub

(Serves: 6 / **Prep Time:** 10 minutes / **Sous Vide Cooking Time:** 120 minutes)

Ingredients

- 1 cup water
- ½ cup honey
- ½ cup balsamic vinegar
- 1 tablespoon freshly grated ginger
- Bourbon whiskey
- Club soda
- Lemon wedges as required

How To

1. Prepare your Sous Vide water bath using your immersion circulator and raise the temperature to 134-degrees Fahrenheit.
2. Take a resealable zipper bag and add the water, vinegar, honey, ginger, and seal it using the immersion method.
3. Submerge and cook for about 2 hours.

4. Once cooked, strain the mixture through a fine metal mesh strainer into a medium bowl.
5. Chill the mixture overnight.
6. Serve with one-part whiskey and one-part club soda in a glass over ice.
7. Garnish with a lemon wedge and serve!

Nutrition Values (Per Serving)

- Calories: 232
- Carbohydrate: 54g
- Protein: 1g
- Fat: 0g
- Sugar: 51g
- Sodium: 19mg

Cherry Bourbon

(Serves: 8/ **Prep Time:** 20 minutes / **Sous Vide Cooking Time:** 120 minutes)

Ingredients

- 1 lb. fresh cherries
- 1½ cup bourbon

How To

1. Prepare your Sous Vide water bath using your immersion circulator and raise the temperature to 135-degrees Fahrenheit.
2. Then, pit the cherries using a cherry pitter. (if using)
3. Add the cherries and bourbon to a resealable zipper bag.
4. Seal using the immersion method and mash the cherries. Cook for 2 hours.
5. Let the mixture cool and strain it to a bowl through a fine metal mesh
6. Pour in the bottles and serve chilled!

Nutrition Values (Per Serving)

- Calories: 441
- Carbohydrate: 65g
- Protein: 4g
- Fat: 18g
- Sugar: 36g
- Sodium: 240mg

Raspberry Cordial

(Serves: 14/ **Prep Time:** 15 minutes / **Sous Vide Cooking Time:** 120 minutes)

Ingredients
- 2 cups fresh raspberries
- 2 cups sugar
- 3 cups vodka

How To
1. Prepare your Sous Vide water bath using your immersion circulator and raise the temperature to 135-degrees Fahrenheit.
2. Add the raspberries and sugar to a resealable zip bag.
3. Mash the berries by hand.
4. Open the bag and add the vodka.
5. Seal using the immersion method.
6. Cook for 2 hours and allow it to come to room temperature.
7. Pour into bottles and serve chilled!

Nutrition Values (Per Serving)
- Calories: 381
- Carbohydrate: 41g
- Protein: 5g
- Fat: 23g
- Sugar: 36g
- Sodium: 55mg

Bacon Vodka

(Serves: 10/ **Prep Time:** 20 minutes / **Sous Vide Cooking Time:** 45 minutes)

Ingredients
- 2 cups vodka
- 8 oz. bacon
- 3 tablespoons reserved bacon grease

How To
1. Prepare your Sous Vide water bath using your immersion circulator and raise the temperature to 150-degrees Fahrenheit.
2. Bake the bacon for 16 minutes at 400-degrees Fahrenheit.
3. Allow the mixture to cool.
4. Add all the ingredients to a resealable bag and seal using the immersion method.

5. Cook for 45 minutes.
6. Strain the liquid into bowl and chill until a fat layer forms.
7. Remove and skim off the fat layer, strain using a cheesecloth once again.
8. Serve chilled!

Nutrition Values (Per Serving)

- Calories: 295
- Carbohydrate: 9g
- Protein: 5g
- Fat: 17g
- Sugar: 4g
- Sodium: 572mg

Spiced Rum

(Serves: 10/ **Prep Time:** 5 minutes / **Sous Vide Cooking Time:** 120 minutes)

Ingredients

- 1 bottle rum
- 1 vanilla bean, split lengthwise
- 2 whole cloves
- ½ cinnamon stick
- 2 whole black peppercorns
- ½ piece star anise
- 2 pieces of 3-inch fresh orange zest

How To

1. Prepare your Sous Vide water bath using your immersion circulator and raise the temperature to 153-degrees Fahrenheit.
2. Add all the listed ingredients to a resealable zipper bag.
3. Seal using the immersion method and cook for 2 hours.
4. Once cooked, transfer it to an ice bath and chill.
5. Strain to bottle and serve the drink!

Nutrition Values (Per Serving)

- Calories: 416
- Carbohydrate: 1g
- Protein: 0g
- Fat: 0g
- Sugar: 0g
- Sodium: 3mg

Mulled Wine

(Serves: 2/ **Prep Time:** 15 minutes / **Sous Vide Cooking Time:** 60 minutes)

Ingredients

- ½ bottle red wine
- Juice of 2 oranges, peel of 1
- 1 cinnamon stick
- 1 bay leaf
- 1 vanilla pod, sliced in half lengthways
- 1-star anise
- 2 oz. caster sugar

How To

1. Prepare your Sous Vide water bath using your immersion circulator and raise the temperature to 140-degrees Fahrenheit.
2. Add all the listed ingredients to a large bowl.
3. Divide the mixture across two resealable zip bags and seal using the immersion method. Cook for 1 hour.
4. Serve chilled!

Nutrition Values (Per Serving)

- Calories: 206
- Carbohydrate: 17g
- Protein: 1g
- Fat: 0g
- Sugar: 11g
- Sodium: 0mg

Hot Spiced Cider

(Serves: 6/ **Prep Time:** 5 minutes / **Sous Vide Cooking Time:** 60 minutes)

Ingredients

- 2 bottles apple cider
- 1 cinnamon stick
- 1 tablespoon maple syrup
- ½ teaspoon black peppercorns
- 2 tablespoons orange juice

How To

1. Prepare your Sous Vide water bath using your immersion circulator and raise the temperature to 140-degrees Fahrenheit.
2. Add all the listed ingredients to a resealable zip bag.
3. Seal using the immersion method.
4. Cook for 1 hour.
5. Strain and serve chilled!

Nutrition Values (Per Serving)

- Calories: 130
- Carbohydrate: 24g
- Protein: 0g

- Fat: 0g
- Sugar: 20g
- Sodium: 9mg

Mint Julep & Coconut Sugar

(Serves: 2/ **Prep Time:** 10 minutes / **Sous Vide Cooking Time:** 90 minutes)

Ingredients

- 2 cups water
- 2 cups bourbon

- 1 ½ cups coconut sugar
- 2 cups fresh mint

How To

1. Prepare your Sous Vide water bath using your immersion circulator and raise the temperature to 135-degrees Fahrenheit.
2. Add the water, coconut sugar, bourbon, and mint to a resealable zip bag.
3. Seal using the immersion method.
4. Cook for 1 ½ hour.
5. Strain and serve chilled!

Nutrition Values (Per Serving)

- Calories: 124
- Carbohydrate: 5g
- Protein: 0g

- Fat: 0g
- Sugar: 4g
- Sodium: 0mg

Grand Marnier

(Serves: 12/ **Prep Time:** 5 minutes / **Sous Vide Cooking Time:** 90 minutes)

Ingredients

- Zest of 8 large orange
- 2 cups brandy
- ½ cup ultrafine sugar

How To

1. Prepare your Sous Vide water bath using your immersion circulator and raise the temperature to 180-degrees Fahrenheit.

2. Add all the listed ingredients to a resealable zip bag.
3. Seal using the immersion method.
4. Cook for 90 minutes.
5. Strain and discard the orange zest.
6. Allow it to chill and serve when needed!

Nutrition Values (Per Serving)

- Calories: 191
- Carbohydrate: 39g
- Protein: 4g
- Fat: 2g
- Sugar: 31g
- Sodium: 31mg

Red Wine Plum Shrub

(Serves: 8/ **Prep Time:** 15 minutes / **Sous Vide Cooking Time:** 90 minutes)

Ingredients

- 2 cups red plum, pitted and diced
- 1 cup ultrafine sugar
- 1 cup red wine
- 1 cup red wine vinegar
- 1 cinnamon stick
- 1 clove
- ½ teaspoon vanilla bean paste

How To

1. Prepare your Sous Vide water bath using your immersion circulator and raise the temperature to 180-degrees Fahrenheit.
2. Add all the listed ingredients to a resealable bag.
3. Seal using the immersion method and cook for 90 minutes.
4. Strain and discard the cinnamon stick, clove, and plums.
5. Chill and serve!

Nutrition Values (Per Serving)

- Calories: 79
- Carbohydrate: 2g
- Protein: 0g
- Fat: 0g
- Sugar: 1g
- Sodium: 0mg

Sous Vide Classic Creamy Eggnog

(Serves: 8/ **Prep Time:** 10 minutes / **Sous Vide Cooking Time:** 60 minutes)

Ingredients

- 6 large whole eggs
- 1-quart whole milk
- 1 cup heavy cream
- ½ cup bourbon
- ½ cup brandy
- ½ cup ultrafine sugar
- 1 teaspoon vanilla bean paste
- ½ teaspoon freshly ground nutmeg
- ½ teaspoon freshly ground cinnamon
- A pinch of salt

How To

1. Prepare your Sous Vide water bath using your immersion circulator and raise the temperature to 144-degrees Fahrenheit.
2. Add all the listed ingredients to a blender and puree, pour the mixture to a zip bag
3. Seal using the immersion method
4. Submerge underwater and cook for 1 hour, making sure to agitate a bit
5. Transfer the bag to an ice bath
6. Serve chilled and add a bit of bourbon if you desire.

Nutrition Values (Per Serving)

- Calories: 433
- Carbohydrate: 34g
- Protein: 8g
- Fat: 30g
- Sugar: 34g
- Sodium: 87mg

Tomato Shrub

(Serves: 12/ **Prep Time:** 15 minutes / **Sous Vide Cooking Time:** 1 hour 30 minutes)

Ingredients

- 2 cups diced tomatoes
- 2 cups granulated sugar
- 2 cups red wine vinegar
- 1 cup water

How To

1. Prepare your Sous Vide water bath using your immersion circulator and raise the temperature to 180-degrees Fahrenheit.
2. Add all the listed ingredients to a resealable zip bag and seal using the immersion method.

3. Cook for 1 ½ hour.
4. Once done, remove and strain the contents into a bowl.
5. Discard any solids and transfer to storing jar.
6. Serve as needed!

Nutrition Values (Per Serving)

- Calories: 126
- Carbohydrate: 30g
- Protein: 1g
- Fat: 0g
- Sugar: 28g
- Sodium: 80mg

Strawberry & Rhubarb Shrub

(**Serves:** 12/ **Prep Time:** 15 minutes / **Sous Vide Cooking Time:** 1 hour 30 minutes)

Ingredients

- 2 cups granulated sugar
- 2 cups balsamic vinegar
- 1 cup diced rhubarb
- 1 cup strawberries, diced
- 1 cup water

How To

1. Prepare your Sous Vide water bath using your immersion circulator and raise the temperature to 180-degrees Fahrenheit.
2. Add all the listed ingredients to a large-sized heavy-duty zip bag
3. Seal using the immersion method and cook for 1 ½ hour.
4. Remove the bag and strain the contents to a bowl.
5. Save the fruit for later.
6. Transfer to liquid storage, chill and serve!

Nutrition Values (Per Serving)

- Calories: 256
- Carbohydrate: 30g
- Protein: 4g
- Fat: 1g
- Sugar: 16g
- Sodium: 23mg

Rhubarb & Thyme Syrup

(Serves: 12/ **Prep Time:** 15 minutes / **Sous Vide Cooking Time:** 1 hour 30 minutes)

Ingredients

- 2 cups diced rhubarb
- 1 cup ultrafine sugar
- 1 cup water
- 5 sprigs thyme

How To

1. Prepare your Sous Vide water bath using your immersion circulator and raise the temperature to 180-degrees Fahrenheit.
2. Add all the listed ingredients to a heavy duty zip bag
3. Seal using the immersion method
4. Submerge underwater and cook for 1 ½ hour.
5. Remove the bag and strain the contents to a bowl.
6. Transfer to liquid storage, chill and serve!

Nutrition Values (Per Serving)

- Calories: 190
- Carbohydrate: 47g
- Protein: 1g
- Fat: 0g
- Sugar: 43g
- Sodium: 5mg

Chili Agave Liqueur

(Serves: 8/ **Prep Time:** 10 minutes / **Sous Vide Cooking Time:** 45 minutes)

Ingredients

- 2 cups vodka
- ½ cup water
- ½ cup light agave nectar
- 3 dried Guajillo chili peppers
- 1-piece Serrano pepper, sliced in half and seeded
- 1 Fresno pepper, sliced in half and seeded
- Zest of 1 lemon
- 1 cinnamon stick
- 1 teaspoon black peppercorns

How To

1. Prepare your Sous Vide water bath using your immersion circulator and raise the temperature to 180-degrees Fahrenheit.
2. Add all the listed ingredients to a heavy-duty zip bag.
3. Seal using the immersion method and cook for 45 minutes.

4. Once done, remove the bag and strain the contents to a bowl.
5. Transfer to liquid storage, chill and serve!

Nutrition Values (Per Serving)

- Calories: 139
- Carbohydrate: 37g
- Protein: 1g
- Fat: 0g
- Sugar: 29g
- Sodium: 8mg

Bourbon Grape & Ginger Beer Cocktail

(Serves: 8/ **Prep Time:** 30 minutes / **Sous Vide Cooking Time:** 120 minutes)

Ingredients

- 2-3 cups sliced seedless red grapes
- 1 ¼ cups vanilla sugar
- ½ cup bourbon
- ½ vanilla bean, split
- 1 lemon, peeled
- 1-star anise pod
- 1 cardamom pod
- ½ cup ginger beer per serving
- Fresh mint leaves
- Lemon twists
- Sliced grapes for garnishing

How To

1. Prepare your Sous Vide water bath using your immersion circulator and raise the temperature to 167-degrees Fahrenheit.
2. Add the grapes, sugar, vanilla, bourbon, star anise, lemon peel, and cardamom to a large resealable zip bag.
3. Seal using the immersion method and cook for 2 hours.
4. Once done, remove the bag and transfer to an ice bath, once the grape mix is cool, transfer to the refrigerator and chill.
5. Strain the grape mixture through a metal mesh strainer over a bowl and reserve the fruit for later use.
6. Then, fill a rocks glass with ice and add ½ cup ginger beer, 1 ½ ounce of infused bourbon.
7. Garnish with mint and lemon twist.
8. Serve with a garnish of sliced grapes.

Nutrition Values (Per Serving)

- Calories: 216
- Carbohydrate: 23g
- Protein: 0g
- Fat: 0g
- Sugar: 3g
- Sodium: 17mg

Sous Vide Gin

(Serves: 1/ **Prep Time:** 10 minutes / **Sous Vide Cooking Time:** 1 minute 30 seconds)

Ingredients

- 3 oz. vodka
- Zest of small orange
- 8 juniper berries
- 10-12 coriander seeds
- 2 cardamom pods
- 8-10 grains of paradise
- 1 Tasmanian pepper berry

How To

1. Prepare your Sous Vide water bath using your immersion circulator and raise the temperature to 176-degrees Fahrenheit.
2. Add all the listed ingredients to a resealable bag and seal using the immersion method.
3. Cook for 90 seconds.
4. Once done, take the bag out from the water bath and transfer it to an ice bath.
5. Massage the bag to infuse the gin carefully.
6. Cool down the mixture and strain the mixture through a metal mesh strainer and pour it to a medium-sized bowl
7. Serve!

Nutrition Values (Per Serving)

- Calories: 173
- Carbohydrate: 17g
- Protein: 0g
- Fat: 0g
- Sugar: 16g
- Sodium: 14mg

Limoncello Vodka Cocktail

(Serves: 5/ **Prep Time:** 20 minutes / **Sous Vide Cooking Time:** 180 minutes)

Ingredients

- 1 bottle vodka
- Grated zest/peel of 10-15 thoroughly washed lemons
- 1 cup granulated sugar
- 1 cup water

How To

1. Prepare your Sous Vide water bath using your immersion circulator and raise the temperature to 135-degrees Fahrenheit.

2. Add the vodka and lemon zest to a large zip bag and seal using the immersion method. Cook for 2-3 hours.
3. Take a saucepan and put it over medium-high heat
4. Add the sugar and water and stir until the sugar dissolves to prepare the syrup
5. Once done, take the bag out from the water bath and strain through metal mesh into a bowl.
6. Stir in syrup.
7. Pour Limoncello into bottles and serve!

Nutrition Values (Per Serving)

- Calories: 430
- Carbohydrate: 61g
- Protein: 1g
- Fat: 0g
- Sugar: 53g
- Sodium: 8mg

Swedish Rosemary Snaps

(Serves: 10/ **Prep Time:** 10 minutes / **Sous Vide Cooking Time:** 120 minutes)

Ingredients

- 1 bottle vodka
- 3 sprigs fresh rosemary + plus extra for storage
- 4 strips of fresh orange peel

How To

1. Prepare your Sous Vide water bath using your immersion circulator and raise the temperature to 135-degrees Fahrenheit.
2. Add the vodka, 3 sprigs rosemary, and 3 strips of orange peel to a resealable zip bag.
3. Seal using the immersion method. Cook for 2 hours.
4. Once done, take the bag out from the water bath and pass through metal mesh strainer into large bowl.
5. Put one fresh sprig of rosemary and one strip of orange peel into bottle.
6. Pour the prepared snaps into bottle.
7. Chill and serve!

Nutrition Values (Per Serving)

- Calories: 236
- Carbohydrate: 14g
- Protein: 0g
- Fat: 0g
- Sugar: 11g
- Sodium: 4mg

Strawberry Basil Shrub

(Serves: 12/ **Prep Time:** 10 minutes / **Sous Vide Cooking Time:** 120 minutes)

Ingredients

- 1 lb. fresh strawberries, trimmed
- 1 lb. ultrafine sugar
- 2 cups balsamic vinegar
- 1 cup water
- 1 cup fresh basil leaves

How To

1. Prepare your Sous Vide water bath using your immersion circulator and raise the temperature to 135-degrees Fahrenheit.
2. Add all the listed ingredients to a resealable zip bag.
3. Seal using the immersion method. Cook for 2 hours.
4. Once cooked, take the bag out from the water bath and pass through metal mesh strainer into large bowl.
5. Chill and serve!

Nutrition Values (Per Serving)

- Calories: 150
- Carbohydrate: 36g
- Protein: 0g
- Fat: 0g
- Sugar: 35g
- Sodium: 6mg

Drambuie

(Serves: 8/ **Prep Time:** 15 minutes / **Sous Vide Cooking Time:** 30 minutes)

Ingredients

- 1 cup scotch
- ½ cup water
- ½ cup honey
- 2 teaspoons fresh rosemary
- 2 teaspoons whole fennel seeds

How To

1. Prepare your Sous Vide water bath using your immersion circulator and raise the temperature to 180-degrees Fahrenheit.
2. Add all the above ingredients to a resealable zip bag.
3. Seal using the immersion method.
4. Cook for 30 minutes.

5. Once done, take the bag out from the water bath and pass through metal mesh strainer into a large bowl.
6. Chill and serve!

Nutrition Values (Per Serving)
- Calories: 184
- Carbohydrate: 24g
- Protein: 0g
- Fat: 0g
- Sugar: 23g
- Sodium: 3mg

Bacon Infused Bourbon

(Serves: 8/ **Prep Time:** 80 minutes / **Sous Vide Cooking Time:** 60 minutes)

Ingredients
- 2 cups bourbon
- 8 oz. smoked bacon, cooked until crisp
- 3 tablespoon bacon fat reserved from cooking
- 3 tablespoons light brown sugar

How To
1. Prepare your Sous Vide water bath using your immersion circulator and raise the temperature to 150-degrees Fahrenheit.
2. Add all the listed ingredients to a resealable zip bag.
3. Seal using the immersion method. Cook for 1 hour.
4. Once done, take the bag out from the water bath and strain the contents through a fine-mesh strainer into a large bowl
5. Transfer the bourbon to the refrigerator and chill until the pork fat solidifies on top. Skim off the fat
6. Then, strain the bourbon a second time through a cheesecloth-lined strainer.
7. Pass it to a storage container and store in the refrigerator.

Nutrition Values (Per Serving)
- Calories: 274
- Carbohydrate: 14g
- Protein: 6g
- Fat: 19g
- Sugar: 13g
- Sodium: 316mg

Lemongrass Syrup

(Serves: 4/ **Prep Time:** 15 minutes / **Sous Vide Cooking Time:** 60 minutes)

Ingredients
- 4 stalks lemongrass, cut into 1-inch pieces
- 1 cup water
- 1 cup ultrafine sugar

How To
1. Prepare your Sous Vide water bath using your immersion circulator and raise the temperature to 180-degrees Fahrenheit.
2. Add all the above ingredients to a resealable zip bag.
3. Seal using the immersion method.
4. Cook for about 1 hour.
5. Once cooked, remove the bag from the water bath and transfer it to an ice cold bath.
6. Strain into a large bowl and transfer to a container
7. Serve chilled!

Nutrition Values (Per Serving)
- Calories: 208
- Carbohydrate: 54g
- Protein: 0g
- Fat: 0g
- Sugar: 50g
- Sodium: 4mg

Thai Basil Drink

(Serves: 4/ **Prep Time:** 15 minutes / **Sous Vide Cooking Time:** 60 minutes)

Ingredients
- 1 bunch of Thai basil rinsed
- 1 cup water
- 1 cup ultrafine sugar

How To
1. Prepare your Sous Vide water bath using your immersion circulator and raise the temperature to 180-degrees Fahrenheit.
2. Add all the listed ingredients to a resealable zipper bag.
3. Seal using the immersion method.
4. Submerge underwater and cook for 1 hour.

5. Once done, take the bag out from the water bath and transfer to an ice bath.
6. Strain into a large bowl and transfer to a container
7. Serve chilled!

Nutrition Values (Per Serving)

- Calories: 197
- Carbohydrate: 19g
- Protein: 0g

- Fat: 0g
- Sugar: 16g
- Sodium: 159mg

Jalapeno Vodka

(Serves: 5/ **Prep Time:** 10 minutes / **Sous Vide Cooking Time:** 120 minutes)

Ingredients

- 2 jalapeno peppers
- 1 bottle vodka

How To

1. Prepare your Sous Vide water bath using your immersion circulator and raise the temperature to 147-degrees Fahrenheit.
2. Cut the peppers and remove the stem, veins and seeds.
3. Add the ingredients to a resealable zipper bag.
4. Seal using the immersion method. Cook for 2 hours.
5. Once done, take the bag out from the water bath and transfer to an ice bath.
6. Strain into a large bowl and transfer to a container
7. Serve chilled!

Nutrition Values (Per Serving)

- Calories: 729
- Carbohydrate: 1g
- Protein: 0g
- Fat: 0g
- Sugar: 1g
- Sodium: 4mg

Apple & Cardamom Gin

(Serves: 4/ **Prep Time:** 10 minutes / **Sous Vide Cooking Time:** 120 minutes)

Ingredients
- 1 cup Gin
- 1 pink lady apple cored, sliced into rings
- 1 green cardamom pod

How To
1. Prepare your Sous Vide water bath using your immersion circulator and raise the temperature to 136.4-degrees Fahrenheit.
2. Add all the above ingredients to a resealable zip bag.
3. Seal using the immersion method. Cook for 2 hours.
4. Once done, take the bag out from the water bath and transfer to an ice bath.
5. Strain into a large bowl and transfer to a container
6. Serve chilled!

Nutrition Values (Per Serving)
- Calories: 152
- Carbohydrate: 22g
- Protein: 0g
- Fat: 0g
- Sugar: 19g
- Sodium: 7mg

Ginger Brandy

(Serves: 4/ **Prep Time:** 10 minutes / **Sous Vide Cooking Time:** 120 minutes)

Ingredients
- 4 ½ oz. fresh ginger
- 1 ½ cup brandy
- 5 oz. sugar
- 1 cup water

How To
1. Prepare your Sous Vide water bath using your immersion circulator and raise the temperature to 135-degrees Fahrenheit.
2. Peel and grate the ginger.
3. Add the ginger and brandy to a resealable zip bag and seal using the immersion method. Cook for 2 hours.

4. Then, take a saucepan and place it over medium heat. Add the water and sugar and allow the sugar to dissolve.
5. Strain the brandy and ginger mixture into a clean bottle and add all the sugar syrup.
6. Serve!

Nutrition Values (Per Serving)

- Calories: 416
- Carbohydrate: 57g
- Protein: 1g
- Fat: 0g
- Sugar: 53g
- Sodium: 7mg

CHAPTER 9 | STOCKS, SAUCES, BROTHS, & SPICE RUBS

Caramel Sauce

(Serves: 10 / **Prep Time:** 5 minutes / **Sous-Vide Cooking Time:** 120 minutes)

Ingredients

- 20 pitted dates
- 1 cup non-dairy milk soy
- 1 teaspoon vanilla
- A pinch of salt

How To

1. Prepare your Sous-vide water bath to a temperature of 135-degrees Fahrenheit.
2. Take your dates alongside the milk, vanilla and add them to a heavy-duty resealable zip bag.
3. Seal the bag using the immersion method.
4. Submerge underwater and cook for about 2 hours.
5. Add the mixture to a blender and blend until you have sauce like consistency
6. Season with a bit of salt and use as needed

Nutrition Values (Per Serving)

- Calories: 258
- Carbohydrate: 28g
- Protein: 2g
- Fat: 15g
- Sugar: 22g
- Sodium: 220mg

Cauliflower & Pepper Chowder

(Serves: 2 / **Prep Time:** 20 minutes / **Sous-Vide Cooking Time:** 120 minutes)

Ingredients

- 2 cups cauliflower florets, chopped
- 1 medium-sized Yukon gold potato, peeled and chopped
- 1 chopped red bell pepper
- 1 tablespoon extra-virgin olive oil
- 1 garlic clove, crushed
- 1 bay leaf
- Kosher salt as needed
- ¼ teaspoon ground coriander

- ¼ teaspoon ground cumin
- 2 cups chicken broth
- 1 cup whole warmed milk
- Freshly grated parmesan cheese
- Fresh ground black pepper

How To

1. Prepare your Sous-vide water bath to a temperature of 185-degrees Fahrenheit.
2. Take a large resealable zip bag and add the cauliflower, bell pepper, olive oil, potato, bay leaf, ½ teaspoon of salt, garlic, ½ teaspoon of cumin, and coriander.
3. Seal using the immersion method. Submerge underwater and cook for 2 hours.
4. Once cooked, remove the bag and transfer the contents to a bowl.
5. Add the chicken broth and milk and whisk them using the immersion blender.
6. Season the mixture with pepper and salt
7. Garnish with a bit of parmesan and serve!

Nutrition Values (Per Serving)

- Calories: 187
- Carbohydrate: 24g
- Protein: 6g
- Fat: 9g
- Sugar: 9g
- Sodium: 553mg

Cauliflower Alfredo

(**Serves:** 4 / **Prep Time:** 5 minutes / **Sous-Vide Cooking Time:** 2 hours)

Ingredients

- 2 cups chopped up cauliflower florets
- 2 crushed garlic cloves
- 2 tablespoons butter
- ½ cup chicken stock
- 2 tablespoons milk
- Salt and pepper as needed

How To

1. Prepare your Sous-vide water bath to a temperature of 181-degrees Fahrenheit.
2. Add all the listed ingredients into a resealable zip bag.
3. Seal using the immersion method.
4. Submerge underwater and cook for 2 hours.
5. Once done, transfer it to a food processor and puree until you have a smooth texture
6. Serve!

Nutrition Values (Per Serving)

- Calories: 90
- Carbohydrate: 21g
- Protein: 9g

- Fat: 3g
- Sugar: 12g
- Sodium: 216mg

Strawberry Rhubarb Jam

(Serves: 4 / **Prep Time:** 15 minutes / **Sous-Vide Cooking Time:** 1 hours 30 minutes)

Ingredients

- 1 cup rhubarb, diced
- 1 cup strawberries, diced
- 2 tablespoons powdered pectin
- 2 tablespoons fresh squeezed lemon juice

How To

1. Prepare your Sous-vide water bath to a temperature of 180-degrees Fahrenheit.
2. Add all the listed ingredients to a resealable zip bag.
3. Seal using the immersion method.
4. Cook for 1 ½ hours.
5. Serve as needed.

Nutrition Values (Per Serving)

- Calories: 35
- Carbohydrate: 10g
- Protein: 0g

- Fat: 0g
- Sugar: 9g
- Sodium: 0mg

Orange-Thyme Maple Syrup

(Serves: 12 / **Prep Time:** 15 minutes / **Sous-Vide Cooking Time:** 60 minutes)

Ingredients

- 2 cups pure maple syrup
- 6 sprigs thyme
- 2 tablespoons orange zest
- ½ teaspoon fine sea salt

How To

1. Prepare your Sous-vide water bath to a temperature of 135-degrees Fahrenheit.
2. Add all the listed ingredients to a resealable zip bag.
3. Seal using the immersion method. Submerge underwater and cook for 1 hour.
4. Discard the thyme and allow the syrup to cool.
5. Serve or you can store in container for up to 2 weeks.

Nutrition Values (Per Serving)

- Calories: 234
- Carbohydrate: 40g
- Protein: 4g
- Fat: 7g
- Sugar: 22g
- Sodium: 121mg

Ancho Chile Oil

(Serves: 12 / **Prep Time:** 15 minutes / **Sous-Vide Cooking Time:** 60 minutes)

Ingredients

- 1 cup canola oil
- 2 dried ancho chilis, with stems and seeds removed and torn into 1-inch pieces
- 1 tablespoon red wine vinegar
- 2 garlic cloves, crushed
- 1 teaspoon of kosher salt

How To

1. Prepare your Sous-vide water bath to a temperature of 180-degrees Fahrenheit.
2. Add all the listed ingredients to a resealable zipper bag.
3. Seal using the immersion method.
4. Submerge underwater and cook for 1 hour.
5. Serve or you can store in container for up to 2 weeks.

Nutrition Values (Per Serving)

- Calories: 196
- Carbohydrate: 11g
- Protein: 3g
- Fat: 17g
- Sugar: 0g
- Sodium: 417mg

Mango Chutney (Indian Mango Sauce)

(Serves: 4 / **Prep Time:** 10 minutes / **Sous-Vide Cooking Time:** 6 hours)

Ingredients

- 1 large ripe mango, peeled and cut up into small dices
- ¼ cup Granny Smith Apple, cored, peeled, and cut up into small dices
- ¼ red onion, finely chopped
- ¼ cup packed light brown sugar
- 1 ½ tablespoons malt vinegar
- 1 finely chopped chili
- ½ teaspoon grated fresh ginger
- A pinch of salt

How To

1. Prepare your Sous-vide water bath to a temperature of 185-degrees Fahrenheit.
2. Add all the listed ingredients to a resealable zip bag.
3. Seal using the immersion method.
4. Submerge underwater and cook for 6 hours.
5. Transfer to an ice bath and allow it to cool.
6. Transfer the cooled chutney to jars and use as needed, or you can store in container for up to 1 week.

Nutrition Values (Per Serving)

- Calories: 450
- Carbohydrate: 116g
- Protein: 0g
- Fat: 0g
- Sugar: 90g
- Sodium: 490mg

Hollandaise Sauce

(Serves: 4 / **Prep Time:** 20 minutes / **Sous-Vide Cooking Time:** 30 minutes)

Ingredients

- 1 cup dry white wine
- 3 tablespoons champagne vinegar
- 2 tablespoons shallots, minced
- 2 sprigs fresh thyme
- 6 large egg yolks
- 1 cup unsalted butter, warm and melted
- 1 tablespoon freshly squeezed lemon juice

How To

1. Prepare your Sous-vide water bath to a temperature of 145-degrees Fahrenheit.
2. Take a medium-sized saucepan and bring the vinegar, wine, shallot and thyme to a boil over medium heat.
3. Bring the mixture to a simmer by lowering down the heat to low and let it simmer for 10 minutes until you have syrup-like mixture.
4. Strain the wine through a fine mesh into blender.
5. Add the egg yolks and puree for 30 seconds.
6. Transfer to a resealable zip bag and seal using the immersion method.
7. Let it cook for 30 minutes.
8. Once done, transfer the contents to a blender and blend for 30 seconds with warm butter and lemon juice.
9. Season and serve!

Nutrition Values (Per Serving)

- Calories: 67
- Carbohydrate: 1g
- Protein: 1g
- Fat: 7g
- Sugar: 0.6g
- Sodium: 44mg

Mezcal Cream

(**Serves:** 8 / **Prep Time:** 15 minutes / **Sous-Vide Cooking Time:** 30 minutes)

Ingredients

- ½ cup heavy cream
- ½ cup mezcal*
- ½ cup ultrafine sugar
- 4 large egg yolks
- 1 teaspoon vanilla extract
- A pinch of kosher salt

How To

1. Prepare your Sous-vide water bath to a temperature of 180-degrees Fahrenheit.
2. Add everything to your blender and puree for 30 seconds.
3. Then, transfer the mixture to a large resealable bag.
4. Seal using the immersion method and cook for 30 minutes.
5. Transfer to an ice bath and serve once cooled.

Nutrition Values (Per Serving)

- Calories: 791
- Carbohydrate: 101g
- Protein: 12g

- Fat: 33g
- Sugar: 66g
- Sodium: 625mg

(**Note: Mezcal*** - Mezcal is a distilled alcoholic beverage made from any type of agave plant native to Mexico. The word mezcal comes from Nahuatl mexcalli metl and ixcalli which means "oven-cooked agave.)

Béarnaise Sauce

(**Serves:** 10 / **Prep Time:** 20 minutes / **Sous-Vide Cooking Time:** 45 minutes)

Ingredients
- ¼ cup white wine vinegar
- ¼ cup white wine
- 2 tablespoons chopped fresh tarragon
- 1 tablespoon scallion, chopped
- Salt as needed
- Fresh ground black pepper as needed
- 4 large egg yolks
- 6 tablespoons unsalted butter

How To
1. Prepare your Sous-vide water bath to a temperature of 174-degrees Fahrenheit.
2. Add the vinegar, wine, tarragon, and scallion to a large saucepan.
3. Sprinkle some salt and pepper to the mixture and bring it to a boil over high heat.
4. Lower down the heat to medium-low and allow it to cook for 5 more minutes.
5. Once done, strain the mixture through a fine metal mesh and allow it to cool for 5 minutes.
6. Mix the egg yolks in a medium-sized bowl.
7. Add the cooled vinegar mixture and mix.
8. Keep mixing constantly and drizzle in the melted butter. Keep mixing until smooth.
9. Transfer the mixture to a resealable zipper bag and seal using the immersion method.
10. Cook for 45 minutes.
11. Once cooked, take the bag out from the water bath and transfer to a medium-sized bowl, blend using immersion blender.
12. Stir in tarragon and serve!

Nutrition Values (Per Serving)
- Calories: 1327
- Carbohydrate: 5g
- Protein: 7g
- Fat: 145g
- Sugar: 1g
- Sodium: 78mg

Meyer Lemon Infused Olive Oil

(Serves: 8 / **Prep Time:** 10 minutes / **Sous-Vide Cooking Time:** 180 minutes)

Ingredients
- 2 cups olive oil
- Peels of two Meyer Lemon, twisted

How To
1. Prepare your Sous-vide water bath to a temperature of 131-degrees Fahrenheit.
2. Add the listed ingredients to your resealable zip bag and seal using the immersion method.
3. Cook for 3 hours.
4. Once done, transfer the bag to an ice bath and allow it to cool.
5. Discard the peels.
6. Store in airtight container and serve as needed.

Nutrition Values (Per Serving)
- Calories: 201
- Carbohydrate: 0g
- Protein: 0g
- Fat: 0g
- Sugar: 0g
- Sodium: 2mg

Hot Chili Oil

(Serves: 8 / **Prep Time:** 10 minutes / **Sous-Vide Cooking Time:** 180 minutes)

Ingredients
- 2 habanero peppers, sliced up crosswise
- 2 jalapeno peppers, sliced up crosswise
- 2 cups olive oil

How To
1. Prepare your Sous-vide water bath to a temperature of 131-degrees Fahrenheit.
2. Add the listed ingredients to your resealable zip bag and seal using the immersion method. Submerge underwater and cook for 3 hours.
3. Once cooked, transfer the bag to an ice bath and allow it to cool.
4. Discard the peppers.
5. Store in airtight container and serve as needed.

Nutrition Values (Per Serving)

- Calories: 227
- Carbohydrate: 18g
- Protein: 8g
- Fat: 13g
- Sugar: 1g
- Sodium: 512mg

Champagne Citrus Vinegar

(Serves: 8 / **Prep Time:** 10 minutes / **Sous-Vide Cooking Time:** 180 minutes)

Ingredients

- Peels of 2 lemon
- Peels of 2 orange
- 17 oz. champagne vinegar
- 1 thick sliced of lemon
- 1 thick sliced of orange
- 1 tablespoon granulated sugar

How To

1. Prepare your Sous-vide water bath to a temperature of 153-degrees Fahrenheit.
2. Twist the citrus peels.
3. Add the lemon slice, vinegar, sugar, orange slice and peels to your resealable zip bag.
4. Seal using the immersion method. Cook for 3 hours
5. Once done, take the bag out from the water bath and strain the contents through a cheesecloth into a storing jar with lid.
6. Serve as needed or you can store in a fridge for up to 6 weeks.

Nutrition Values (Per Serving)

- Calories: 35
- Carbohydrate: 10g
- Protein: 4g
- Fat: 0.6g
- Sugar: 0.8g
- Sodium: 6mg

Lemon Ginger Vinegar

(Serves: 10 / **Prep Time:** 15 minutes / **Sous-Vide Cooking Time:** 180 minutes)

Ingredients

- Peel of 1 lemon
- 17-ounce white wine vinegar
- 1-inch piece of fresh ginger root peeled up and sliced into ¼ inch
- 1 thick slice lemon
- 1½ tablespoon granulated sugar

How To

1. Prepare your Sous-vide water bath to a temperature of 153-degrees Fahrenheit.
2. Twist the lemon peels.
3. Add the vinegar, lemon peel, lemon slice, ginger, sugar, and seal using the immersion method.
4. Submerge underwater and cook for 3 hours.
5. Strain through cheesecloth into a jar with lid.
6. Serve as needed.

Nutrition Values (Per Serving)

- Calories: 320
- Carbohydrate: 55g
- Protein: 18g
- Fat: 4g
- Sugar: 15g
- Sodium: 470mg

Blackberry Lavender Balsamic Vinegar

(**Serves:** 10 / **Prep Time:** 15 minutes / **Sous-Vide Cooking Time:** 180 minutes)

Ingredients

- 17 oz. balsamic vinegar
- 2 cups fresh blackberries
- 5 sprigs lavender
- 1 tablespoon granulated sugar

How To

1. Prepare your Sous-vide water bath to a temperature of 153-degrees Fahrenheit.
2. Add all the listed ingredients to Sous Vide zipper bag and seal using the immersion method.
3. Submerge underwater and cook for 3 hours.
4. Halfway through your cooking, make sure to squeeze the bag to soften them up
5. Once cooked, strain the contents through a cheesecloth into a clean bottle.
6. Serve as needed!

Nutrition Values (Per Serving)

- Calories: 364
- Carbohydrate: 30g
- Protein: 23g
- Fat: 15g
- Sugar: 1g
- Sodium: 415mg

Shallot Confit

(Serves: 8 / **Prep Time:** 10 minutes / **Sous-Vide Cooking Time:** 120 minutes)

Ingredients

- 4 pieces' shallots, peeled and quartered
- 3 tablespoons extra-virgin olive oil
- 3 tablespoons granulated sugar
- 1 teaspoon kosher salt

How To

1. Prepare your Sous-vide water bath to a temperature of 190-degrees Fahrenheit.
2. Add all the above ingredients to a large resealable zipper bag and seal using the immersion method.
3. Submerge underwater and cook for 2 hours.
4. Once cooked, transfer to a storage and use as needed.

Nutrition Values (Per Serving)

- Calories: 109
- Carbohydrate: 25g
- Protein: 4g
- Fat: 0g
- Sugar: 12g
- Sodium: 18mg

Garlic Confit

(Serves: 8 / **Prep Time:** 10 minutes / **Sous-Vide Cooking Time:** 2 hours)

Ingredients

- 1 cup peeled garlic cloves
- ¼ cup extra-virgin olive oil
- 1 tablespoon kosher salt

How To

1. Prepare your Sous-vide water bath to a temperature of 190-degrees Fahrenheit.
2. Add the listed ingredients to a large resealable zip bag and seal using the immersion method.
3. Submerge underwater and cook for 2 hours.
4. Once cooked, transfer to a storage and use as needed

Nutrition Values (Per Serving)

- Calories: 148
- Carbohydrate: 28g
- Protein: 5g

- Fat: 2g
- Sugar: 1g
- Sodium: 416mg

Apricot Jam

(Serves: 8 / **Prep Time:** 10 minutes / **Sous-Vide Cooking Time:** 2 hours)

Ingredients

- 12 oz. dried apricots
- 1 ½ cup granulated sugar

How To

1. Prepare your Sous-vide water bath to a temperature of 190-degrees Fahrenheit.
2. Add the listed ingredients to your bag and seal using the immersion method.
3. Submerge underwater and cook for 2 hours.
4. Once done, remove from the bag and transfer to a bowl.
5. Smash any large pieces.
6. Serve or you can store up to 3 weeks and use as needed.

Nutrition Values (Per Serving)

- Calories: 276
- Carbohydrate: 69g
- Protein: 2g

- Fat: 1g
- Sugar: 66g
- Sodium: 2mg

Pineapple Compote with Rum & Mint

(Serves: 8 / **Prep Time:** 10 minutes / **Sous-Vide Cooking Time:** 60 minutes)

Ingredients

- 1 lb. fresh pineapple, peeled, cored and diced
- 1 cup granulated sugar
- ½ cup dark rum
- Zest of 1 lime
- 2 sprigs fresh mint

How To

1. Prepare your Sous-vide water bath to a temperature of 190-degrees Fahrenheit.
2. Add all the listed ingredients to a resealable bag and seal using the immersion method.
3. Submerge underwater and let it cook for 1 hour.
4. Once done, transfer to airtight container and use as needed or you can store for up to 2 weeks.

Nutrition Values (Per Serving)

- Calories: 196
- Carbohydrate: 33g
- Protein: 1g
- Fat: 0g
- Sugar: 29g
- Sodium: 12mg

Balsamic Fig-Jam

(Serves: 8 / **Prep Time:** 10 minutes / **Sous-Vide Cooking Time:** 120 minutes)

Ingredients

- 12 oz. dried mission figs
- 1 cup water
- 1 cup granulated sugar
- ½ cup balsamic vinegar
- 2 sprigs fresh rosemary

How To

1. Prepare your Sous-vide water bath to a temperature of 190-degrees Fahrenheit.
2. Add the listed ingredients to Sous-vide zip bag and seal using the immersion method.
3. Cook for 2 hours.
4. Once done, remove from the bag and transfer the jam to a bowl.
5. Smash using a spatula.
6. Serve and enjoy!

Nutrition Values (Per Serving)

- Calories: 330
- Carbohydrate: 67g
- Protein: 1g
- Fat: 0g
- Sugar: 60g
- Sodium: 37mg

Smoked Cranberry Relish

(Serves: 8 / **Prep Time:** 15 minutes / **Sous-Vide Cooking Time:** 60 minutes)

Ingredients
- 17 oz. cranberries
- 12 oz. brown sugar
- Juice of ½ orange
- ½ cinnamon stick
- 3-stars anise
- ½ grated nutmeg
- 150 ml port wine
- 2 cloves

How To
1. Prepare the Sous-vide water bath to a temperature of 203-degrees Fahrenheit.
2. Add all the above ingredients to a resealable zipper bag and seal using the immersion method.
3. Submerge underwater and let it cook for 1 hour.
4. Once done, remove the cranberries from pouch and discard the cinnamon, cloves, and star anise.
5. Transfer to an air right container and stir.
6. Serve and use as needed.

Nutrition Values (Per Serving)
- Calories: 509
- Carbohydrate: 130g
- Protein: 1g
- Fat: 0g
- Sugar: 118g
- Sodium: 4mg

Strawberry & Rosemary Compote

(Serves: 8 / **Prep Time:** 10 minutes / **Sous-Vide Cooking Time:** 2 hours)

Ingredients
- 1 lb. freshly diced strawberries, stemmed and quartered
- 1 cup granulated sugar
- Zest of 1 lemon
- 2 sprigs fresh rosemary
- 1 teaspoon kosher salt

How To
1. Prepare your Sous-vide water bath to a temperature of 190-degrees Fahrenheit.
2. Add all the listed ingredients to Sous-vide zip bag and seal using the immersion method.

3. Cook for 2 hours.
4. Once done, remove from the bag and transfer it to a bowl.
5. Smash using a spatula.
6. Serve!

Nutrition Values (Per Serving)

- Calories: 149
- Carbohydrate: 31g
- Protein: 2g
- Fat: 1g
- Sugar: 22g
- Sodium: 4mg

Fresh Ginger Syrup

(Serves: 8 / **Prep Time:** 10 minutes / **Sous-Vide Cooking Time:** 90 minutes)

Ingredients

- 13 oz. caster sugar
- 4 cups water
- ¼ cup vodka
- 3-inch fresh ginger root, peeled and grated

How To

1. Prepare your Sous-vide water bath to a temperature of 142-degrees Fahrenheit.
2. Add the listed ingredients to the resealable zip bag except for the vodka, seal using the immersion method.
3. Cook for 90 minutes.
4. Strain the liquid of the zip bag through a fine metal mesh into a large bowl, add the vodka and mix
5. Pop into clean bottle and use as needed.

Nutrition Values (Per Serving)

- Calories: 284
- Carbohydrate: 72g
- Protein: 1g
- Fat: 0g
- Sugar: 67g
- Sodium: 14mg

Peach Chutney

(Serves: 8 / **Prep Time:** 20 minutes / **Sous-Vide Cooking Time:** 40 minutes)

Ingredients

- ½ cup granulated sugar
- ½ cup water
- ¼ cup white wine vinegar
- 1 clove garlic, minced
- ¼ cup white onion, finely chopped
- 1 lime juice
- 2 teaspoons grated fresh ginger
- 2 teaspoon curry powder
- Pinch of red pepper flakes
- Salt and black pepper as needed
- 4 large peaches, slice, pitted, and peeled into ¼ inch thick wedges
- ¼ cup chopped fresh basil
- Several whole basil leaves for garnishing

How To

1. Prepare your Sous-vide water bath to a temperature of 167-degrees Fahrenheit.
2. Add the sugar, white wine vinegar, water and garlic in a medium-sized saucepan and place it over medium-high heat.
3. Bring the mixture to a boil. Dissolve the sugar.
4. Add the onion, curry powder, lime juice, ginger, red pepper flakes and season with salt and pepper. Stir well.
5. Add the sliced peaches in a large resealable zip bag and pour vinegar mixture over the peach.
6. Seal using the immersion method. Cook for 40 minutes.
7. Transfer to an ice bath and cool.
8. Once done, transfer the contents to a storage container and stir in basil.
9. Serve.

Nutrition Values (Per Serving)

- Calories: 204
- Carbohydrate: 42g
- Protein: 2g
- Fat: 4g
- Sugar: 37g
- Sodium: 462mg

Hot Pepper Sauce

(Serves: 8 / **Prep Time:** 10 minutes / **Sous-Vide Cooking Time:** 20 minutes)

Ingredients

- 1 ½ lbs. fresh red jalapeno peppers, chopped
- 9 garlic cloves, peeled and smashed
- 1 teaspoon sea salt
- 1/3 cup rice vinegar
- 3 tablespoons syrup

How To

1. Prepare your Sous-vide water bath to a temperature of 210-degrees Fahrenheit.
2. Add the chopped peppers, garlic and sea salt to food processor and puree.
3. Pour the mixture into resealable zip bag and seal using the immersion method.
4. Submerge underwater and cook for 20 minutes.
5. Once done, remove from the bag and pour into a bowl.
6. Stir in rice vinegar and syrup.
7. Serve as needed

Nutrition Values (Per Serving)

- Calories: 326
- Carbohydrate: 80g
- Protein: 2g
- Fat: 0g
- Sugar: 71g
- Sodium: 2mg

Provencal Tomato Sauce

(Serves: 8 / **Prep Time:** 20 minutes / **Sous-Vide Cooking Time:** 45 minutes)

Ingredients

- 1-pint cherry tomatoes
- ½ small onion, peeled and chopped up finely
- 1 shallot peeled and minced
- 5-6 large chopped basil leaves
- 2-3 sprigs fresh thyme stripped
- A handful of fresh parsley, fully stemmed and chopped up
- ½ teaspoon sea salt
- ¼ teaspoon ground black pepper
- 1 tablespoon olive oil

How To

1. Prepare your Sous-vide water bath to a temperature of 182-degrees Fahrenheit.
2. Add all the listed ingredients to your resealable zip bag and seal using the immersion method.

3. Submerge underwater and let it cook for 30-45 minutes.
4. Remove the pouch and knead the sauce through the pouch.
5. Serve as needed.

Nutrition Values (Per Serving)

- Calories: 117
- Carbohydrate: 26g
- Protein: 5g
- Fat: 1g
- Sugar: 14g
- Sodium: 520mg

Chicken Stock

(Serves: 8 / **Prep Time:** 10 minutes / **Sous-Vide Cooking Time:** 6-8 hours)

Ingredients

- 10 lbs. chicken bones
- 1 lb. yellow onion peeled and cut in half
- 8 oz. carrots, chopped
- 8 oz. celery, chopped
- ½ teaspoon black peppercorn
- 10 sprigs fresh thyme
- Small handful parsley stem
- 1-piece bay leaf

How To

1. Roast your chicken bones for about 1 ½ hours at 400-degrees Fahrenheit in your oven.
2. Add the roasted chicken bones, onion, and the rest of the ingredients to a resealable zipper bag
3. Add the water (reserve 1 cup) and seal using the immersion method.
4. Prepare the water bath to a temperature of 194-degrees Fahrenheit using your immersion circulator
5. Submerge underwater and cook for 6-8 hours.
6. Strain the mixture from the zip bag through a metal mesh into a large-sized bowl
7. Cool the stock using an ice bath and place it in your oven overnight
8. Scrape the surface and discard fat.
9. Use as needed.

Nutrition Values (Per Serving)

- Calories: 83
- Carbohydrate: 31g
- Protein: 173g
- Fat: 137g
- Sugar: 13g
- Sodium: 561mg

Cinnamon-Apple Flavored Balsamic Vinegar

(Serves: 10 / **Prep Time:** 10 minutes / **Sous-Vide Cooking Time:** 180 minutes)

Ingredients

- 17 oz. balsamic vinegar
- 2 medium apples, sliced
- 2 cinnamon sticks
- 1 tablespoon sugar

How To

1. Prepare your Sous-vide water bath to a temperature of 153-degrees Fahrenheit.
2. Add all the listed ingredients to your resealable zip bag and seal using the immersion method.
3. Submerge underwater and cook for 3 hours.
4. Once done, strain the contents through a cheesecloth into a clean bottle.
5. Serve as needed!

Nutrition Values (Per Serving)

- Calories: 232
- Carbohydrate: 54g
- Protein: 1g
- Fat: 0g
- Sugar: 51g
- Sodium: 19mg

Strawberry & Blueberry Coulis

(Serves: 8 / **Prep Time:** 10 minutes / **Sous-Vide Cooking Time:** 30 minutes)

Ingredients

- 1 cup strawberries, stemmed, washed, and quartered
- 1 cup fresh blueberries, stemmed and washed
- ¼ cup granulated sugar
- 1 lemon juice

How To

1. Prepare the Sous-vide water bath to a temperature of 180-degrees Fahrenheit.
2. Add the berries, sugar and alongside the lemon juice into a resealable zipper bag and seal using the immersion method.
3. Cook for 30 minutes.
4. Mash through the pouch for a smoother consistency.
5. Once done, transfer it to a food processor and puree until you have a smooth texture
6. Chill and use as needed!

Nutrition Values (Per Serving)

- Calories: 128
- Carbohydrate: 30g
- Protein: 3g
- Fat: 1g
- Sugar: 13g
- Sodium: 20mg

Summer Corn Salsa

(Serves: 8 / **Prep Time:** 10 minutes / **Sous-Vide Cooking Time:** 30 minutes)

Ingredients

- 4 ears fresh corn, shucked and washed
- Salt, and pepper as needed
- 2 cloves garlic, chopped and peeled
- 1 deseeded and finely chopped jalapeno
- 2 tomatoes, chopped
- 2 limes, juiced
- 1/4 cup extra-virgin olive oil
- 2 avocados, peeled, chopped, and seeded
- 1 bunch coriander, chopped up
- Tortillas for serving

How To

1. Prepare the Sous-vide water bath using your immersion circulator and raise the temperature to 182-degrees Fahrenheit.
2. Season the corn with salt and pepper.
3. Place the corn in a resealable zip bag and seal using the immersion method. Cook for 30 minutes.
4. Take a large bowl and mix the finely chopped garlic, tomatoes, jalapenos, lime juice, avocado, coriander, and olive oil.
5. Once cooked, remove the corn and allow it to cool.
6. Cut the kernels and mix in the salsa. Season.
7. Serve with tortillas.

Nutrition Values (Per Serving)

- Calories: 362
- Carbohydrate: 77g
- Protein: 10g
- Fat: 7g
- Sugar: 5g
- Sodium: 1975mg

Grand Marnier Cranberry Sauce

(Serves: 8 / **Prep Time:** 10 minutes / **Sous-Vide Cooking Time:** 120 minutes)

Ingredients

- 1 cinnamon stick
- 1 teaspoon allspice berries
- 3 cloves garlic
- 12 oz. fresh cranberries
- 1 cup granulated sugar
- ¼ cup Grand Marnier Orange Liquor
- Juice and zest of 1 orange

How To

1. Prepare your Sous-vide water bath to a temperature of 175-degrees Fahrenheit.
2. Bundle the cinnamon stick, cloves, and allspice in a cheesecloth and tie using a string.
3. Add the sachet of spices, sugar, cranberries, Grand Mariner, orange juice and zest to a resealable zip bag.
4. Seal using the immersion method. Cook for 2 hours.
5. Once done, remove the spice sachet and discard.
6. Transfer the bag of cranberry sauce to an ice bath.
7. Allow it to cool.
8. Enjoy!

Nutrition Values (Per Serving)

- Calories: 207
- Carbohydrate: 52g
- Protein: 1g
- Fat: 0g
- Sugar: 42g
- Sodium: 84mg

Lemon Ginger Marmalade

(Serves: 8 / **Prep Time:** 15 minutes / **Sous-Vide Cooking Time:** 180 minutes)

Ingredients
- 4 pieces thinly sliced Meyer lemons
- 4 cups granulated sugar
- ¼ cup chopped crystallized ginger
- 1 tablespoon grated fresh ginger

How To
1. Prepare your Sous-vide water bath to a temperature of 190-degrees Fahrenheit.
2. Add the above-listed ingredients to your resealable zipper bag and seal using the immersion method. Cook for 3 hours.
3. Once done, transfer the bag to an ice bath and allow it to cool.
4. You can store in an air tight container and serve as needed.

Nutrition Values (Per Serving)
- Calories: 455
- Carbohydrate: 119g
- Protein: 1g
- Fat: 0g
- Sugar: 110g
- Sodium: 11mg

Cooking Time and Temperature Charts

Vegetables				
Food	**Thickness**	**Cooking Temp**	**Min.Time**	**Max.Time**
Beets	Up to 1 inch	183 degrees F	1-2 hours	4 hours
Carrots	Up to 1 inch	183 degrees F	1-2 hours	4 hours
Celery	Up to 1 inch	183 degrees F	1-2 hours	4 hours
Parsnips	Up to 1 inch	183 degrees F	1-2 hours	4 hours
Potatoes	Up to 1 inch	183 degrees F	1-2 hours	4 hours
Turnips	Up to 1 inch	183 degrees F	1-2 hours	4 hours
Asparagus	Up to 1 inch	183 degrees F	45 minutes	1 and ½ hours
Broccoli	Up to 1 inch	183 degrees F	45 minutes	1 and ½ hours
Cauliflower	Up to 1 inch	183 degrees F	45 minutes	1 and ½ hours
Corn	Up to 1 inch	183 degrees F	45 minutes	1 and ½ hours
Eggplant	Up to 1 inch	183 degrees F	45 minutes	1 and ½ hours
Green Beans	Up to 1 inch	183 degrees F	45 minutes	1 and ½ hours
Onions	Up to 1 inch	183 degrees F	45 minutes	1 and ½ hours
Peas	Up to 1 inch	183 degrees F	45 minutes	1 and ½ hours
Squash	Up to 1 inch	183 degrees F	45 minutes	1 and ½ hours

Fruits				
Food	**Thickness**	**Cooking Temp**	**Min.Time**	**Max.Time**
Apples	Up to 1 inch	183 degrees F	45 minutes	2 hours
Pears	Up to 1 inch	183 degrees F	45 minutes	2 hours
Peaches	Up to 1 inch	183 degrees F	30 minutes	1 hour
Apricots	Up to 1 inch	183 degrees F	30 minutes	1 hour
Plums	Up to 1 inch	183 degrees F	30 minutes	1 hour
Mango	Up to 1 inch	183 degrees F	30 minutes	1 hour
Nectarines	Up to 1 inch	183 degrees F	30 minutes	1 hour
Strawberries	Up to 1 inch	183 degrees F	30 minutes	1 hour

Eggs (Chicken)				
Food	**Thickness**	**Cooking Temp**	**Min.Time**	**Max.Time**
Soft-Cooked In Shell (Quick)	***	167 degrees F	15 minutes	18 minutes
Soft-Cooked In Shell (Slow)	***	146 degrees F	45 minutes	1 and ½ hours
Hard-Cooked In Shell	***	160 degrees F	45 minutes	1 and ½ hours
Scrambled	***	167 degrees F	20 minutes	*
Pasteurized In Shell	***	135 degrees F	1 and ¼ hours	2 hours

Meat and Seafood

Food	Thickness	Cooking Temp	Min.Time	Max.Time
Beef or Lamb Tenderloin	1 inch	134 degrees Fahrenheit or Higher	1 Hour	4 Hours
Beef or Lamb Tenderloin	2 inch	134 degrees Fahrenheit or Higher	2 Hours	4 Hours
Beef Or Lamb Sirloin	1 inch	134 degrees Fahrenheit or Higher	1 Hour	4 Hours
Beef Or Lamb Sirloin	2 inch	134 degrees Fahrenheit or Higher	2 Hours	4 Hours
Beef Or Lamb Ribeye	1 inch	134 degrees Fahrenheit or Higher	1 Hour	4 Hours
Beef Or Lamb Ribeye	2 inch	134 degrees Fahrenheit or Higher	2 Hours	4 Hours
Beef T-Bone Steak	1 inch	134 degrees Fahrenheit or Higher	1 Hour	4 Hours
Beef T-Bone Steaks	2 inch	134 degrees Fahrenheit or Higher	2 Hours	4 Hours
Lamb Chops	1 inch	134 degrees Fahrenheit or Higher	1 Hour	4 Hours
Lamb Chops	2 inch	134 degrees Fahrenheit or Higher	2 Hours	4 Hours

Bison	1 inch	134 degrees Fahrenheit or Higher	8- 10 Hours	12 to 24 Hours
Roast Leg of Lamb	2.75 inch	134 degrees Fahrenheit or Higher	10 Hours	24 to 48 Hours
Beef Spare Ribs	2 inch	176 degrees Fahrenheit	24 Hours	48-72 Hours
Flank Steak	1 inch	134 degrees Fahrenheit or Higher	8-10 Hours	24 to 30 Hours
Brisket	2 inch	134 degrees Fahrenheit or Higher	8-10 Hours	48 to 72 Hours
Pork Tenderloin	1.5 inch	134 degrees Fahrenheit or Higher	1 and ½ Hours	24 to 30 Hours
Baby Back Ribs	1 inch	165 degrees Fahrenheit	4-8 Hours	24 to 30 Hours
Pork Chops	1 inch	134 degrees Fahrenheit or Higher	2-4 Hours	6 to 8 Hours
Pork Chops	2 inch	134 degrees Fahrenheit or Higher	4-6 Hours	8 to 10 Hours
Pork Roast	2.75 inch	160-167 degrees Fahrenheit	12 Hours	30 Hours
Spare Ribs	2.75 inch	160-167 degrees Fahrenheit	12 Hours	30 Hours

Chicken Breast, Bone In	2 inch	146 degrees Fahrenheit or Higher	2 and ½ Hours	4 to 6 Hours
Chicken Breast, Boneless	1 inch	146 degrees Fahrenheit or Higher	1 Hour	2 to 4 Hours
Chicken Leg/Thigh		160 degrees Fahrenheit or Higher	4 Hours	4 to 6 Hours
Split Game Hen	2.75 inch	160 degrees Fahrenheit or Higher	6 Hours	8 Hours
Turkey/Duck Leg		176 degrees Fahrenheit	8 Hours	10 Hours
Duck Breast	1 inch	134 degrees Fahrenheit or Higher	2 and ½ Hours	6-8 Hours
Lean Fish	0.5	Desired Serving Temperature	30- 40 minutes	*
Fatty Fish	1 inch	Desired Serving Temperature	40-50 minutes	*
Lobster	1 inch	140 degrees Fahrenheit	45 minutes	*
Scallops	1 inch	140 degrees Fahrenheit	40-60 minutes	*
Shrimp	Large	140 degrees Fahrenheit	30 minutes	*

*Cooking to maximum may result in soft and unevenly-textured meals

**Make sure to prevent vacuum packaging eggs that are still in shells

***Possible to cook 12 eggs (still in shell)/ 5 scrambled eggs

Measurement Conversion Charts

The charts you are seeing below will help you to convert the difference between units of volume in US customary units.

Please note that US volume is not the same as in the UK and other countries, and many of the measurements are different depending on your country

It's very easy to get confused when dealing with US and UK units! The good thing is that the metric units never change!

All the measurement charts below are for US customary units only!

We have gone to great length in order to make sure that the measurements on the following Measurement Charts are accurate.

American and British Variances					
Term	Abbreviation	Nationality	Dry or liquid	Metric equivalent	Equivalent in context
cup	c., C.		usually liquid	237 milliliters	16 tablespoons or 8 ounces
ounce	fl oz, fl. oz.	American	liquid only	29.57 milliliters	
		British	either	28.41 milliliters	
gallon	gal.	American	liquid only	3.785 liters	4 quarts
		British	either	4.546 liters	4 quarts
inch	in, in.			2.54 centimeters	
ounce	oz, oz.	American	dry	28.35 grams	1/16 pound
		n	liquid	see OUNCE	see OUNCE
pint	p., pt.	American	liquid	0.473 liter	1/8 gallon or 16 ounces
			dry	0.551 liter	1/2 quart
		British	either	0.568 liter	
pound	lb.		dry	453.592 grams	16 ounces
Quart	q., qt, qt.	American	liquid	0.946 liter	1/4 gallon or 32 ounces
			dry	1.101 liters	2 pints
		British	either	1.136 liters	
Teaspoon	t., tsp., tsp		either	about 5 milliliters	1/3 tablespoon
Tablespoon	T., tbs., tbsp.		either	about 15 milliliters	3 teaspoons or 1/2 ounce

Volume (Liquid)

American Standard (Cups & Quarts)	American Standard (Ounces)	Metric (Milliliters & Liters)
2 tbsp.	1 fl. oz.	30 ml
1/4 cup	2 fl. oz.	60 ml
1/2 cup	4 fl. oz.	125 ml
1 cup	8 fl. oz.	250 ml
1 1/2 cups	12 fl. oz.	375 ml
2 cups or 1 pint	16 fl. oz.	500 ml
4 cups or 1 quart	32 fl. oz.	1000 ml or 1 liter
1 gallon	128 fl. oz.	4 liters

Volume (Dry)

American Standard	Metric
1/8 teaspoon	5 ml
1/4 teaspoon	1 ml
1/2 teaspoon	2 ml
3/4 teaspoon	4 ml
1 teaspoon	5 ml
1 tablespoon	15 ml
1/4 cup	59 ml
1/3 cup	79 ml
1/2 cup	118 ml
2/3 cup	158 ml
3/4 cup	177 ml
1 cup	225 ml
2 cups or 1 pint	450 ml
3 cups	675 ml
4 cups or 1 quart	1 liter
1/2 gallon	2 liters
1 gallon	4 liters

Oven Temperatures

American Standard	Metric
250° F	130° C
300° F	150° C
350° F	180° C
400° F	200° C
450° F	230° C

Weight (Mass)

American Standard (Ounces)	Metric (Grams)
1/2 ounce	15 grams
1 ounce	30 grams
3 ounces	85 grams
3.75 ounces	100 grams
4 ounces	115 grams
8 ounces	225 grams
12 ounces	340 grams
16 ounces or 1 pound	450 grams

Dry Measure Equivalents

3 teaspoons	1 tablespoon	1/2 ounce	14.3 grams
2 tablespoons	1/8 cup	1 ounce	28.3 grams
4 tablespoons	1/4 cup	2 ounces	56.7 grams
5 1/3 tablespoons	1/3 cup	2.6 ounces	75.6 grams
8 tablespoons	1/2 cup	4 ounces	113.4 grams
12 tablespoons	3/4 cup	6 ounces	.375 pound
32 tablespoons	2 cups	16 ounces	1 pound

About the Author

As one of seven children, Rachel Collins grew up in Cleveland, Ohio before moving to the mountains of Colorado in her early teens. From a young age she dreamed of moving to LA and becoming a fashion stylist. But when Rachel was fifteen, her only sister was born. Ever determined to rein in the chaos of her big family...and have dinner on the table before midnight...Rachel began doing the cooking. She eventually discovered a new found freedom and a creativity she hadn't known existed. She began chronicling her fresh takes on old favorites and coupling them with her styling skills - only this time on tables and cutting boards - on her blog.

Since then, lots of people have fallen in love with her unique recipes, stunning photography, and charming life in her barn, which she has made into her home, high up in the snow-capped mountains.

Finally, before you go, I'd like to say "thank you" for purchasing my book and I hope that you had as much fun reading it as I had writing it.

I know you could have picked from dozens of books on Sous Vide Recipes, but you took a chance with my guide. So, big thanks for purchasing this book and reading all the way to the end.

Now, I'd like to ask for a *small* favor. Could you please take a minute or two and leave a review for this book on Amazon by returning to your order history, the top right-hand side of your screen.

This feedback will help me continue to write the kind of books that will help you get results and help me to compete with other big publishers and authors.

I bid you farewell and encourage you to move forward and find your true Sous Vide cooking spirit!

Thank you and good luck!

—Rachel Collins

RECIPE INDEX

Made in the USA
Columbia, SC
05 December 2019